BEING JEWISH

THE SPIRITUAL AND CULTURAL PRACTICE OF JUDAISM TODAY

ARI L. GOLDMAN

Simon & Schuster Paperbacks
New York London Toronto Sydney

SIMON & SCHUSTER PAPERBACKS
1230 Avenue of the Americas
New York, NY 10020

First Simon & Schuster trade paperback edition October 2007

SIMON & SCHUSTER PAPERBACKS and colophon are registered trademarks of Simon & Schuster, Inc.

For information about special discounts for bulk purchases, please contact Simon & Schuster Special Sales at 1-800-456-6798 or business@simonandschuster.com.

Dedicated to the memory of my Mother and my Father

Designed by Jeanette Olender
Manufactured in the United States of America

1   3   5   7   9   10   8   6   4   2

The Library of Congress has catalogued the hardcover edition as follows:
Goldman, Ari L.
Being Jewish : the spiritual and cultural practice of Judaism today / Ari L. Goldman.
p.   cm.
Includes bibliographical references and index.
1. Judaism—Customs and practices.   2. Fasts and feasts—Judaism.
3. Jewish way of life.   4. Life cycle, Human—Religious aspects—Judaism.   I. Title.
BM700.G616 2000
296.4—dc21   00-044047

ISBN-13: 978-684-82389-8
ISBN-10: 0-684-82389-6
ISBN-13: 978-1-4165-3602-4 (pbk)
ISBN-10: 1-4165-3602-7 (pbk)

Dedicated to the memory of

my Mother and my Father

ACKNOWLEDGMENTS

Work, family, synagogue.

This book would not have been possible without the cooperation of all three of those elements in my life. I want to thank my dean, Tom Goldstein, and my colleagues at Columbia for encouraging me to write. And I am indebted to my synagogue, Ramath Orah, led by Rabbi Steven Friedman and Mr. Leo Chester, for inspiring me.

My brother Shalom read through the work in progress several times, questioning and challenging my assumptions and conclusions. My brother Dov was afraid that in presenting my own theories and stories, I'd forget some of the essentials. That's why, at his suggestion, each chapter ends with a section called "The Basics."

Several friends read the manuscript or parts of it at various points along the way. They include Jack Nelson, Michael Shapiro, Sam Freedman, Peter Steinfels, Steven Bayme, and a small conclave of rabbis, including Yair Silverman, Michael Paley, and Elie Spitz. I mention their names to offer public thanks but in no way to hold them accountable for what is in these pages. Indeed, I often rejected their counsel. Ultimately, this book reflects my perspective.

A good part of this book was written during a sabbatical year that I took in 1997–1998 with my family in Israel. I want to thank the Fulbright Educational Exchange Program for making that year possible. During my year in Israel, and in the time since my return, I tried out many of the ideas in this book on two valuable men's groups in which I take part, one in Jerusalem and the other in New York. I would like to thank the Israeli group, which was made up of Ray Lederman, Elli

Wohlgelernter, Elie Spitz, Winston Pickett, Joel Fish, Sid Slivko, and Jeff Kamins. And thanks to my New York men's group, known as the *tertulia,* a group that includes Jack Nelson, Robert Spira, Henry Anhalt, Dan Victor, Allan Kozinn, Neal Rosen, Enrique Levy, Steve Greenberg, Larry Heligman, Jonathan Mark, Fred Polaniecki, Ken Prager, Yakov Stern, Michael Miller, Mark Sarna, and Ike Herschkopf.

It wasn't all men. I also drew inspiration and wisdom for this book from a number of amazing women, among them Blu Greenberg, Haviva Ner-David, Amy Lederman, Fiona Sharpe, Helen Spielvogel, Linda Kaplan, Arlene Agus, Rolinda Schonwald, Marga Hirsch, Laurie Patton, Babette Kamins, and Rabbi Rachel Cowan.

I owe a great debt of gratitude to my talented editor, Constance Herndon, for her wisdom, grace, and patience, and to my ever-inspiring agent, Robert Markel. I am also grateful for the support of my in-laws, Henry and Rochelle Dicker. I am lucky in having friends like Mark Podwal, who helped with the art in this book, and Joseph Telushkin, who helped me think through the ideas in countless informal sessions at our *shul.*

And last but not least, my immediate family. From the very beginning, my wife, Shira, knew how important this project was and lovingly supported me every step of the way. I also want to thank our children, Adam, Emma, and Judah, for providing sustaining hugs and laughter when the task seemed daunting.

I lovingly dedicate this book to the memory of my mother, Judith Goldman, and my father, Marvin Goldman. Each in his and her own way continues to guide and shape me. I never knew I would miss them so much.

Ari L. Goldman
Manhattan

CONTENTS

7

CONTENTS

FOREWORD

When I completed *Being Jewish* in the early days of 2000, the world—and the Jewish world in particular—was a very different place. Nine-one-one were the numbers one dialed to summon the police in an emergency, not a shorthand for a cataclysm that would shape the new century. The greatest national security concern was something called Y2K, the fear that somehow our computers couldn't handle the transition to four new digits. Senator Joseph Lieberman of Connecticut, an observant Jew, was the Democratic Party nominee for the vice presidency, running with Vice President Al Gore in a race against George W. Bush that the pollsters said was too close to call. One hundred and twenty thousand United States troops were not mired in a hopeless conflict in Iraq.

The world was also different place in another part of the Middle East in 2000. Israel was engaged in a peace process with its Arab neighbors that gave many people reason to hope that the long Arab-Israel conflict could be settled. Treaties were in place between Israel and Egypt and between Israel and Jordan. A permanent peace with a new reinvigorated Palestinian Authority led by Yassir Arafat seemed close at hand. In a decade that saw the collapse of the Soviet bloc and the end of apartheid in South Africa, the Middle East seemed the next great frontier for peace.

I tasted this late-twentieth-century optimism both as an American Jew and as a temporary resident of Israel in 1997–98 when I was on sabbatical as a Fulbright scholar in Israel writing *Being Jewish*. In many ways, *Being Jewish* embodies the optimism of that time. This is a book that on every page celebrates the vibrancy and variety of Jewish thought and practice. As Alan M. Dershowitz of Harvard put it when I asked him for an endorsement, *Being Jewish* is about the "joy rather than the 'oy'" of contemporary Jewry.

From the beginning of this project I wanted *Being Jewish* to be more than a how-to book. It seemed that there were a host of good books out there, many of them written by rabbis, about how to celebrate Jewish holidays and life-cycle events—by the rules. I wanted to do something different. I wanted to show how the faith is lived. And so I took the approach of the journalist, employing scores of anecdotes to demonstrate how people create a Judaism that works for them. I drew both on my own Jewish life and on my thirty years as a journalist. This is not a how-to book but a what-do-they-do book.

What I've found since the book was published in 2000 is that the new political realities, however distressing they may be, have not dampened the varieties of Jewish religious creativity and commitment. In my book, I rely on the 1990 National Jewish Population Survey to demonstrate the persistence of American Jewish observance (page 30). That sense of creativity is also evident in the updated 2000 Jewish Population survey. In almost every category, there was an increase in the number of Jews who observed particular rituals. Thus, there was hard evidence that more Jews were attending Passover seders, fasting on Yom Kippur, visiting Israel, and lighting Sabbath candles.

What's more, the widely quoted dire statistic from the 1990 survey, namely that 52 percent of American Jews were choosing non-Jewish spouses—a statistic that was particularly shocking because it was easy to summarize as "most Jews marry out"—later turned out to be a statistical error. Subsequent analyses of the 1990 data showed the inter-marriage rate was 43 percent, still alarmingly high but far from "most."

The intermarriage rate inched up to 47 percent in the 2000 survey, which is a curious trend given that several behavioral indicators suggested a greater commitment to Jewish practice. Clearly two factors were at play in American Jewish life: (1) a greater integration into

American life that meant old ethnic barriers between Jew and gentile had fallen; and (2) a growing interest in exploring and experiencing Jewish religious identity. As the sociologist Steven M. Cohen observed in analyzing the survey data, Jewish religion is "in" and Jewish ethnic identity is "out."

"On average," Cohen wrote in a 2006 essay called "A Tale of Two Jewries," "American Jews are decreasingly ethnic in the sense that fewer are engaged in formal and informal associations. . . . At the same time, they are no less inclined religiously. This dimension relates to congregational membership, ritual observance, and participation in Jewish education."

Cohen found that Jewish membership in such well-established "ethnic" organizations as B'nai B'rith, Hadassah, and Jewish Federations has declined. At the same time, he said, affiliation with religious organizations, namely synagogues, remained steady and even experienced some growth.

In promoting *Being Jewish* before synagogue and book fair audiences over the last few years, I saw some of the themes of my book come to life. When I recounted stories from *Being Jewish* about Jews who honored the Sabbath in quirky ways, such as not eating shellfish on Friday night, they'd come back with their own stories. One woman in Miami greeted me with a big smile and said, "I don't floss on Shabbos."

Every story I threw out to them they matched with an even better story. I told an audience about the Passover meal of matzah and shrimp, they told me about the Yom Kippur fast broken with a cheeseburger. "At least we fasted," they said.

Jewish religious creativity knows no bounds, I learned.

Along the way, I heard a wonderful Torah thought from Rabbi Nachman of Bratzlav, the eighteenth-century Hasidic master whose irrepressibly positive attitude was a challenge to the rabbis of his time—and even to some rabbis today. I loved the thought so much I wished I had included it in *Being Jewish*. Now I have the chance to.

Rabbi Nachman worried in his day about the Jewish propensity to claim fault. "We have sinned," Jews say in a public confessional prayer on Yom Kippur, the holiest day of the year. The liturgy then demands that we go on to enumerate our sins: I lied, I cheated, I committed adultery (even if only in my heart), I was dishonest in business, etc.

Rabbi Nachman said that just as one is required to confess sins, so must one confess good deeds: I gave to charity, I kept the Sabbath, I ate kosher, I paid my taxes, I was faithful to my wife, etc.

Each good deed, Rabbi Nachman said, is a musical note on your soul. Take one note and another and another, he added, and soon you have a Jewish song. Each Jew, he said, has his or her own special song.

When you meet Jews, Rabbi Nachman said, don't look at their faults. Instead, listen for their particular songs, made up of all the good deeds they have done.

I hope that as you turn the pages of *Being Jewish* you, too, will hear the song of American Jewry.

INTRODUCTION

Gabriel's Helper

There is a medieval Jewish legend, "Gabriel and the Infants," that goes like this: In the months before a Jewish child is born, it is visited in the womb by the Angel Gabriel. There, in the warmth and silence of the mother's body, the angel teaches the baby all of Jewish learning—the Torah, the rituals, the holidays, the deepest truths of Jewish wisdom. The baby absorbs it all, just as it takes nourishment from its mother. But suddenly, as the baby is about to be thrust into the world to eat and breathe on its own, the angel presents it with a similar intellectual challenge. Right before birth, Gabriel strikes the child on the upper lip, and all the teachings are instantly forgotten.

I loved hearing this story as a child. For one thing, it explained that otherwise useless indentation above my upper lip. For another, it gave me a timeless relationship with all Jewish knowledge. The process of living a Jewish life seemed to have more to do with remembering what is inherently mine rather than learning anew. As I encountered Jewish rituals and holidays, Jewish ideas and philosophies, they seemed to have a familiar ring. Sometimes the image of Gabriel flashed before my eyes.

The legend of Gabriel also provided me with something else: company. I knew that as a Jew I was not alone. From my earliest beginnings, there was someone there—teaching, coaxing, and guiding. This notion of a Gabriel in one's life is built into virtually all of the Jewish life cycle events. At the first initiation rite, the *brit,* there is the *sandek,* the man who holds the baby during the cutting. A bar or bat mitzvah cannot take place without a teacher who passes on the ancient words and melodies to a new generation. At a wedding, the bride and groom are traditionally given *shomrim,* or royal guards, who escort them to the wedding canopy. And even in death, Jewish law ensures that the body is not left alone from the time of death until the moment of burial. It is customary for family members or friends to take turns standing watch at the bier.

Judaism provides community. It does so in the major life cycle events as well as in the more mundane moments of the day, the week, the month, and the year. Daily, Sabbath and festival services ring out from synagogues across America and the world in a variety of styles and beliefs. Home rituals, from Sabbath candle lighting to Passover seder meals, connect the individual with the Jewish community at large and with practices both ancient and modern.

In American society, there is no coercion to be a religious person. Freedom of religion means that we are as free to do *with* religion as we are to do without. Those who convert to Judaism are nowadays called Jews by choice. But, as has often been said, every Jew today is, in fact, a Jew by choice. We can go to synagogue or not go to synagogue, pray or not pray, mark the life cycle events or ignore them. Judaism is out there, something external, something we can choose to partake of— or dismiss.

But the legend of Gabriel and the Infants provides another model. Gabriel teaches us that Jewish knowledge is not external, removed from life, but something inside: the very stuff of life that must be reckoned with and rediscovered. And, just as important, Gabriel reminds us that built into Judaism are guides, companions, and teachers who can help both those born Jewish and others who want to learn about the faith. These lessons, I believe, are ones that American Jews desperately need. Judaism can help ease the modern sense of isolation and loneliness, providing a sense of belonging in the present and a sense of connection with the past.

A third lesson I take from Gabriel is that Jewish teaching is not monolithic. What is good for one person may not be the answer for others. Gabriel visits each of us with a personalized lesson. Of course, there is Sinai, with its dramatic revelation for all the faithful, but there is also the awareness that each Jew has to forge an individual relationship with the divine.

In this book, I will lead the reader through the process of Jewish discovery, moving first from birth rituals to funeral rites, and then through the Jewish months, from one Jewish New Year to the next. Along the way, I will take a look at how different Jews have found meaning, richness, and variety in the tradition and made it their own.

The book is divided into three sections, each representing a cycle of Jewish life. The first section will demonstrate how Judaism responds to the natural events of life, looking at the ceremonies associated with birth, the coming of age, marriage, and death.

The second section will deal with the major milestones of the Jewish calendar—the classic holidays, such as Rosh Hashanah and Yom Kippur, Hanukkah and Passover—as well as the minor fast days and holidays created in the twentieth century to respond to the tragedy of the Holocaust and the creation of the modern State of Israel.

The third and final section will explore the rhythm of the Jewish day, in which time is marked with prayers and blessings. This section will look at Jewish prayer, the laws of *kashrut,* and Jewish ethical behavior in everything from charitable giving to family life.

BEING JEWISH IN AMERICA
AND IN ISRAEL

This book grew out of a rethinking and reexamination of Jewish life during a sabbatical I took with my family in Jerusalem in 1997–1998. My previous sabbatical, taken over a decade earlier, was spent at Harvard Divinity School exploring the religions of the world. The literary product of that year, my book *The Search for God at Harvard*, struggles with concepts of pluralism and belief. It deals with the question of how someone Orthodox, like myself, can embrace and appreciate the truths of other religions. *The Search* gained widespread acclaim, with one reviewer calling me "a kind of Gulliver of faith," but there was criticism too, perhaps the most stinging from a rabbi in a right-wing Jerusalem yeshiva who "caught" one of his students reading my unorthodox book. He was dismissive, telling the student: "Why does Goldman run off and study Christianity and Islam when he barely knows Judaism?" This new book is my effort to examine not the faiths of others but my own faith, to look deep into its practices and history and try to invigorate it with new meaning and purpose. I undertake this examination not as the yeshiva boy I once was but with the insight of a Gulliver who has seen the lives of others and can now reflect better on his own.

This book is not a right-wing or even Orthodox approach. While Orthodoxy is my home, I believe that Judaism can and should be celebrated in a variety of ways. I am that rare breed: an Orthodox pluralist, someone who believes that the right answer for me is not the answer for everyone. After all, if I embrace pluralism in my approach to other religions, I must embrace it as well within my own faith. In these pages, I will demonstrate a variety of Jewish practices: some traditional, some innovative, and—many of the best of them—a combination of the two.

In recent years, the pietistic ArtScroll Series of books has enjoyed enormous popularity in Orthodox circles. Riding a wave of Orthodox fundamentalism, ArtScroll has found a niche in a community obsessed with unbending adherence to halacha, Jewish law. Every aspect of life, from the bedroom to the synagogue to the kitchen stove, has found regulation in ArtScroll's three hundred volumes. Often lost in this effort, however, has been much of the nuance, subtlety, poetry, and flexibility of traditional Judaism. To put it plainly, Judaism is much more fun than the ArtScroll Series would have you believe.

To me, the way in which people live their Judaism tells as much about Judaism as what is legally required in the halachic system. I have tried to enrich this volume with stories—stories from my own life and from the lives of other Jews who, while far from perfect, are striving to live a meaningful Jewish life.

This is not a comprehensive religious text on Jewish observance. Do not look at this book as a manual, but as a beginning. There are many places to turn—even to ArtScroll—for greater depth and knowledge. In these pages, I want to demonstrate how Judaism developed over the centuries and provide a snapshot of how it is observed at the turn of the new millennium.

During my year in Jerusalem, I studied with some of the greatest teachers of Judaism at the Shalom Hartman Institute and at the Jerusalem Fellows. I read in the finest libraries of Jewish law and literature at the Hebrew University of Jerusalem and at the campus of Hebrew Union College in Jerusalem. I dipped into the cacophonous and exuberant study halls at the Mir Yeshiva, Aish Hatorah, and Chabad-Lubavitch. I availed myself of the riches of the stately Diaspora Museum on the campus of Tel Aviv University. But I probably gained the most from extended conversations with several pulpit rabbis from around the world—people who, like me, were on sabbatical for the year in Jerusalem. They represented all the major modern movements in contemporary Jewry—Orthodox, Conservative, and Reform—and helped root my academic inquiry in the reality of contemporary Jewish practice.

My study of Judaism was also set against the backdrop of a year of extraordinary political and security developments. I arrived with my wife, Shira, and our three children on August 1, 1997, the day after two Arab suicide bombers killed fifteen people at the busy outdoor market in Jerusalem known as Machane Yehudah. Less than a month later, Shira was a block away when three Arab terrorists killed themselves and four others on the pedestrian walkway of Ben Yehudah.

The year 1998 arrived with renewed fear of chemical attacks by Iraq's Saddam Hussein. The fears were rooted in the 1991 Persian Gulf

War, when Saddam rained thirty-nine Scud missiles on Israel. With concerns about a renewed conflict, we were sent scurrying to find gas masks in adults' and children's sizes. We sealed a room of our Jerusalem apartment in fear of an attack. At the last moment, the threat of war was averted after a settlement brokered by the United Nations Secretary General, Kofi Annan.

It wasn't until a year after we left Israel that a new prime minister, Ehud Barak, ushered in an era of new hopes (and fears) by reopening long-dormant negotiating channels with the Palestinians and Syrians.

While the issues of survival are always paramount in Israel, the issue of religion was never deep beneath the surface during our visit. Until I lived there, I never understood what power religion had in Israel, in both good ways and bad. I had read so much about the deep division over religion—how the secularists hated the ultra-Orthodox, known as the *haredim,* and vice versa. I saw much evidence of this on the streets of Tel Aviv and Jerusalem. But, living in Israel, I came also to see something else: how much the Orthodox and secular have *in common.* Judaism is a central part of the identity of the non-Orthodox. For virtually all Israeli Jews, religion serves as a common denominator when it comes to life cycle events and holiday celebrations. Regardless of whether you are religious or secular, you don't work on Yom Kippur. That doesn't mean you go to synagogue—many Israelis go to the beach (and some go to both). But for all it is a festival. Nearly all Israeli Jews (95 percent) circumcise their sons, and virtually all are married under a *chuppah,* a Jewish wedding canopy. There are problems, to be sure. Israelis have no choice when it comes to religion. The only religious Judaism that is officially recognized in Israel is Orthodoxy. About 15 percent of Israeli Jews are Orthodox, but the Orthodox grip on the religious establishment is absolute. There is no formal sanction (and little government support) for the non-Orthodox movements. During our year in Israel, Conservative and Reform Jewry struggled to gain some recognition but made little headway in the face of the powerful Orthodox political parties.

Clearly, the Israeli's life is governed by the religious calendar and

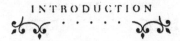

shaped by Jewish life cycle events. There is no such guarantee for American Jews, many of whom have no relationship to the Jewish calendar on either a communal or a personal level. What came through clearly to me during our year in Israel is how different American Jewry is from Israeli Jewry. American Jews have many options when it comes to Judaism—they can choose between the three major religious movements, the smallest of which is Orthodoxy. But on a day-to-day level, most American Jews have little relationship with or knowledge of the Jewish cycle of life.

Today, there are more Jews in America than there are in Israel (although demographers say that within the next ten years Israel's Jewish population will surpass America's). Of the 15 million Jews currently in the world, roughly 6 million live in the United States, and about 5 million live in Israel. There remain about 1.5 million in the former Soviet Union and more than 1 million in Western Europe, principally in France and Great Britain. In addition there are 300,000 in Canada, 233,000 in Argentina, 120,000 in South Africa, and 130,000 in Brazil. The remaining 5 percent are scattered throughout the world.

WHAT DO ALL JEWS HAVE IN COMMON?

What connects this dispersed people? Some say a common history. We all share a story that includes both triumph and tragedy. While we all have our personal Gabriel, the tradition teaches that all Jews stood at Sinai thirty-five hundred years ago when God gave the Torah to the Jewish people. The souls of Jews for all time were there, the rabbis state, when the Jews answered God's charge with the words *na'asheh v'nishma:* "We will do and we will listen." By placing all Jews at Sinai, the rabbis argue that all are included in the covenant. History is a strong bond.

Others say that all Jews are connected by a common wisdom, as embodied in Jewish writings, both sacred and secular. We are guided by the Torah, the Talmud, and the codes of Jewish law developed over the centuries, as well as by the genius of Maimonides, the Baal Shem Tov, Herzl, Freud, and Einstein. Still others point to our ancestral home and the imperative to keep modern Israel a safe and thriving nation. When Israel is at risk, Jews everywhere feel endangered. All of these are powerful connections.

Last, Jewish ritual serves as a powerful connection between all Jews. It occupies a special place because it sanctifies all these elements—our history, our ideas, and our land—through acts that unite us in common practice.

Ritual acts are *mitzvot*, acts of obligation, more commonly known in the singular form, *mitzvah*. By the count of the rabbis of the Talmud, there are 6 1 3 *mitzvot*. There are two kinds of *mitzvot*, those that involve human relations and those that involve relation with the divine. Examples of the former include "Thou shalt not steal," and the imperative to "love the stranger." Examples of the latter—between humankind and God—include "keep the Sabbath" and the obligation to pray.

GOD AS FATHER? MOTHER? LOVER?

Each of the modern branches of Judaism sees God in a different way. And its God-view shapes the ritual. The Orthodox, it might be argued, see God as Father, demanding and exacting. God loves us, the Orthodox say, but it is a conditional love, dependent on our actions. For the Orthodox, ritual reigns supreme, especially the rituals between God and man. The Orthodox punctiliously watch what they eat (kosher only), what they wear (modest garb), and how often they pray (three times a day).

For the Reform, God is Mother, whose love is unconditional. The details of the *mitzvot*, are not important; if she cares about ritual, it is only in a nostalgic way. The important thing is that we're good to our fellow human beings and try to leave the world a better place than we found it. Reform emphasizes the *mitzvot* involving human relations, such as helping the poor, rather than *mitzvot* involving obligations to God.

The Conservatives, however, see God as a lover. According to this approach, Jews are in a partnership with God in which God listens and we listen. God wants us to do God's will, but that will is not static. It changes as we change. The Conservatives believe that God's law is modified to fit the modern circumstance. Hence, ritual is an elastic phenomenon that changes with the times.

In this book I will deal for the most part only with the three major branches, but let me just extend this analysis to one other branch: the small Reconstructionist group. Reconstructionism sees God as neither Mother, Father, nor Lover. The Reconstructionists do not see God as a noun at all, but as a verb. God is the catalyst that enables us to actualize who we are as people and as a nation. We can use ritual to take us where we need to go. It is an instrument for our use.

My friend Elie Spitz, a West Coast rabbi who was on sabbatical with me in Jerusalem, likens the denominations to a deck of cards. My ritual summary above emphasizes the top card—the ritual-bound Orthodox, the ritual-free Reform, the ever-changing Conservatives, and the utilitarian Reconstructionists. "All too often they play only their top card," Rabbi Spitz would say of the branches. In fact, the decks of all the denominations include the ritual card, just as all the denominations include love, change, and acts of charity. These days, ritual might be seen as the wild card. In all the denominations, including the Reform, the ritual card is moving higher and higher in the decks. In May 1999, the Reform movement—which for more than a hundred years had stood squarely against ritual observance—took the extraordinary step of encouraging its members to reconsider traditional observances, such as embracing the dietary laws and observing the Sabbath. The movement's rabbinical body, the Central Conference of American Rabbis, issued the challenge using the words *mitzvah* and *mitzvot*—terms more often utilized by the Orthodox. *Mitzvot*, the Reform rabbis said, "demand renewed attention as the result of the unique context of our times." Among all branches of Judaism, there is a growing awareness that ritual acts that are specifically Jewish have the power to create and preserve the Jewish community.

Take lighting candles on Friday night to usher in the Sabbath, an act traditionally performed in the home by Jewish women. The four denominations might have a different explanation for the act, but they all would see it as having great merit. The Orthodox say that women must light the candles because on Sinai that is what God told Moses that Jews must do in perpetuity. It is a practice that goes back to our matriarch Sarah, who lit candles in Abraham's tent, the Orthodox explain. The Conservatives would say that yes, we are commanded to light, either by Sinai or by the tradition. But it is not only women who must light; men have the obligation too. Times change. The Reconstructionists might talk about how lighting chases away the darkness and ennobles our spirits. And the Reform would argue that lighting candles on Friday night is a matter of personal choice, but certainly it is a ritual of great beauty.

To my mind, the important thing is not why you light, just that you light. What is the value of ritual? There are many answers. On a fundamental level, a ritual act connects you with all the others who have done that ritual, both past and present. Light the Sabbath candles and think of all the candles being lit by members of your congregation that night. Then think about all the candles in your city, in your country, in the world. Then think of all the candles ever lit by Jewish women and men through the ages, back to the matriarch Sarah. Now that's a lot of light.

On another level, doing a ritual act connects the Jew to a power larger than ourselves. If we are to believe on some level that God—whether Mother, Father, Lover, or Catalyst—wants us to do this act, then lighting the candle or keeping the Sabbath or having a *brit* or attending a seder or helping the poor connects us with the Divine. On a vertical level we are connected to God; on a horizontal level, to others who have done these acts, both past and present. What emerges for me is a web of light.

BEING JEWISH MEANS
HAVING JEWISH CHILDREN

How do we pass Judaism on to our children? For the Israeli, it is easy. Judaism is there as part of the atmosphere—in the language, in the food, and in the music as well as in the events of the year and one's life. For the American Jew, who lives in a place where Judaism is a minority culture, education is essential: we can teach our children our history and our wisdom and our love for the land. But nothing makes it more concrete than ritual.

I recently heard a Reform rabbi talk to a group of parents of teenagers about intermarriage. Alarmed by statistics showing that more than 50 percent of Jews are marrying out of the faith, the rabbi encouraged us not to send our kids off to college without "the talk." "Tell them that they can have friends from all over, but the person they marry should be Jewish," he said. I remarked that I've been working on it since my children were born. "How?" he asked. I explained that every night before I put my children to sleep, I have them say *sh'ma,* the Jewish creed: "Hear O Israel, the Lord Our God, the Lord is One." They're all still young, but they could no more go to sleep without *sh'ma* than without a pillow. It gives them comfort and closure on their day. Now, I don't pretend to think that my children won't intermarry because they say a Jewish prayer before nodding off. But in this way and in hundreds of others, I have given them a practice, a ritual, that reminds them they are Jewish—and not just in synagogue but in school, in the playground, at home, in the kitchen, and even in bed.

In recent years, several authors, from Alan Dershowitz to Herman Wouk, have written about a crisis in American Jewry. While Jewish political and economic power appears secure, our numbers are shrinking; "disappearing" is Dershowitz's word. The intermarriage rate—as high as 52 percent marry out of Judaism, according to the 1990 Jewish Population Survey—shows no sign of reversing its upward trend, and our birthrate is below the replacement rate. Several solutions have been advanced. For some, the solution is to open up Judaism by relaxing its rules and making conversions to the faith easier. Others say, target efforts toward the non-Jewish spouses of intermarried couples to bring them into Judaism. Others say, concentrate instead on the "core Jews"—those already members of the faith; build walls and fortify the faithful. Still others say, strengthen Jewish community centers where Jews can both study and socialize; others say, concentrate on improving and building synagogues. Others say that a fund must be supported to guarantee that every Jewish teen gets a trip to Israel; clearly, it is an experience that ties one to the land and the people. Still others talk about strengthening Jewish educational and social programs for college youth.

I say, start simple. Do a ritual. Light a candle, visit a synagogue, attend a seder, celebrate life in a Jewish way. I believe there is something intrinsically valuable about Jewish observance. Take the Sabbath. In our house, we do not watch television or cruise the Internet or even talk on the telephone from sundown Friday until the stars come out Saturday night. For some this deprivation might seem like a punishment, but for me it is bliss. Our week is so filled with outside intrusions that it is a blessing to have one day without them. It is one thing to do that alone, or even as a family, but to do it in connection with others all around the world can transform and enrich.

YOU DON'T HAVE TO DO IT ALL

To my mind, it is not necessary to shut out all intrusions; even dropping one of them has its benefits. Turn off the television, and you just might finish that book you've been reading. Forget the telephone, and you just might spend more time at the dinner table talking to your family and guests.

I've spent my life observing Jews. As a child from a divorced family, I grew up at the tables of my aunts and uncles, in kosher hotels with one parent or the other, and in the synagogue, which often served as a home away from home. I've always been a student of the many variations in religious practice. In my twenty years at the *New York Times*—ten of them spent covering religion—I made a living out of watching these different ways of practicing Judaism. I covered New Age Jewish retreats, staid rabbinical conventions, and exuberant Hasidic gatherings known as *farbrengens*. In addition, with this book in mind, I've conducted interviews with hundreds of Jews about their religious practices—both on the Internet and in person—in every denomination and in every region of the country. From all my years of observing Jews, I find one common thread: Jews are not consistent. Jews pick and choose from among the wide panoply of religious practices. In the words of the late Jacob Rader Marcus, the preeminent historian of American Jewry, who died in 1995 at the age of ninety-nine: "There are six million Jews in America and six million Judaisms."

Jews are not alone in their selective observance. American Roman Catholics, in fact, have a name for it: Cafeteria Catholicism. The image is of Catholics walking down the line with their cafeteria tray, taking what suits them. Some will agree with the Church on birth control but not on abortion. Some will want to see women as priests but not gays. Many revere the office of the Pope but vehemently disagree with the man in office.

Instead of Cafeteria Catholics, we are Smorgasbord Jews. No orderly cafeteria line for us. I use the term smorgasbord because the Jewish choices are so much greater. Traditional Judaism makes demands that Christianity, from its very start, dismissed: circumcise, eat only kosher meats, pray three times a day, don't mix milk and meat, don't work on the Sabbath, and on and on. American Jews come to the great table of Jewish observance and take what best suits them. No two buffet plates are the same.

There are Jews who keep kosher at home but not outside the home. Some observe the Sabbath by not working, and others keep it by going to synagogue. There are those who observe neither the kosher laws nor the Sabbath, but wouldn't dream of eating bread on Passover. Some won't keep any rituals but wouldn't think of buying a German car, listening to a Wagner opera, or reading Ezra Pound.

Even the Orthodox are subject to these variations. There are those who eat kosher and those who eat only *glatt* kosher (a higher level of kosher supervision). Some Orthodox men go to their jobs wearing large black hats; others go bareheaded. There are some married Orthodox women who cover their hair all the time—some with wigs, others with hats—and there are others who cover their hair only in the synagogue. There are Orthodox men who will not shake hands with women other than their wives, and there are those who do. Some go to synagogue for prayer twice a day; others go only on Saturdays and festivals.

One of the nation's leading sociologists of Judaism, Dr. Bethamie Horowitz, has conducted hundreds of in-depth interviews with Jews around the nation. Getting a precise picture of Jewish practice is difficult, she said, because Jewish religious practice is fluid and idiosyncratic, and reinvents itself constantly throughout the life of the believer. Dr. Horowitz added, "We need to widen the way we define Jewish identification to include the idiosyncratic things people relate to Jewishly."

REACHING FOR THE HOLY

I like to think of these inconsistencies as the Jewish attempt to reach for the holy. As we stand at the smorgasbord we take the items that are most meaningful to us, and that will make us better Jews. All of this makes Jews a very quirky people. There is no single way to be Jewish in America today. Let me give some examples from my "quirk file":

• Joe, a high school teacher and a big Red Sox fan from Boston, always has a hot dog on opening day at Fenway. Hot dogs at Fenway are not kosher, but that doesn't bother Joe, who considers himself an

American first and a Jew a distant second. One year, however, when opening day landed on Passover, Joe bought his hot dog, took it off the bun, and put it on a piece of matzah he had brought along just for that purpose.

• Phil works for a major weekly magazine that goes to press on Saturdays. He can't observe the Sabbath in the traditional manner, so he makes his own—beginning Monday night; for twenty-five hours, he does not work.

• Sam is an orthodontist with a busy practice in New Jersey. He neither prays, goes to synagogue, nor keeps any ritual laws, with one exception. Every morning, he puts on *tzitzit*, the four-cornered fringed undergarment worn by pious Jews. He wears the garment all day while he sees patients and while he eats his non-kosher meals. Why does he wear *tzitzit?* "I feel naked without them," he says.

• Katherine, a convert to Judaism, can't fast on Yom Kippur. She gets sick if she doesn't eat. So she spends the day with a fast of another kind: she doesn't speak for twenty-five hours.

• Charlie and his wife, Susan, do not keep kosher. But on the Sabbath they never eat bacon or shellfish. "It's our way of keeping Shabbos," Charlie explains.

• The Weinstein family in Detroit keeps a kosher home; there are separate dishes for meat and milk. But there is also a third set—Chinese—which they use only for non-Kosher takeout.

All of these are true stories; about real people. What has been changed here are their names. In fact, the vast majority of them did not want their names used—they consider these quirky practices to be private. Several admitted to being downright ashamed at their behavior, but for very different reasons. In some cases they felt they were doing too little; in other cases they felt they were doing too much. Perhaps the most poignant story for me came from my friend Bill (not his real name). Bill, a book editor, is not otherwise observant on a daily basis, but before he goes to sleep each night, he whispers the *sh'ma*. "I don't even think my wife knows," said Bill. "It's my own little private prayer."

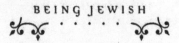
BEING JEWISH BY THE NUMBERS

Attend a Passover seder	85 percent
Don't have a Christmas tree	82 percent
Fast on Yom Kippur	61 percent
Light Hanukkah candles	77 percent
Light Sabbath candles	44 percent
Maintain synagogue or temple membership	41 percent
Have visited Israel	31 percent
Eat kosher meat exclusively	17 percent
Attend weekly religious services	11 percent

Source: The 1990 National Jewish Population Survey, based on telephone interviews with twenty-five hundred households. The survey became widely known for another finding, one that had to do with intermarriage. In the years 1985 to 1990, the survey found, 52 percent of marriages involving Jews were to a non-Jewish partner. This compared with statistics from the 1950s showing that 9 percent of Jewish marriages were to non-Jews.

I had known Bill for decades and never knew this about him. As a regular *sh'ma* sayer myself, I felt a new connection. "Do you say it with your kids?" I asked hopefully. "No," he said. "I never thought of it."

What has happened is that religious idiosyncrasies have gotten such a bad name that people don't want to talk about them, let alone pass them on to their children. I know this mind-set; I was brought up with it. The Orthodox rabbis of my youth did not subscribe to the more popular notion we find today that Judaism is a matter of choice for both converts and those born Jewish. They spoke about the "yoke of the kingdom of heaven," an obligation to follow the precepts of Torah right down to rigorous daily observances. Feeling good was not part of the system. To allow people to do what they felt good about Jewishly was to invite a kind of religious free-for-all that allows people to pick and choose what feels good to them.

Today, even some outside of the Orthodox world worry about this kind of anarchy. Writing recently in *Commentary* magazine, Jack Wertheimer, provost of the Conservative Jewish Theological Seminary, warned of those who advocate a "Judaism without limits," where a variety of choices and practices are incorporated into Judaism simply because they are trendy or they feel good. "Instead of setting clear lines," he wrote, "they enjoin Jews to lower the barriers between Jewish and non-Jewish religion. . . . This way lies not pluralism but anarchy, and self-extinction."

I'm not advocating extinction, but I do think a little anarchy can be healthy. Being Jewish *is* about feeling good. It *is* about finding meaning. For some, that might mean the ArtScroll *Shabbos Kitchen Guide,* but for others, it might mean eating lox and bagel or even a non-kosher hot dog on matzah. It might mean not talking on Yom Kippur, or having three sets of dishes, or saying the *sh'ma* silently on your bed.

The young assistant rabbi in my Manhattan Orthodox synagogue might not put it the way I do, but he, too, sees virtue in idiosyncratic practice. "Judaism gives you 613 opportunities to find God," said Rabbi Yair Silverman, referring to the 613 *mitzvot,* or commandments. "For each one you do, you do good."

"People are afraid of looking like hypocrites" by observing some laws and ignoring others, Rabbi Silverman added. "But they shouldn't be afraid. You should strive to be as great a Jew as you can be. Inconsistencies are part of human nature." He noted that the Jewish festivals, periods during which greater ritual observance is required, are meant to "highlight the extremes." The festivals "modulate the monotony of everyday life," he explained. "You don't live at the extremes. You climb to the top of the mountain to see the view. But you don't necessarily stay there."

Throughout this book, in sections labeled "variations on a theme," I will give other examples of how Jews live their Judaism—on their own terms. I will describe both what the tradition demands and what people actually do in their lives. My purpose is to elevate these practices and show how indeed they are all efforts to reach for the holy. Only if people are proud of them and have confidence in their idiosyncrasies will they endure.

WHERE DOES ONE BEGIN?

I believe that quirks reveal a desire on the part of American Jews to act in a Jewish way. While some may ask why they go to so much trouble, I wonder why they don't do more. Why doesn't Joe find a kosher hot dog? Why doesn't Sam go to synagogue? Why doesn't Bill say the *sh'ma* with his children? One rabbi told me that fear keeps many American Jews from performing rituals—fear of doing the wrong thing, fear of sitting in the wrong place, fear of not knowing the words to the prayer. I understand this fear. Many Jews, well educated at the best universities, know Homer and Shakespeare but never read Maimonides. They can order food at the best French restaurants but can't read the Passover haggadah. We've forgotten the lessons of the Angel Gabriel. Gabriel reminds us that we have a relationship with ritual that goes back to our very beginnings. And whether or not we want to believe that all that is part of our distant past, Gabriel reminds us that there are mentors and teachers and stories that can help us make Judaism a greater part of our lives.

My hope is to be one of those mentors—Gabriel's helper, if you will—by making Jewish ritual accessible for American Jews and others interested in the faith. I will explain what the tradition demands, what the rabbis allow, and what people actually do in their daily practice. In these pages, I offer a "toolbox" of Jewish ritual that I hope readers will open, explore, and experiment with. These are not magic incantations or rites. Lighting a candle is no more meaningful than picking up a hammer. What is important is how you use that candle to build a Sabbath experience in your home. Ritual has the power to take the mundane and make it holy and, with time, open the heart.

To my mind, the greater debate on the Jewish destiny can wait. What is important is to start with acts that proclaim that Jews are a people with a land, a history, wisdom, and a heart. Doing ritual acts makes those ideas concrete and connects us with our past, our God, and our people.

BOOK ONE

The Jewish Life

INTRODUCTION

Judaism has prescribed ways to mark the major life cycle events. Rites, rituals, and liturgies mark birth, the coming of age, marriage, and death. Rabbis can perform these straight out of the synagogue manual; each denomination has one. What is common to all the life cycle liturgies is that they are relatively short, especially compared with Sabbath and holiday synagogue services, which can stretch on for hours. Each of these life cycle ceremonies is liturgically simple, as if these moments are almost beyond words. Rabbi Judith Abrams, who runs a Talmud Web site, Maqom, once told me that the more important the event, the shorter the service. I wouldn't dare to rank the importance of the four life-cycle events in this section, but they are all short: a few blessings and a prayer of hope. The traditional wedding has seven blessings, a *brit* four, a bar mitzvah two, and a funeral one.

Blessings in Jewish liturgy tend to start with a formula: "Blessed art thou, Lord our God, King of the universe, who has sanctified us with Thy commandments, and commanded us . . ." The ending of the phrase depends on the ceremony at hand, i.e., "to marry," "to circumcise," "to study Torah." It is all methodically laid out.

What shapes these events beyond the liturgy is what the participants bring to the table. A family's values should be reflected in these events. The birth ceremonies are really about the hopes and dreams of parents; the bar and bat mitzvah represent a work in progress, a young man or woman emerging as an individual but still under the wing of parents; the wedding represents the dreams of a couple and their families; and the funeral reflects on a life.

There is enough flexibility in these rites for individual expression. While virtually every bar mitzvah boy reads the Torah, each one will do it in a different voice. While there is a manual, that doesn't mean you have to do it by the book. In the chapters that follow, I discuss the history and contemporary practice of these rituals and show how American Jews have succeeded in making them their own.

CHAPTER ONE

Beginnings

Judaism, from its beginnings, has been obsessed with fertility. Abraham, as the first Jew, knew that his discovery of the Oneness of God would amount to little if he did not have a child with his wife, Sarah. But "Sarah was barren," Genesis reports; "she could not give birth." Yet, God promises Abraham offspring "as numerous as the stars" and "as plentiful as the sands of the earth." When three visitors appear and promise Abraham a child through Sarah, she laughs with a mixture of disbelief and delight. It is a great moment—one of the only times in the Bible that anybody laughs. The name she gives her son, Isaac, comes from the Hebrew *tzechok*, laughter. Isaac's wife Rebecca is also barren, and so is Rachel, the favorite wife of Jacob. But in response to their prayers, God intervenes there too; they bear children and, through them, the Jewish people.

In Judaism, the birth of a child is a fulfillment of a dream. In a sense, every Jewish child is an Isaac, worthy of being welcomed with laughter and celebration. In birth ceremonies, we give the child a Jewish identity by giving a Jewish name. In the case of boys, the identity is cut into the flesh in the act of the *brit*, or circumcision. Boys are named at their *brit*; girls, either in a special naming ceremony, known as a *simchat bat*, or when one or both of their parents are called to the Torah in the synagogue. The formal naming is so significant that traditionally the name

of the child is not revealed until the moment of the religious ceremony. For that reason, you will often see bassinets in maternity wards
with a last name and the word "Baby" filled in where the first name
should be, as in "Baby Rabinowitz." These are often the babies of Orthodox parents who are waiting for the formal ceremony to give the
name. The official Hebrew name, usually an analogue of the English
(Yosef for Joseph, Rivka for Rebecca) is completed not with the family
name but with the name of the parents. Thus, it would be Yosef ben
Avraham V'Sorah (Joseph the son of Abraham and Sarah), or Rivka bat
Yitzchak V'Rachel (Rebecca the daughter of Isaac and Rachel). While
it is not required, children are often named after relatives, although
there is a difference of opinion as to which relatives are so honored.
Jews of Middle Eastern origin name children after their living or deceased relatives; most European Jews name them only for relatives
who have died.

A name is a powerful legacy. Our youngest child, Judah, was born
just five weeks after the death of my mother, Judith Goldman, from
cancer at the age of seventy. Giving Judah my mother's name provided
enormous comfort—and a lasting connection to her. My mother
would want to be remembered first as a religious woman, but she also
believed in adventure, in love, and in life. She had two homes, one
in Manhattan and the other in the tony Connecticut town of
Westport. On Saturdays, you'd find her with her head covered in the
women's balcony of the Fifth Avenue Synagogue in Manhattan, but
during the week, she'd be driving around Westport in her white con-
vertible, the top down and the radio blaring. Judah, an energetic
preschooler who does cartwheels down the halls of our Manhattan
apartment, has much of her spirit. Sometimes I even find myself calling him "Judy."

THE *BRIT*

Boys are circumcised on the eighth day, just as Abraham circumcised
his son Isaac, some four thousand years ago. "This is my covenant," God

tells Abraham in Genesis, "which you shall keep, between me and you and your offspring after you: Every male among you shall be circumcised . . . when he is eight days old."

A circumcision can be postponed if the child is sick or otherwise at risk, such as in the case of a premature baby, but the tradition to perform the ritual on the eighth day is strong, even if the eighth day turns out to be the Sabbath or Yom Kippur, the holiest day of the year. To be considered a ritual act, the circumcision—the removal of the foreskin that covers the penis—must be done in a religious ceremony. A circumcision performed by a doctor in the hospital without the attendant blessings and intentions is not considered a religious rite. Religious circumcisions are often performed by a trained practitioner, known as a *mohel,* at a celebration that is held in either the home, the hospital, or the synagogue.

The popularity of circumcision, once a standard practice in America for most of the twentieth century, is apparently on the wane. Thirty years ago, about 90 percent of boys in the United States were circumcised; the most recent figures from the National Center for Health Statistics show that the rate has fallen to 62 percent. The American Academy of Pediatrics, which for decades favored the procedure on the grounds that it had medical benefits, reversed itself in 1999. "Circumcision is not essential to a child's well-being at birth," the group, with fifty-one thousand members, said.

Individual doctors take positions one way or the other. Some health authorities say that to circumcise is to ensure a cleaner, healthier male who will have greater pleasure during sex. Circumcision is said by these authorities to reduce the risk of contracting urinary tract infections. Uncircumcised males have a higher incidence of penile cancer as well as a higher risk of contracting HIV infections and other sexually transmitted diseases, they say. Other health authorities say that the traumas and dangers of such surgery are so great that any positive byproducts are to be discounted. The risks of infection can be effectively reduced by proper hygiene. Besides, they add in direct contradiction of circumcision advocates, sex is better with a foreskin.

"For every health argument, you can find a counterargument," said Rabbi Jeffrey Kamins of Sydney, Australia, who was on sabbatical in Israel with me. His congregation is Reform, but still, most members opt for circumcision. "Every once in a while you get a couple who doesn't want one. I go through the arguments with them. I'm not going to say that it's painless. It hurts, but isn't it better to do it now than for your child to grow up and want one? It's a lot simpler in infancy. As for trauma, ask any Jewish man if he's had surgery, and chances are, unless he's had his appendix out, he'll say no. Who remembers their *brit*? There are no lasting harmful effects. Sure, it's tough to do, but part of being a parent is making tough choices."

It is significant that a Reform rabbi advocates for *brit*. One hundred fifty years ago, in the early days of the Reform movement, some of its theologians argued that circumcision should be rejected as a bloody throwback to antiquity. In 1843 in Germany, where Reform Judaism was founded, some of its leaders attempted to abolish the practice on several grounds, including the fact that there is no parallel initiation rite in Judaism for girls. Abraham Geiger, an early Reform leader, described circumcision as "a barbaric, bloody act, which fills the father with fear."

Over the years, Reform Judaism softened its opposition and today recommends that parents circumcise their sons. In Reform and Reconstructionist Judaism, however, *brit* is not required, as it is among the Orthodox and Conservative branches.

Rabbi Kamins tells the parents that whether or not they opt for the *brit*, "your child will still be Jewish," an opinion shared even by the Orthodox. But he adds, "Think about where your son stands regarding the Jewish community." To be a Jewish male is to be circumcised. In ancient times an uncircumcised male could not fully participate in the seder by eating the Passover sacrifice. Some religious authorities today say that someone without a *brit* should not be called to the Torah in synagogue.

Both of those acts—eating at the Passover sacrifice and being called to the Torah—demonstrate one's attachment to the Jewish people.

"*Brit* links the child to the Jewish community," said Rabbi Elie Spitz, the head of a Conservative congregation near Irvine, California. "It's not simply a tribal act, but a statement of linkage to God. What makes the Jewish people a religious people is that we live our life moments in God's embrace. In this moment of *brit* the child is given an identity in covenant with God."

Creating a child involves not only mother and father, he adds, "but a presence of God that makes the moment transcendent, providing miracle and meaning. At a *brit,* all these things come together: the wonder and fear of being a parent, the sense of discovery of who this child is, and the wonder that out of an act of sex comes a human being."

For me, *brit* is not only a statement of Judaism but a declaration that one is not a Christian. God's covenant with Abraham still stands despite what was once a pervasive Christian theology that said that the Jews lost the covenant because they failed to live up to it. What's important, Paul says in the New Testament book of Romans, is "to be circumcised in the heart, not in the flesh."

For a Jew to affirm circumcision at the beginning of the third millennium, then, means much as it did four thousand years ago when Abraham circumcised Isaac. Back then, Abraham was just breaking with his clan; but today, the act of ritual circumcision is a counterpoint to Christianity. To circumcise today is to proclaim publicly and boldly that we are still circumcised in the flesh, bound to the everlasting Covenant of Abraham.

THE CEREMONY FOR BOYS

Preparations for the ritual begin when the baby is born. The parents have to find a *mohel* and decide whether to hold the circumcision in the home or the synagogue. Arrangements must be made for the *seudah*, a light celebratory meal that follows the circumcision. A time must be set. By tradition, the *brit* is held early in the morning on the eighth day.

On the night before the *brit*, some families gather around the newborn's bassinet to observe a special night of watching, in German *Wachnacht*. In Jewish folklore—a world populated by spirits, some of them good, most of them bad—the uncircumcised male is particularly vulnerable. He does not yet bear the sign of the covenant and therefore can fall prey to the mightiest female demon, Lilith. Sometimes identified as the first wife of Adam before the creation of Eve, Lilith is said to prey on males, women in childbirth, and especially newborn babies. Even a full-grown man should be wary of sleeping alone, lest Lilith seduce him. From his nocturnal emissions, she bears an infinite number of demonic sons.

In some Sephardic homes, candles are lit throughout the house and incense is burned. Among the Jews of Greece, the mother stays awake all night. Among Ashkenazic Jews, the mother sleeps, but the father stays up late into the night studying sacred texts. Brothers and sisters will sing lullabies to comfort the infant. Among the Jews of Yemen, a white lamb is slaughtered the morning of the *brit*, both as a symbolic sacrifice in which one soul is given for the safety of another and, on a more practical level, to provide food for the celebratory *seudah*. Most

American Jews will just order lox and bagels. The *brit* is bloody enough without a slaughtered lamb.

A *brit* is a community celebration. Traditionally, one does not invite friends to a *brit* but just informs them that the *brit* is taking place. The parents might call and say "The *brit* will be held Wednesday at eight," rather than "You're invited to join us." There's no time for RSVPs. It is understood that all are welcome. According to the Talmud, the religious obligation to circumcise falls on the father, just as it fell on Abraham. If the father is unable to perform the rite, it is the responsibility of the Jewish community; if the community fails to step in and the child grows to manhood without being circumcised, the obligation falls on the man himself to fulfill the commandment.

It is a tough thing to do, to cut the foreskin of your son, shed his blood for what you believe. Here, too, the ancient figure of Abraham serves as an inspiration. Abraham fulfilled his obligation to circumcise his son Isaac, but God wanted more. The same God who had promised to multiply Abraham's children like the sands and the stars, later in Genesis tells Abraham to sacrifice his beloved Isaac. "Take your son, your only son Isaac, whom you love, and go to the land of Moriah, and offer him there as a burnt offering upon one of the mountains of which I shall tell you." Abraham wastes no time in the pursuit of God's will. "So Abraham rose early in the morning," the story continues. He takes Isaac, a knife, and firewood, and marches to the top of Mount Moriah and prepares the sacrifice. As everyone knows, Abraham was lucky. An angel stayed his hand.

I think every Jewish father, in the moments before his son's *brit*, secretly wishes for another visitation by God's angel. Happily, Jewish law allows for a surrogate in the person of the *mohel*, a professional with a steady hand specially trained in the art of circumcision. In the traditional ceremony, the *mohel*, with the scalpel in his hand, turns to the father and asks, "Do you designate me as your messenger?" With the father's assent, the cutting begins.

The place that is cut is at once the most sensitive and most potent part of the male body. As in any operation, there is risk, but there is also great symbolism. The child is connected to Jewish history through the cutting of his reproductive organ, an organ through which he will some day pass his Judaism on to another generation. The moment of the *brit*, then, is a link between the Jewish past and the Jewish future.

To represent this continuity between the generations, older members of the family take a central role in the ceremony. The *kvaterin*, a grandmother or other senior member of the family, brings the baby into the room, passing the child from one relative to another until it reaches the *sandek*, the grandfather or other elder of the family. The *sandek* holds the infant during the operation but first gently places the child on a special chair called *kesai shel Eliyahu*, the chair of Elijah, symbolizing that, like Elijah, every child has the potential to bring the Messiah—or to be the Messiah.

After the operation, a blessing is said over a cup of wine, and the baby is given a name. It is customary to dip a piece of gauze in the wine and let the baby suck; just a drop, I've found, always eases the baby's crying. A prayer is then offered that the child grow "to Torah, the wedding canopy, and good deeds." The prayer sets an agenda for life and reminds me of what one older friend once told me about being a parent. "You're not raising children," he said. "You're raising adults." The *brit* is the first step.

THE CEREMONY FOR GIRLS

A baby girl's entry into the Jewish community was traditionally marked by her father's being called to the Torah in the synagogue on the Sabbath after the birth. The father would first make a blessing for the health of the girl and the recovery of the mother and then bestow a Hebrew name on the newborn. The mother and daughter were rarely present.

Since the advent of the women's movement in the 1970s, ceremonies celebrating the birth of a daughter have become more popular. But they didn't have to start from scratch. In the traditional Jewish

PIDYON HA'BEN

When a firstborn son reaches the age of thirty days, a special ceremony called *pidyon ha'ben* takes place in the presence of a *kohen*, a Jew who is a descendant of the priestly family of Aaron, the brother of Moses. The *pidyon ha'ben*, which is mentioned in the book of Numbers, derives from the idea that the first and best of everything we possess belongs to God. In the *pidyon ha'ben*, the father redeems the firstborn from the *kohen* by giving him five silver coins, as mentioned in the Torah (Numbers 18:15–16): "The first born of man you shall redeem . . . and their redemption money shall be . . . five shekels of silver."

Not everyone qualifies for a *pidyon ha'ben*. It is a ceremony only for boys, and I know of no corollary for girls; the Torah is quite explicit that this is a rite for males. Also, the boy must be the first fruit of the womb, delivered naturally and not by cesarean section. And a *pidyon ha'ben* is not performed if the child's mother or father is either a *kohen* or a *levi*, the tribe that assisted the priestly class in its temple work.

Most who are experienced in this rite have on hand five silver coins that they then transfer to the father of the newborn before the ceremony. The ceremony itself is quite simple. The father brings the newborn before the priest and proclaims that the baby is the first fruit of the mother's womb. The *kohen* then asks the father, "Which do you prefer, to give me your son or to redeem him?" Luckily, the *pidyon ha'ben* takes place when the baby is just thirty days old. A year or two later, this might be a harder question to answer. The father says, "To redeem him." The father then hands the silver coins to the *kohen* and recites a blessing to the God "who commanded me to redeem my son."

The priest then blesses the newborn with the priestly blessing, and the father says a prayer of thanksgiving called *shehecheyanu*.

communities of Yemen, for example, women for centuries held a service called the *zebed habat,* the Gift of a Daughter. Women of the community would come and sit with the mother and child to admire both with songs of praise. Women would bring gifts of incense and candles and fertility symbols, such as live chickens and "star water" (water exposed to the heavens for seven nights). This was to ensure the continued fertility of the mother and the eventual fertility of the newborn.

Today's ceremonies for girls are focused less on fertility, and both men and women participate. Known as the *simchat bat,* the Joy of the Daughter, the ceremony is a time to welcome the newborn into the community of Israel, both male and female. The practice can today be found in all the branches of Judaism.

Rather than hold the *simchat bat* on the eighth day, a time when the mother may not have fully recovered and the infant is still fragile, families decide on the most convenient time, usually within a month of the birth. Some will wait for the beginning of the next Jewish month, known in Hebrew as Rosh Hodesh, a time that coincides with the cycle of the moon, which is of special significance to Jewish women. The new moon is traditionally seen as a special holiday for women, whose bodies are biologically in tune with the cycles of nature.

Simchat bat ceremonies by their very nature are more relaxed and spontaneous than the *brit* ceremony. I've seen grown men faint and most men admit to feeling a little weak at the knees at the sight (or even mention) of a circumcision. The baby boy's cry when he is cut has no echo at the *simchat bat.*

While the liturgy for the *brit* ceremony can be found in any prayer book, the ceremony for girls is constantly updated. The Jewish feminist Arlene Agus has collected a whole file of these ceremonies, some of them handsomely printed on glossy paper but most written by hand and photocopied for the participants. A ritual guide published by the Jewish Women's Resource Network, a national group based in Manhattan, suggests that the ceremonies include songs, blessings, wine, and a celebratory meal. "And not to be forgotten," the guide adds, "the ceremony should be fun." Rabbi Kamins told me that in his community

VARIATION ON A THEME: GENTILE CIRCUMCISION

Ben is Jewish. His wife, Alicia, is not. When their son Jeremy was born, Ben told the obstetrician that he wanted Jeremy circumcised. "Oh, I can do it," the doctor volunteered. But Ben resisted. "I wasn't going to let that *Gentile* do it," he confided to me. I was surprised that he used the term with such derision—after all, both his wife and his son were Gentiles. Instead of using the Gentile doctor, Ben called a *mohel*. When the *mohel* asked if the mother was Jewish, Ben lied and said yes. The *mohel* said that he'd be there on the eighth day of the child's life, as is customary. But Ben had to go out of town and said he wanted to do it sooner. The *mohel* explained that the ritual circumcision takes place on the eighth day unless there is a medical problem, in which case the circumcision can be postponed. So Ben fessed up. "Okay, I lied," he said. "My wife is not Jewish. Can you come tomorrow?" The *mohel* agreed. He performed the circumcision but without the blessings that are said when the ceremony is a *brit*. When Ben thanked him, the *mohel* said, "You know, you didn't really need a *mohel*. Any Gentile could do this just as well."

in Sydney, the women bring their Sabbath candlesticks to the *simchat bat* and light them to serve as a backdrop to the ceremony. The newborn is passed from woman to woman, but instead of being handed over for surgery, she is placed on a bed of flowers and is formally named by her parents.

Haviva Ner-David, an Orthodox Jewish feminist who lives in Israel, took her newborn daughters to the *mikveh*, the ritual bath, to mark their entrance into the Covenant of Abraham. She based the custom on the commentary of Rabbi Menachem ben Solomon, who lived in Provence in the late thirteenth century. Rabbi ben Solomon, known as the Meiri, suggested that Abraham's wife, Sarah, immersed herself in the *mikveh* as a sign of her connection to God when Abraham was circumcised. In her book *Life on the Fringes*, Ner-David writes: "There can be no more appropriate ritual to bring our daughter, the product of our love and partnership with God, into the Jewish people. There can be no more appropriate means than *mikvah*, the ritual bath in which women throughout Jewish history have been immersing themselves after the cessation of their menstrual flow, for me to initiate my daughter into Jewish womanhood, with all its joys and conflicts, trials and responsibilities."

Ner-David was nervous about putting her newborn underwater, but was assured by her doctor and her husband that it would be all right. She concludes: "I blew into her face so that she would instinctively hold her breath, and then I dunked her. . . . I put what is most precious to me in the hands of God."

The trip to the *mikveh* might work for Ner-David, but some rabbis feel that it smacks of Christian baptism and should be avoided. An alternative that I heard about at a meeting of Orthodox feminists involves holding a special ceremony for the infant girl during which her ears are pierced. The act of cutting the ear has echoes in the Bible—in Exodus, a Jewish servant is permanently bound with such an act to his master. In this context, piercing the ears can be a sign of the newborn's attachment to God. And such a ceremony outdoes the *brit*, if only because there are two ears.

A SIGN OF THE COVENANT

The Bible refers to the mark of male circumcision as "*ot brit*"—a sign of the covenant. The guide from the Jewish Women's Resource Network comments: "Since women do not have a permanent sign of the covenant cut into them, some parents like to supply their daughter with an external sign." The *simchat bat* is a time to make a public presentation by the parents of a gift that will be a reminder of the day.

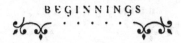
Among the suggested gifts are Sabbath candlesticks, a silver wine goblet, or a Hebrew Bible.

One enduring gift that parents can give a child, boy or girl, on the day of the baby's naming is a letter in which they detail their decision to give the child a particular name. Parents often use the occasion of the ceremony to give a short talk on the name. They tell the assembled who the child is named for or what attributes of the name they especially identify with. Rabbi Stuart Kelman, who leads a Conservative congregation in Berkeley, California, urges parents to write down their thoughts in a letter and save it for the child. Who wouldn't love to have such a letter from his or her parents? he asks. Each new life brings a hope so pure and horizons unlimited. Jewish ritual helps you capture and preserve those feelings.

The Basics

BIBLICAL ORIGINS "Every male among you shall be circumcised. And you shall be circumcised in the flesh of your foreskin, and it shall be a token of a covenant between Me and you. And he that is eight days old shall be circumcised among you, every male throughout your generations" (Genesis 17:11–12).

THE OPERATION The foreskin is surgically removed from the head of the penis.

VOCABULARY In Hebrew, the circumcision is called a *brit,* which literally means covenant. The man who performs the *brit* is a *mohel* (plural: *mohalim*). A woman is known as a *mohelet* (plural: *mohalot*). If a man is already circumcised surgically and wants a ritual circumcision as well, a *mohel* makes a symbolic incision in the head of the penis in a procedure known as *hatafat dam brit.*

PURPOSE The Bible is silent on any motive. In Jewish history, the *brit* has served to distinguish Jews from others. The operation was also a deterrent against conversion into Judaism. Some see in the act a message of sexual restraint.

FIRST RECORDED CIRCUMCISION Abraham, at age ninety-nine.

SECOND Ishmael, at age thirteen.

THIRD Isaac, at eight days.

CODE OF JEWISH LAW (*Shulchan Aruch*) It is a father's duty to have his son circumcised. If the father does not act, the community must step in and ensure that the boy is circumcised. If the boy grows to adulthood without a circumcision, the duty falls on the man himself. When possible, the circumcision should be done on the eighth day of life. If the *brit* would endanger the child, the operation can be postponed. The ritual is so sacred that it can even be performed on the Sabbath if it is the eighth day.

BLESSINGS The father (or sometimes both parents) makes two blessings, acknowledging that he is initiating this act to bring the child "into the covenant of Abraham our father." Those gathered respond: "Even as he has been introduced into the covenant, so may he be introduced to the Torah, the marriage canopy, and to a life of good deeds." The *mohel* makes two additional blessings, one on the act of cutting and another on a glass of wine.

HONORS *Sandek*, a man who holds the child during the circumcision. *Kvaterin*, a woman who presents the infant for the ritual.

WHO CAN CIRCUMCISE According to tradition, a Jewish man. If there is no one else available, the tradition allows a woman to do the *brit*.

MODERN INNOVATIONS The *simchat bat* celebration for girls, a new custom found in all the branches of Judaism. Among the non-Orthodox, there is also a movement to involve women in the boy's circumcision. Women (usually pediatricians or gynecologists) are trained in the non-Orthodox movements to act as *mohalot*.

CHAPTER TWO

Coming of Age

Parents have no greater responsibility in Judaism than to educate their children. They are supposed to forsake every spiritual and material comfort so that a child learns Torah. "You shall teach your children," the Torah commands. The Talmud adds that one may not neglect teaching children, even in order to fulfill the highest communal aspirations: the rebuilding of the Holy Temple in Jerusalem. The Talmud tells the story of the mother of the third-century sage Rabbi Joshua ben Hananiah, who took him in his cradle to the house of study "so that his ears would become attuned to the words of Torah." There is a moment when childhood learning comes into full flower and passes from preparation to obligation. That moment is the bar mitzvah for a boy and a bat mitzvah for a girl, when the young person becomes a full member of the community.

Bar mitzvah is marked at the thirteenth birthday; bat mitzvah at either the twelfth or the thirteenth. The ceremony roughly coincides with the arrival of puberty, but it assumes much more than the onset of sexual maturity. The bar mitzvah boy or bat mitzvah girl takes his or her place in the synagogue with an act that only adults can perform: an *aliyah* to the Torah.

What is an *aliyah?* Four times a week in the synagogue—on Mondays, on Thursdays, and twice on Saturdays—the Torah scroll is taken from the ark, placed on a table, and publicly chanted in Hebrew. Adult members of the community are called to the Torah to make a blessing on the portion to be read. This is called an *aliyah*, literally a going up, as one rises to the Torah scroll.

"Rise up," the cantor begins and calls a Jew by the name he or she is given at birth. The bar mitzvah boy or bat mitzvah girl approaches and says the blessings over the Torah that recall the chosenness of the Jewish people and Judaism's promise of "everlasting life." To varying degrees, Hebrew is the language of bar and bat mitzvah. In some congregations, the ceremony is wall-to-wall Hebrew, and in others a minimum of Hebrew is used, but virtually all bar mitzvah boys and bat mitzvah girls will chant the blessings in Hebrew beginning with the words "*Barchu et Adonai Hamevorach*," Bless the Lord who is blessed.

The Torah blessings end with the Hebrew words "*notein ha Torah*," acknowledging God, the "Giver of the Torah." There is significance in the use of the present tense. It is not that God gave the Torah thousands of years ago on Sinai but that God repeatedly gives the Torah in each generation and to each person. At the bar and bat mitzvah, children accept the commandments as their own.

With bar mitzvah, all the obligations of Jewish adulthood fall on the new teenager, such as fasting on Yom Kippur, observing the Sabbath, and keeping the kosher laws. Above all, becoming a bar or bat mitzvah requires that one keeps the *mitzvah* of studying Torah. Coming of age is a beginning, not an end.

THE TRAINING

After the recitation of the first blessing, the child often reads from the Scripture. How much he or she reads depends on the child's skills and the congregation's custom, and can range anywhere from three verses to several hundred. The readings can be from the Torah portion, taken from the five books of Moses, or from the Haftorah, taken from the

prophetic books of the Bible. To prepare for this moment, Jewish boys and girls study for months or even years.

Some children prepare for bar and bat mitzvah on two tracks. First, they study Hebrew and Jewish custom together with other bar and bat mitzvah candidates at their synagogue, temple, or Jewish day school. Second, they have a private tutor to prepare their particular biblical portion. Their portion is determined by the date of their twelfth or thirteenth birthday on the Hebrew calendar. Usually families try to schedule the bar or bat mitzvah for the Sabbath immediately after the birthday.

The portion is chanted in a system of cantillation called *ta'amei hamikra* (known as *layning* in Yiddish), which was developed over centuries and codified in tenth-century Tiberias by a scholar named Aaron ben Moses Ben-Asher. Each word in the Torah has a graphic symbol over or under it that indicates how it is to be read.

Some parents forgo the tutor and teach their children the reading and cantillation themselves. I've kept up my Torah skills since my bar mitzvah enough to enable me to teach my elder son, Adam, his bar mitzvah portion. I am now preparing my daughter Emma for her bat mitzvah. Although there have been moments of struggle, it has been an important bonding experience. My most effective threat to get their attention has been, "Listen, if you don't make progress with me, I'll have to get you a bar mitzvah teacher."

Bar mitzvah tutors have a bad name, but there are some marvelous ones out there. Several years ago, I wrote an article for *The New York Times* about a cantor in New Rochelle, New York, Lawrence Avery, who was much loved by his bar and bat mitzvah students. I caught up with him while he was teaching his one thousandth student, thirteen-year-old Pamela Bookman. Pamela's mother couldn't get over the attention that the cantor lavished on her daughter. "It's not like Pamela is his first student, it's like she's his only one," said Arlene Bookman.

Although popular Jewish literature is replete with stories of bar mitzvah boys who panic and flee the synagogue (it's always the boys, never the girls), Cantor Avery told me that everyone rises to the challenge. "There is no such thing as a kid who can't sing," he said, pausing for effect. "They may not sing on pitch, but they can sing."

Some boys and girls also give a short discourse on their Torah reading to demonstrate that they have mastered not just the words and chants but the meaning. A parent or teacher usually helps prepare these, but it is still impressive that the kid can deliver it. Depending on the congregation, the discourse might be delivered in the synagogue or at the festive meal or party that follows.

I remember my own bar mitzvah fondly. It was held in Queens at the Young Israel of Jackson Heights in 1963. My bar mitzvah teacher had taught me how to incorporate Hebrew and Hasidic songs into the prayer service. It was held right before my voice changed, so I hit all the high notes with ease. I sang my little heart out. My Torah and Haftorah readings were also impeccable. The one disaster was my bar mitzvah speech. It was written in Hebrew as a joint effort of my father and my rabbi. I didn't understand a word, but I had practiced hard and committed it to memory. I was so confident that I showed up in *shul* without the text. But when I got halfway through the speech, my mind went blank. I couldn't remember the rest. I paused for a moment, collected my thoughts, and then started all over again. I delivered the first half of the speech again and then sat down. Nobody seemed to notice.

THE MEANING

The bar mitzvah or bat mitzvah rite represents a new stage of religious and personal development for the child. At this stage, the child is given the intellectual tools to engage the tradition on his or her own. Ideally, reading the Torah is not simply mouthing the words that one has heard before but adding something to them and ultimately changing them in the process. Like fingerprints, every voice is different; by chanting the ancient text, you make it your own. Once you master your portion, it becomes yours. And once you master one, you can prepare other portions.

Many children learn Hebrew just for the bar or bat mitzvah (and forget it soon afterward). Yet, some familiarity with Hebrew is key. Although the Roman Catholic Church abandoned the idea of a universal language for prayer in the 1960s as one of the reforms of the Second Vatican Council, the language of Jewish prayer remains Hebrew. Latin may be dead, but Hebrew is very much alive, and knowing it means that you can pray in any Jewish congregation in the world.

There is also an important element of public witness in bar and bat mitzvah. Unlike other life cycle events, the coming-of-age ceremony occurs in a service that would happen even without the child who is being celebrated. *Brit*, wedding, and funeral are all special events for which friends and family gather. But a bar mitzvah comes in the middle of the regular synagogue service. The bar mitzvah boy or bat mitzvah girl joins the congregation, not the other way around. In a significant balance, the boy or girl is at once the center of attention and part of the regular flow of the Sabbath service.

CHILDREN OF DIVORCE

Bar mitzvah is a difficult rite of passage for any twelve- or thirteen-year-old. If the child is from a divorced family, the challenge is even greater. In most cases, parents who divorce don't want to have much to do with each other, but here they are being asked to coordinate a public event in the synagogue and a party for their child. All sorts of issues are raised: Who pays? Who gets an *aliyah*? Who speaks? If the parents have remarried, the questions multiply: How are the stepparents recognized? If one of the stepparents is not Jewish, there are even more questions: How are they acknowledged in what is primarily a Jewish event?

There are no simple answers, except for one: Focus on the child. Under no circumstances allow the child to be caught in the middle. Possibly the worst thing you can do is make two bar or bat mitzvah events, one for the mother's family and one for the father's family. Remember, there is one child—and he or she is what is important. It may be uncomfortable for the adults, but celebrating the child together is what is central.

Such events must be carefully negotiated. In the best of cases, the bar or bat mitzvah can be an opportunity for healing in which the parents show that they can put their personal animosities aside for the sake of the child. Divorced parents may not be able to make it all sweet, but they can demonstrate to the child that he has two sets of parents who love him and want to see him come of age as a Jew.

In so doing, the child makes a public statement that he or she is part of a larger Jewish community. The celebrant also makes a statement to those outside the Jewish community who have come to the synagogue for the occasion: the child's schoolmates and the parents' friends, neighbors, and business associates.

To the non-Jewish schoolmate, the whole spectacle is exotic. The visitor may be thinking, "Here's my friend, the boy I play soccer with, and he wears this funny thing on his head and a shawl with fringes and is speaking in a foreign language."

In effect, the bar mitzvah boy or bat mitzvah girl is saying, "Yes, I'm different. I may go to the same school as you and play on the same soccer team, but this is also part of my life. I am a Jew—and I'm a Jew who reads Torah."

If in *brit* the parents declare the child a Jew as part of the Covenant of Abraham, at bar mitzvah the child himself or herself makes the declaration, accepting the second Jewish covenant: the Covenant of Moses at Sinai.

One's fundamental responsibilities as a Jew change with bar and bat mitzvah. According to tradition, if a minor sins, the parents bear the responsibility for the transgression. It is only after bar or bat mitzvah that the child is held fully accountable for his or her actions. This shift is articulated in a prayer said in Orthodox congregations when a boy rises for his first *aliyah*. The father of the bar mitzvah says: "Blessed is the one who has freed me from the responsibilities for this" child.

This prayer, with its emphasis on sin and responsibility, is not said in most Conservative and Reform congregations. Many of these congregations, however, give the mother and father of the bar or bat mitzvah the opportunity to say a few words to their child. Rabbi Kelman of Berkeley urges parents not to squander the occasion by simply saying how great the child is and how much they love him or her ("they should have done that already") but to use it as a teaching moment. Some parents will use religious texts or family histories to talk about the importance of this moment.

With the rise in Jewish-Christian marriages, there are an increasing number of non-Jewish parents of bar mitzvah boys and bat mitzvah girls. By and large, these are parents who agreed to raise their children as Jews. While the non-Jewish parents are not able to get an *aliyah* to the Torah, some rabbis do allow them to address the child in the synagogue. Rabbi Kelman recalled giving one non-Jewish father the opportunity to speak—"It's his kid too," he reasoned. The rabbi added that he was delighted when he found that the father, a Christian, chose to talk to his son about the importance of being Jewish. "This is your heritage," the father said. "And in a very real sense, it is mine also."

THE HISTORY

There is no explicit mention of bar or bat mitzvah in the Torah. But according to Jewish folklore, thirteen is the age of moral and spiritual choices, even among Biblical characters. In a rabbinic elaboration on Genesis, Abraham smashes his father's idols on the way to declaring his belief in the oneness of God. One rabbi suggests that he was thirteen at the time. In a rabbinic elaboration on Exodus, Miriam, the older sister of Moses, tells her parents they must continue to have children despite Pharaoh's decree that infant boys be thrown into the Nile. Miriam insists that they sleep together. She too must have been thirteen, another rabbi suggests.

The first explicit reference in sacred texts about an age of obligation comes in a passage from the *Mishna Avot*. In this text, a second-century scholar, Judah ben Temah, comments on the stages of a man's life: "At five, one should study Scripture; at ten, one should study *Mishna;* at thirteen, one is ready to do *mitzvot;* at fifteen, one is ready to study Talmud; at eighteen, one is ready for the wedding canopy; at twenty, one is responsible for a family."

The "one" mentioned here is clearly a boy. Thirteen is the age of obligation, both on a personal and on a communal level. With the coming of age, a boy can be called to the Torah and be counted as a member of a *minyan,* the quorum required for public prayer. For girls, the Talmud adds, the passage to religious maturity occurs at the age of twelve. But the girl's obligations, as outlined in the Talmud, are more of a private than of a public nature. She is personally responsible to keep many of the commandments, but she cannot conduct any of the synagogue rituals that are open to a boy.

There is no evidence in the early literature, however, that any special ceremony was held to mark this passage into religious adulthood for either boys or girls. Curiously, the first reference is not about an *aliyah* to the Torah but about food. The sixteenth-century code of law, the *Shulchan Aruch,* declares: "It is the obligation of the father to tender a festive meal in honor of his son's bar mitzvah, just as he might do when the boy marries." In seventeenth-century Germany, boys who had a good voice were invited to lead part of the Sabbath service. And in the eighteenth century, also in Germany, boys delivered a public discourse, a *d'var Torah,* on their Torah portion.

THE FIRST BAT MITZVAH

There is no record of a bat mitzvah ceremony until the twentieth century. The first one occurred in 1922 when Rabbi Mordecai Kaplan, the founder of the fourth branch of Judaism, Reconstructionism, held a bat mitzvah for his daughter, Judith, at his Manhattan synagogue, the Society for the Advancement of Judaism. This break with tradition was consistent with Kaplan's philosophy that Judaism was not a static set of rules but, to use his word, an evolving "civilization." On the seventieth anniversary of that first bat mitzvah, I spoke with Kaplan's daughter, Judith Kaplan Eisenstein, as she was being honored by Jewish feminists at a dinner in New York City. She recalled that on the Friday night before the event, her father still had not decided the exact form of the ceremony. When the day dawned, Rabbi Kaplan ran a traditional service. The Torah and Haftorah were read by men, as always. His daughter was not called to the Torah. But after the reading, she stood and recited the blessing and read the scripture from her prayer book from what she recalled as "a very respectable distance."

Later, she added, "The scroll was returned to the ark with song and procession, and the service was resumed. No thunder sounded, no lightning struck. The institution of bat mitzvah had been born without incident."

The idea of a bat mitzvah for girls took many years to catch fire. It did not gain force until it met up with the feminism of the 1970s. When I was preparing for my bar mitzvah in 1962, a parallel rite for girls was virtually unheard of. Even my wife, who is eleven years my junior and the daughter of a Conservative rabbi, didn't have a bat mitzvah when she turned thirteen in 1973. But in the late 1970s, bat mitzvahs began to be popular. Today they are widely practiced. Most families that have a bar mitzvah for a son would have a bat mitzvah of equal magnitude for a daughter.

THE ORTHODOX

The one exception is the Orthodox. In keeping with the traditions laid down in the Talmud, the Orthodox accept a girl as an adult member of the community when she reaches the age of twelve. Among the Orthodox, women continue to have a secondary role in the synagogue. They do not read from the Torah or represent others in prayer. In fact, they sit separately from men, behind a barrier called a *mechitza*. As a consequence, when an Orthodox girl turns twelve, she assumes the personal rights and responsibilities of a Jew but assumes no public role.

In some Orthodox synagogues, the girl's father is called to the Torah and offers a blessing for his daughter to mark her bat mitzvah. Among the rigorously Orthodox, the father's blessing is in some cases the entire event. But even the Orthodox have not escaped the advent of feminism. In recent years, there has been a growing trend among the modern Orthodox to give girls more of a celebration, albeit within the limits of Orthodoxy. For example, some Orthodox girls will give a short sermon on the Torah reading, just as boys have long done as part of their celebration.

A handful of modern Orthodox rabbis allow special women's services, where bat mitzvah girls can read Torah to a congregation of women. A small group of men (fewer than ten) is permitted to attend, but they must stand off to the side behind a *mechitza* so as not to distract the women. The modern Orthodox will also host a party for the girl, but it is not unusual for these events to be more muted than the parties given for boys.

My son had his bar mitzvah in an Orthodox congregation in Israel; my wife looked on (unhappily) from the women's balcony. But for my daughter, I'll step momentarily out of Orthodoxy so that she can have an *aliyah* and read from the Torah. This would not be possible in the Orthodox *shul* I normally attend, where men and women sit separately and have different roles. Emma, who attends a modern Orthodox day school, will have her bat mitzvah in a congregation of both men and women when she turns twelve at a Conservative summer camp in Massachusetts.

A FAMILY EVENT

Religious distinctions between boys and girls do not exist in the Reform, Reconstructionist, and Conservative movements. Both boys and girls are celebrated at the age of thirteen. Bar and bat mitzvah are central to these non-Orthodox branches. A good chunk of their membership, in fact, is made up of couples with youngsters ranging in age from ten to fifteen. Clearly, a major impetus for couples to join a synagogue is the approaching bar or bat mitzvah of a child. Many couples drop out of congregational life a year or two later.

Congregations use the approaching bar or bat mitzvah as an op-

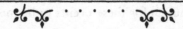

ON THE IMPORTANCE OF A JEWISH EDUCATION
"If there are no little ones, there will be no disciples. If there are no disciples, there will be no sages. If there are no sages, there will be no elders. If there are no elders, there will be no prophets. If there are no prophets, there will be no holy spirit. If there is no holy spirit, the Holy One will not cause his presence to rest upon Israel" (Palestinian Talmud, Sanhedrin 10:2).

portunity to teach the youngster—and their family—some basic Hebrew and familiarize them with the prayer book and the synagogue service.

"It is the key focus of their life in seventh grade," said Rabbi Spitz of California. In a system that has become fairly typical among non-Orthodox congregations, Rabbi Spitz's synagogue requires that children attend six hours a week of Hebrew school in the years leading up to the bar or bat mitzvah. In addition, in the year preceding the occasion, the child must attend the synagogue's weekly Saturday morning services. The boys and girls also take on a social action project of their choosing, such as cleaning beaches, collecting food for the poor, or volunteering to visit with residents of a nursing home.

But the reading of the Torah is the crowning moment. "When you ask adults what they remember from their bar mitzvah, it is not the party and not the presents, it's the synagogue service," Rabbi Spitz says.

Many congregations use the occasion as an attempt to involve the entire family in synagogue life, even if the family's initial impetus for joining was the approaching bar or bat mitzvah of a child. Some require that parents accompany the children to special bar mitzvah classes and to synagogue services. "If Dad drops his son off at synagogue Saturday morning and proceeds to the tennis court, what can you expect the kid will do as soon as he's able?" asks Rabbi Kamins of Australia.

Another trend is to involve the entire family in the Torah service—not simply as observers but as participants. Bar mitzvah is not about performance but participation. Many rabbis encourage all the teenage and adult members of the child's family to also read publicly from the Torah. Many Torah portions are long, so there is plenty of reading to go around. For some fathers and mothers, this may be the first opportunity they've had to read Torah since their own bar and bat mitzvahs. In many cases, the teenager may bolt afterward, but the family remains connected and involved in synagogue life.

IMAGINE YOU ARE A TORAH

Rabbi Spitz talks about one role-playing exercise that he does with youngsters in his congregation. "Imagine you are a Torah," he tells the class. "How are you dressed?"

The children talk of being clothed in velvet and satin, about wearing silver adornments and bells that tinkle when they are carried from the ark.

"How does it feel to be in the ark all week?"

"Lonely," says one. "It's dark," says another. "Sad," says a third.

"How does it feel when the doors of the ark are opened and you are brought out among the members of the synagogue?"

"Joy." "Love." "Light." "Everyone kisses me," says another.

Now he shifts the focus and asks the children to imagine what it feels like to be reading the Torah. "They say the most beautiful things," Rabbi Spitz adds. "I feel like I am speaking for God." "I feel competent." "I feel like my grandfather is standing beside me."

He asks the youngsters to remember those thoughts when they read from the Torah for the first time. Many remember it then and for many years after.

OVERDOING IT VS. DOING IT RIGHT

In my 1992 interview with Judith Eisenstein, she lamented that bar mitzvah celebrations for boys and bat mitzvah celebrations for girls have become virtually indistinguishable. "A lot of us hoped it would be different," she said. "One of my worries is that all the bad aspects of the bar mitzvah institution have been taken over by the bat mitzvah."

The "bad" aspects of bar mitzvah are what often get emphasized—lavish spending on catering halls; chopped liver shaped like swans; parties with themes like Star Wars, Mark McGwire, or the Back Street Boys; an overemphasis on gifts and strapless gowns on thirteen-year-old girls. More "bar" than mitzvah, the lament goes.

The prize for opulent bat mitzvah of the decade went to a thirteen-year-old named Lisa from Pittsburgh, who in 1998 got the party of her dreams when a hotel ballroom was transformed into a scene from the movie *Titanic*. There were twelve-foot steaming smokestacks at the buffet tables, phosphorescent artificial icebergs, and a "steerage" section for children. A gigantic photo, rising ten feet above the floor, featured Lisa's face superimposed over the actress Kate Winslet's body on the prow of the luxury liner, with Leonardo DiCaprio smiling over her shoulder. Lisa's father, a physician, said: "Anyone can go down at any time. We didn't want to wait to show how much we love one another."

In recent years, there has been a significant backlash against the culture of ostentatious bar mitzvahs. Many parents want the bar or bat mitzvah to reflect their values by turning them into social action projects that are also fun and memorable for their children. One youngster in New York, Shira Rockowitz, took her friends to the Lower East Side to help clean and polish an old synagogue. Her parents handed out T-shirts that said "I Shined with Shira." Afterward, the group feasted on blintzes and latkes at another neighborhood institution, Ratner's. Some families eschew the party altogether and save the money for a family trip to Israel. Other youngsters will designate a percentage of their bar mitzvah gifts for a charitable cause. One popular charity is Mazon, a Los Angeles–based organization that suggests a voluntary 3 percent tax on what a family spends on a bar mitzvah to be given to programs for the hungry.

According to Talmudic tradition, parental responsibilities end with bar mitzvah, but we all know that it's only a beginning. Attaining religious adulthood is a step in the right direction. If done right, the bar or bat mitzvah can leave the child with a tremendous sense of accomplishment. A challenge has been met. I hear again and again from non-Jewish parents that they envy the bar mitzvah ceremony. "My son was floored," said a colleague at Columbia after her son attended his first bar mitzvah. "He kept saying that they gave his friend such honor." It is an opportunity for youngsters to shine. They do well not because they're smarter than other kids but because more is expected of them. The Jewish coming-of-age ceremonies are demanding, but kids rise to the occasion.

The Basics

BIBLICAL ORIGINS None.

TALMUD A passage from the tractate *Avot:* "Judah ben Temah says: At five, one should study Scripture; at ten, one should study Mishna; at thirteen, one is ready to do *mitzvot;* at fifteen, one is ready to study Talmud; at eighteen, one is ready for the wedding canopy; at twenty, one is responsible for a family."

PURPOSE Public rite of passage into adulthood, in which the child publicly assumes the responsibilities, obligations, and privileges of Jewish life. This passage is marked by calling the young man or young woman to the Torah as an adult member of the community. The rite for boys comes at the age of thirteen. For girls, it comes at either twelve or thirteen.

VOCABULARY *Mitzvah* means "commandment"; there are 613 of them embodied in the Torah, the five books of Moses. *Bar* means "son of" and *bat* "daughter of." The public acknowledgment of passage into bar and bat mitzvah occurs when a boy or girl recites blessings before the Torah in a ritual called an *aliyah*. The boy or girl might also read from the Scriptures in an ancient musical system called *ta'amei hamikra;* in Yiddish this is known as *layning*. At the Sabbath morning service, there are two opportunities for the child to read; one is the Torah portion of the week, and the other is Haftorah, readings from the prophetic books of the Bible.

FIRST BAR MITZVAH Unknown.

FIRST RECORDED BAT MITZVAH Judith Kaplan in 1922. She was the daughter of Rabbi Mordecai Kaplan, the founder of Reconstructionist Judaism.

BLESSINGS The child says, "Bless the Lord who is blessed." The congregation responds, "Blessed be the Lord who is blessed forever and ever." The child adds two blessings on the Torah, one before and one after the public reading.

ASSOCIATED CUSTOMS Bar or bat mitzvah gives a speech known as a *d'var Torah*. A celebratory meal is given for family and friends. Some families use the occasion to organize a family trip to Israel.

MODERN INNOVATION Adult bar and bat mitzvahs. These are for men and women, including converts to Judaism, who missed it the first time around. Many synagogues have classes for adults to prepare them for this belated public rite of passage.

CHAPTER THREE

Wedding

Forty days before the birth of a child, the Talmud states, a heavenly voice announces: "The son of this person is destined for the daughter of so-and-so" (Sotah 2a). There is a good chance that the intended is not even born yet, but heaven knows just who it will be.

With this kind of predestination, one wonders why dating and courtship can be so trying. Shouldn't it be obvious to us as it is to heaven? And why do so many marriages fail? Did heaven make a mistake?

Apparently, heaven has a plan for us, but we have to discover it for ourselves. We may fail numerous times before we discern the plan. Or we may altogether miss our opportunity. A delightful rabbinic passage expands on the notion of heavenly matchmaking with the following story: The wife of a Roman nobleman asks Rabbi Yossi ben Halaphta, "What has God been doing since He created the world?" "He has been arranging marriages," the rabbi responds. Rabbi Yossi says that matchmaking is a difficult task—as difficult as one of God's great miracles, the splitting of the Red Sea." The matron scoffs. "That is something even I can do," she declares. The woman demonstrates by ordering her manservants to marry her maidservants. The next morning, the couples come to her—one with a cracked skull, one with a missing eye, a third with a broken leg. "I don't want this woman," one shouts. "I can't stand this man," another declares. The Roman matron returns to the rabbi and says: "Your Torah is right, and what you have told me is absolutely true." "That is precisely what I have been telling you," the rabbi says. "You might think the arranging of marriages is an easy task. But for God, it is as difficult as the splitting of the Red Sea" (Pesikta d'Rav Kahana, 2:4). As anyone who's tried their hand in matchmaking knows, bringing the right two people together is a major miracle. The Zohar, the classic mystical Jewish text written in the thirteenth century, explains that marriage is, in fact, a reuniting of two parts that were once one. The soul, the Zohar says, descends from heaven with two characteristics, one male and one female. But the two parts become separated as they enter different bodies. The world is made up of these millions of broken souls, each longing to be completed by its lost piece. In marriage, they are rejoined.

In Judaism, marriage is the natural state. "It is not good that man should be alone," God says in Genesis. "I will make a helpmeet for him." Devotion to the spouse is so great, the Bible adds, that it surpasses filial loyalty. "Therefore shall a man leave his father and mother, and shall cleave unto his wife, and they shall be one flesh."

No sooner are Adam and Eve created in the Genesis account than God gives them a commandment, the very first *mitzvah* of the Torah: "Be fruitful and multiply" (Genesis 1:28). In so commanding, God constantly re-creates the world, the Zohar explains. "In what way?" the Zohar asks rhetorically. "By causing marriages to take place." Men and women join with God to complete creation.

Not to marry is to be incomplete. "He who has no wife is not a proper man," the Talmud in Yevamot (63a) states. And marriage is not only for procreation; it is for companionship and fulfillment as well. A person who does not marry lives "without joy, blessings, goodness . . . Torah, protections . . . and peace" (Yevamot 62b). Although there were some early Jewish sects, like the Essenes, who practiced celibacy, these groups (not surprisingly) died out in the early days of the Common Era. There is no tradition of celibacy in rabbinic Judaism.

In Judaism, marriage is so esteemed that it is a metaphor for God's attachment to Israel. "As a bridegroom rejoices over his bride, so will your God rejoice over you," says Isaiah (62:5). The imagery of marriage is again used in describing the relationship between the Jews and the Sabbath. In the Friday night prayers, the Sabbath is welcomed with the song, "Come, my beloved, to meet the Sabbath bride; let us welcome the Sabbath."

Real marriage can't possibly live up to the idealized versions, but Jews try, beginning with the wedding. If the *brit* ceremony represents bringing a child into the Covenant of Abraham, and bar and bat mitzvahs are about the child accepting the Covenant of Moses, then in marriage the child enters into a new, voluntary covenant, one that mirrors the sacred covenants between God and Israel.

THE HISTORY

My favorite wedding story in the Bible comes in Genesis 28 and 29, when Isaac sends Jacob from Canaan to Paddan-aram to find a wife. The story has acts of chivalry, love at first sight, and a great deception. And it begins with a warning against marrying outside the clan. In some respects, the wedding of Jacob provides a model for generations of Jewish weddings. Why does Isaac send Jacob away to find a wife? Apparently, he doesn't like the local girls. "You shall not marry one of the Canaanite women," Isaac tells his son. Go instead to the house of Laban, your mother's brother, and marry one of his daughters. When Jacob first sets eyes upon his cousin Rachel, he is smitten. She is a shepherd girl, approaching the public well in Paddan-aram with her sheep. Jacob "rolled the stone from the mouth of the well and watered the flock." He wastes no time. "Then Jacob kissed Rachel." After a brief negotiation with Laban, he agrees to work for seven years for the hand of Rachel in marriage. The time flies by. "They seemed to him but a few days because of the love he had for her." When the time comes for the wedding "Laban gathered together all the people of the place and made a feast," the first recorded wedding party. Everyone who's read

the Bible knows that it is not until the next morning that Jacob discovers that it is the older sister Leah, not his beloved Rachel, whom he has wed. Jacob has been deceived. But notice what Laban says: "Complete the week of this one [for the wedding feast], and we will give you the other also in return for serving me another seven years."

Some of the lessons: Marry within the clan. Celebrate with a week-long feast. Love and marriage go together. But even if there is no love, the marriage vows stand.

It is also clear from the Jacob saga that polygamy is allowed in Judaism. But there is a difference between permitted and encouraged. In the Bible, polygamy is at best a compromise and at worst a disaster. As Rabbi Joseph Telushkin, the author of *Jewish Literacy*, points out, every polygamous marriage in the Bible is troubled. Jacob's two wives, Rachel and Leah, are bitterly jealous of each other. King Solomon is criticized for having too many wives. Judaism upholds not only monotheism but monogamy as the ideal. Historians say that polygamy has always been rare among Jews. But it was not formally outlawed until the tenth century by a decree of Rabbi Gershom ben Yehudah of Germany. The ban was widely honored by Ashkenazic (Northwest European) Jewry, probably because the population lived among Europe's Christians, who saw polygamy as a pagan and uncivilized practice. Interestingly, Rabbi Gershom's ban was not accepted among the Sephardic (Spanish and Eastern) Jews, who tended to live in Muslim societies that approved of a man having more than one wife. In the 1950s, the Sephardic Chief Rabbinate of Israel banned polygamy for Sephardic Jews as well.

BETROTHAL

There are two aspects to the Jewish wedding: *erusin*, or the betrothal, and *nissu'in*, the marriage proper. In Talmudic times, these two ceremonies were done a year apart. At the betrothal, the groom would give the bride an object of value, usually a ring, and recite this formula: "Behold, you are consecrated to me with this ring according to the law of Moses and Israel." On this occasion, two blessings were recited, one over a cup of wine and the other on the betrothal itself. What followed was a year-long period of limbo, in which the couple was forbidden to have sex with anyone else—or with each other. Cohabitation came a year later after the second ceremony, the *nissu'in*. Here the bride would be led to the groom's house, where seven additional blessings would be said over a cup of wine. The marriage would then be consummated.

Over time, the two ceremonies—*erusin* and *nissu'in*—were collapsed into one, generally known as *kedushin*. The unified ceremony came into practice around the twelfth century, owing in part to the danger and uncertainty under which the Jews lived in the Middle Ages. There was little time for leisurely engagements when the Crusaders were at the door. The system also proved onerous to couples, giving, as it did, all the restrictions of marriage without any of the protections. Both ceremonies were brought under the *chuppah*, the wedding canopy, which symbolizes the groom's domain.

THE *CHUPPAH*

The *chuppah* is the locus of the Jewish wedding ceremony. It can be bedecked with flowers and rooted in the earth or just be a simple prayer shawl held aloft with four poles. Rife with symbolism, it faces the holy city of Jerusalem, and all four sides are open to represent the hospitality of the biblical Abraham, whose open tent is described in Genesis as a place for all wayfarers. Among some groups, notably the Hasidim, the *chuppah* is placed outdoors at night in full view of the stars to remind the couple of the promise God made to Abraham: that God will make Abraham's descendants as numerous as the stars of the heavens. It is one of the many fertility reminders in the ceremony.

The Talmud (Gittin 57a) records a charming custom about the *chuppah*. "When a boy was born, a cedar tree is planted and when a girl is born, a pine tree. When they grow up and get married, the wedding canopy is made of branches taken from both trees." In a modern variation on the custom, some couples prepare for their wedding by giving friends and family members swatches of cloth and asking them to decorate them with a drawing or a message. They then weave the swatches together to create a canopy brimming with the good wishes of loved ones.

By tradition, the *chuppah* represents the man's domain; the woman enters and is, in essence, acquired by the man. "The woman is acquired in three ways," the Talmud says (Kedushin 2a): "through money, contract, and sexual intercourse." Only one of these is transacted under the *chuppah*. Money is represented by the wedding ring that the groom gives the bride and marriage by contract is no longer performed. A document called the *ketubah*, which spells out the responsibilities of the husband to the wife, is read under the *chuppah*. But this is not all business. In Hebrew, the ceremony is called *kedushin*, which comes from the word *kadosh*, which means "holy." Marriage is a holy act, blessed by God and performed in the sight of the community, which takes great pains in safeguarding the rights of the woman.

While the traditional Jewish wedding is, at its very essence, an inequitable ceremony, most of its elements have been preserved, even by the non-Orthodox. It is easy enough to transform the symbols. The *chuppah* becomes the new home of both, not just the man's domain. The *ketubah* can be more equitably rewritten, and both the bride and groom can give each other rings so that no one is "acquired."

Despite the changes, the ceremony retains its aura of holiness. Rabbi Spitz tells me that most of the weddings he performs in southern California are for couples who are already living together. David Nelson, the rabbi of a large Conservative congregation in Detroit, insists that couples separate for a week before the wedding. "You may live together, but for the wedding, you come to the synagogue from your parents' homes," he tells the couples.

The notion that couples are chaste until their wedding night is almost quaint in many sectors of our society other than the Orthodox. But having a Jewish wedding is more than an occasion for a party.

"Through Judaism, they are transforming their relationship," said Rabbi Spitz. "A justice of the peace can help them enter into a contract. But the *chuppah* elevates the union to one in relationship with God."

THE *BADEKEN*

In the Orthodox tradition, the bride and groom are kept apart for a week before the wedding. They do, however, get a chance to see each other once before they meet under the *chuppah* in a brief veiling ceremony called the *badeken*. In the hour before the wedding, the bride, surrounded by her female friends and family, sits on a special bridal chair in one room. In a room nearby, the groom witnesses the signing of the marriage contract, the *ketubah*. When the signing is done, he is escorted to his bride by his father and the bride's father. The Orthodox feminist Blu Greenberg calls what happens next the most romantic moment of the wedding. "Their eyes meet," she writes, "and the groom gently draws the veil over his bride's face." The term *badeken* is Yiddish for "the covering." At that moment, the bride and the groom look at each other and see the future.

At the *badeken*, it is customary for the bride's father and the groom's father to put their hands on the bride's head and give her a blessing, again invoking the matriarchs. "May God make you like Sarah, Rebecca, Rachel, and Leah," they begin. The rabbi adds another blessing with a fertility theme: "Oh, my sister, may you become a multitude of thousands" (Genesis 24:60). It is the blessing that is given to Rebecca, who had only two children but a multitude of descendants.

From the *badeken*, the groom is escorted to the wedding canopy.

THE PROCESSIONAL

By tradition, the groom is the first to arrive at the *chuppah*. He is usually escorted by his parents or other close relatives. In some families, the parents carry a candle to remember the spirits of family members who have died. Brothers, sisters, ring bearers, flower girls, and bridesmaids follow until it is the bride's turn. She is last, and she too is accompanied by her parents. All of these close relatives gather around the *chuppah*, creating a scene that is surprising to those accustomed to church weddings, where the solitary couple stands with the priest at the altar. The Jewish ceremony is more of a family affair.

When the bride arrives under the *chuppah*, she encircles the groom by walking around him seven times, often followed by her mother and the groom's mother, who hold the train of her gown. "Some modern people tend to think of this as sexist," writes Blu Greenberg, "but to me it has always seemed a most wonderfully sexy ritual, as if she were wrapping him up in the train of her gown to take him home with her." Another explanation offered is that the woman is circling the man as the biblical Joshua circled Jericho. She's breaking down the walls that separate them.

In weddings performed by the late Jewish songwriter Rabbi Shlomo Carlebach, additional generations yet to be born were added to the circuit. "Look closely, my dear friends," the rabbi would say. "Behind the holy bride walks her children and behind them their children, down through the generations." The imaginary parade that he conjured was a wonderful reminder of the significance of marriage not just for the couple but for all times.

Some couples skip the seven circuits. Others preserve it but give it a new twist. For example, some couples walk together around the perimeter of the *chuppah*, demonstrating their commitment to build a new and secure environment. After everyone is settled under the *chuppah*, the rabbi recites the two betrothal blessings over a cup of wine from which the bride and groom take a sip. Next comes the giving of the ring, the core ritual of the ceremony. The groom places the ring on the index finger of the right hand and says the following: "*Harei at mekudeshet li b'tabaat zoo k'dat Moshe V'Yisrael.*" It means, "Behold, you are sanctified to me with this ring according to the Law of Moses and Israel." Now that the ring is on the bride's finger, she needs the wedding contract in her hand. The rabbi reads the contract out loud in the original Aramaic, giving a brief explanation in English, and then hands it to the groom, who gives it to his bride. While the bride will hand off the *ketubah* to a parent or friend at this point, the document remains hers, a sign of her new status. Next, the officiating rabbi may address the couple. Rabbis take the occasion to talk about the attributes of the bride and groom. They'll often remind the guests that they are not just passive observers but participants in the wedding themselves. They are there to rejoice with the bride and groom and to be part of a supportive community that will sustain the new marriage.

In the final section of the ceremony, a second cup of wine is poured and the marriage blessings are recited. There are seven in all, and they serve to lift the wedding out of the present and put it in the context of Jewish history. The blessings evoke creation, the land of Israel, and messianic longings. The seventh blessing is the most exuberant. It goes like this: "Blessed are you, Lord our God, master of the universe, who created joy and gladness, groom and bride, mirth, happy song, pleasure, delight, love, brotherhood."

To the traditional blessings, some rabbis ask the congregation to add blessings of their own. "What is it that you think the couple needs to make their life together a success?" Rabbi Irwin Kula, president of a transdenominational Jewish think tank, the National Jewish Center for Learning and Leadership, says when performing a wedding. "And what can we take away from their happiness to our own lives?" As Rabbi Kula leads the congregation in a joyous tune, one can almost feel the good wishes traveling across the room as the bride and groom silently bless and are blessed.

With all the blessing complete, the ceremony concludes with what is probably the most well known of Jewish wedding rituals: the breaking of the glass. The glass is wrapped in a cloth napkin and placed on the floor, near the feet of the groom. Some couples even have two glass ceremonies, although the woman usually defers to the man on this one. Numerous reasons are offered for the shattering of the glass. The ritual began in Talmudic times as a reminder that, even at our moments of greatest joy, we must remember the destruction of the Temple in Jerusalem. Whatever the reason, the shattering marks the end of the ceremony and the beginning of the procession away from the *chuppah*. Often this is a dignified procession, although in certain Orthodox weddings, now it's time for joyful chaos to break out. Well-wishers mob the bride and groom and, to the accompaniment of the band, dance them out of the room to the next ritual, known as *yichud*. But the dancing stops at the door of the *yichud* room. The bride and groom enter alone and remain there for about fifteen minutes. In ancient times, this was probably the time for the consummation of the marriage, followed by the display of bloody sheets to prove the woman's virginity. Today, *yichud* is more on the level of symbolism as well as an opportunity for the bride and groom to rest and catch their breath—alone—and begin to digest what just happened. Among the Orthodox, the couple refrain from eating earlier on their wedding day as a sign of the seriousness of the day. Food is set out in the *yichud* room for them. Even if they haven't fasted, few couples get to eat at their wedding reception, so this is a good time to grab a bite before the dancing resumes. In traditional weddings, two witnesses are stationed at the door to ensure privacy.

Yichud, which lasts only a few minutes, gives the wedding guests a chance to regroup, grab a drink, and connect before the newlyweds rejoin the party. Dancing is an essential part of a Jewish wedding. The Talmud even records a discussion about how the dancing should be done. "How does one dance before the bride?" the rabbis ask. There are tales of a rabbi who dances with a myrtle branch, another who does a kind of juggling dance, and another who—to the astonishment of the other rabbis—dances with the bride on his shoulders.

Yeshiva students, who may spend their days poring over the holy books, let loose with ecstatic dancing and acrobatic feats at weddings. There are fire-eaters and jugglers among them. At these yeshiva weddings, the men and women dance in separate circles at different ends of the dance floor. In some ultra-Orthodox weddings, men and women also eat separately at the wedding feast, sometimes on separate floors of the wedding hall. The newlyweds, however, get to sit together.

The festive meal ends with one last ritual, the grace after meals, which concludes with a reprise of the seven blessings said earlier under the *chuppah* and a last glass of wine.

JEWISH-CHRISTIAN WEDDINGS

If the bride or groom—or both—is a convert to Judaism, each is considered Jewish in every regard and can have a fully Jewish wedding. But there are significant differences among the branches as to what constitutes a conversion. An Orthodox conversion includes a visit to the ritual bath, a commitment to lead an Orthodox life, and, in the case of males, a circumcision. The other branches are less demanding. As a consequence, an Orthodox rabbi would not accept a Reform convert as fully Jewish. But certainly, an Orthodox rabbi would treat an Orthodox convert as fully Jewish.

Problems arise, however, when one of the couple is not Jewish. The increase in Jewish-Christian marriages is regarded as a danger by some Jewish leaders and as an "opportunity" by others. In the 1950s fewer than 10 percent of Jews married outside the faith, in part as a consequence of anti-Semitism. American society at the time was more stratified, and Jews did not mix easily with Gentiles. There were neighborhoods where Jews could not live and schools where they could not study. By 1990, however, Jews were far more accepted in society. The integration of Jews has been a remarkable success story, but it came with certain consequences. The intermarriage rate soared in those years to more than 50 percent. For traditionalists, the high rate of intermarriage presents a demographic threat to the Jewish future. If Jews do not marry Jews, they warn, there will be no Jewish children to carry on the faith. There are liberal Jews, however, who say that through intermarriage, more American families can be exposed to Ju-

VARIATION ON A THEME: HERE COMES THE BRIDE

A journalism student of mine, Elizabeth, was marrying a young man, José. Elizabeth was Jewish; José was Roman Catholic. When Elizabeth's seventy-five-year-old Aunt Bessie arrived for the wedding, she was rather upset. She pulled Elizabeth aside. "You're not going to play the wedding march by that anti-Semite, are you?" Elizabeth assured her that the Wagner wedding march would not be played. "Good," said Aunt Bessie. "That's all I was worried about."

daism. The traditionalists respond, however, that the statistics do not bear this out. The overwhelming odds are that children of Jewish-Christian marriages will not be Jewish. Reform leaders acknowledge this but argue that mixed marriage is a growing reality and should be dealt with compassionately. Besides, they argue, the numbers of mixed families that identify with Judaism can be increased if the non-Jewish partner is made to feel comfortable in the temple and synagogue. Reform temples in particular have programs to welcome mixed-faith couples.

Orthodox and Conservative rabbis do not perform intermarriages. Neither will they perform a wedding with non-Jewish clergy. To do either would mean to violate the basic precepts of Jewish tradition. There are, however, many Reform rabbis who perform intermarriages. Officially, the Reform rabbinical body, the Central Conference of American Rabbis, is against participating in such ceremonies, but it allows its rabbis to follow the dictates of their own conscience. Informal surveys of the Reform rabbinate show that 30 percent to 50 percent of them will perform mixed marriages.

Among Reform rabbis there are gradations. Many will not perform interfaith weddings at all. Others will perform them only if they are the sole officiating clergy, and still others will co-officiate with Christian clergy. Many Jewish-Christian couples report that it is difficult to find a rabbi to perform their wedding ceremony. There are some unscrupulous rabbis, many of them with questionable rabbinical credentials, who will take advantage of the situation. Officiating at marriages is just one of the many functions of a rabbi, but I've met some who have made a business of officiating at Jewish-Christian weddings only because there is such a strong market for willing rabbis.

Intermarriage wedding rituals vary. Some will combine Jewish and Christian symbols. For example, there are couples who marry under a *chuppah* with both a priest and a rabbi officiating. There are grooms who break the glass at their wedding in Catholic churches. Alternative, interfaith ceremonies have been developed, such as one called the Children of Noah. This ceremony, written by members of Reconstructionist Judaism, does not talk about Moses as much as Noah, who is seen in this instance as the father of all mankind. After the flood, God gave Noah seven commandments for good living and, of course, a rainbow as a promise that God would not again destroy the world. The Children of Noah ceremony draws on these themes. The ideals of monotheism and of kindness to other people and to animals are stressed. Instead of standing under a *chuppah,* the couple in this ceremony stands beneath a colorful arch, reminiscent of the rainbow.

GAY CEREMONIES

Alternative ceremonies have also been created for gay couples. With the growing acceptance of homosexuality in society as a whole, gay Jews have turned to the synagogue for affirmation of their commitment to each other. Here, too, the branches of Judaism differ in their approach. The Orthodox are staunchly against these ceremonies, while the Reform and Reconstructionists allow them. Conservative Jewry is

officially opposed, but there are those in the movement, including many rabbis, who call for allowing such ceremonies.

A Reform rabbi on Long Island, Jerome Davidson of Great Neck, created a controversy in his congregation a few years ago when he agreed to perform a commitment ceremony for two lesbians, one of whom was his assistant rabbi. Some members of his congregation objected, not because of the same-sex marriage but because the same rabbi refused to perform weddings involving Jews and Christians. Many of the couples he had turned away were the children of members of his congregation. "Why can you accommodate homosexuals and not non-Jews?" The rabbi's response was that the lesbian couple were committed to building a Jewish home but that Jewish-Christian marriages rarely lead to the creation of a Jewish family.

Even the Reform don't call these ceremonies weddings, since the union of couples of the same sex are not recognized as marriages by local civil authorities. Rather, they are "commitment ceremonies," sometimes called "Brit Reyut," or Covenant of Love. One such ceremony, developed by a Reconstructionist rabbi in Berkeley, California, uses a *sukkah* rather than a traditional *chuppah*. The *sukkah*—according to tradition, the temporary shelter that the Jews lived in during the Exodus from Egypt—recalls the love and kindness of God. As with interfaith marriages, there is no mention of Moses, but famous friendships of the Bible, like that of David and Jonathan, are recalled. Rings are exchanged, blessings are said, and the ceremony ends with the shattering underfoot of two glasses.

MIKVEH

For centuries, Jewish women have prepared for their weddings by immersing themselves in the *mikveh*, a special ritual bath. The *mikveh* is a pool of fresh water that renders the woman spiritually clean as well as ready for sexual intercourse with her husband. Women who follow this regimen visit the *mikveh* each month after their period. (The laws of *mikveh,* which are highly technical, will be discussed in greater detail later in the book in the chapter on Jewish home life.) Orthodox Jews will pick a date for the wedding that coincides with the end of this "forbidden" time so that the woman can go into the marriage in a state of readiness.

But it is not only the strictly observant Orthodox who perform these pre-wedding ablutions. Women who have no intention of continuing the practice of *mikveh* in their married lives often decide that this rite of passage into the married state is one they do not want to miss. In that sense, it is like the white wedding gown. They may not wear a white dress every day of their married life, but they want to get married in one. Many feel the same way about *mikveh.* Many Jewish brides want to start their marriage in a state of ritual purity.

For reasons of modesty, the monthly visit to the *mikveh* is traditionally performed quietly and without much fanfare. *Mikvehs* are busiest at night. But some women have turned the first visit into a cause for celebration. One woman I know had a beach party for her women friends on the eve of her wedding. She swam out a respectable distance and then slipped out of her bathing suit for the formal ablutions. Afterward, her bathing suit back on, she sat on the beach with her friends in a circle and talked with them about her dreams for her marriage.

DIVORCE

The Torah provides greater details about divorce than it does about marriage. "When a man takes a woman, and marries her . . . if she find no favor in his eyes . . . then he shall write her a bill of divorcement and sends her out of his house" (Deuteronomy 24:1). It is a harsh system that leaves the woman vulnerable. The rabbis soften it somewhat by including in the *ketubah,* the marriage contract, a guarantee that the man will pay a substantial alimony to the wife in the event of a divorce. Still, the Orthodox and Conservative branches require that marriages

be dissolved through "a bill of divorcement," known as a *get*. The Reform do not require a *get*, saying that a civil divorce given by the secular courts serves the same legal purpose. The giving of the *get* is a formal procedure performed in front of a panel of rabbis, known as a *bet din*. Just as a Jewish marriage begins with a legal document, the *ketubah*, so must it end with one. The *get*, however, is a far more complicated document than the *ketubah*. Each *get* is handwritten by a scribe in Hebrew in a form that is almost an anti-sonnet: exactly twelve lines of Hebrew text. The husband (or a proxy) must put the *get* in the hands of the woman (or her representative). An Orthodox or Conservative rabbi who is asked by a couple to perform the wedding will ask for evidence of a *get* if either the man or the woman was previously married. Without a *get*, the children of the second marriage will be considered illegitimate under Jewish law—*mamzerim* is the technical term.

I have been to hundreds of Jewish weddings, but never to a divorce until a friend in Israel asked me to accompany him to his *get* proceedings. Formally, I was there to attest before the rabbinical court to the fact that my friend was who he said he was. (Drivers' licenses or passports don't pass muster in a rabbinic court; witnesses are necessary.) More important, I was there for moral support. My friend and his wife had been married for twenty years and had produced two wonderful children. The letting-go of that relationship, no matter how flawed, was a devastating moment. For the first time, I understood the Talmud when it says that "when a man divorces the wife of his youth, even the very altar sheds tears because of him" (Gittin 90b).

The Basics

BIBLICAL ORIGINS Marriage is the ideal human state, established by God at creation. "It is not good that the man should be alone. I will make a helpmeet for him. . . . Therefore shall a man leave his father and his mother, and shall cleave unto his wife, and they shall be one flesh" (Genesis 2:18,24).

FIRST WEDDING PARTY When Jacob married Leah, Laban, Leah's father, "gathered all the people of the place and made a feast" (Genesis 29:22).

TALMUDIC REQUIREMENTS "A woman is acquired in three ways: through money, a contract, and sexual intercourse" (Kedushin, 2a).

VOCABULARY *Kedushin*, the act of marriage, derived from the word *kadosh*, which means "holy"; *chuppah*, the canopy under which the ceremony takes place; *ketubah*, the wedding contract; *yichud*, the private time the bride and groom have together after the ceremony.

THE CEREMONY Under the *chuppah*, the groom gives the bride a ring, the marriage contract is read, the bride and groom share a cup of wine, and blessings are said in their honor.

BLESSINGS Seven blessings are said under the *chuppah*, evoking creation, the land of Israel, and messianic yearnings. The most exuber-

CHAPTER FOUR

Mourning

Judaism believes there is a world of the living and a spiritual realm of those who once lived. Death, the Talmud states in a lovely phrase, is where the two worlds kiss. Everyone must pass from one realm to the other. The image of a kiss is a comforting one.

Heaven, in Judaism, is not the ideal—the world of the living is the true purpose of creation. "The dead cannot praise the Lord," the Psalmist says (Psalm 115:17). There are stories in the Talmud in which the great rabbis cry on their deathbeds—not out of fear, they explain, but out of sadness that they will no longer be able to perform God's commandments. As Moshe Hayyim Luzzatto, the eighteenth-century kabbalist, wrote: "Whoever fails to take account of his deeds in this world will not have time to take account of them in the next world. Whoever has not acquired wisdom in this world will not acquire it in the grave."

Unlike Christianity and Islam, Judaism has no elaborate explanation of just what it is that the dead do. The whole area of life after death is left shrouded. (Angels exist in Jewish lore, but they tend not to be the dead; rather, they are special spiritual emissaries of God.) Like other faiths, Judaism does hold out the promise that the dead will be resurrected at a time known as the "end of days" when all humankind will accept the one God. The Biblical prophets Isaiah, Ezekiel, and Daniel speak about this time metaphorically, but details about just how this will happen are few.

Human life, then, is not all there is to existence. In the first chapters of Genesis, man is formed by two elements: clay and spirit. At the end of life, when the physical form deteriorates, the spirit remains and returns to God. The promise of resurrection indicates that even the spirit has a destiny. By linking the life of individuals to both creation and the "end of days," Judaism says that our existence is not finite, but is, in fact, timeless and bound to the fate of the universe.

HISTORY

In the Bible, there is great concern about where a person is buried. The burial place of significant Biblical characters is almost always mentioned. In the Genesis accont, Abraham is beside himself with worry because he does not have a burial place for his beloved Sarah. He buys a plot in Kiryat-arba and goes to "mourn for Sarah and to weep for her." Abraham is later buried in the same plot. Jacob and Joseph are so worried that they not be buried in Egypt that they extract a promise from their descendants to return their bones to the Holy Land. In the early Jewish sources, providing a decent burial is tantamount to giving food and lodging to the wayfarer. The Talmud refers to the kindness offered to the dead—such as assisting the burial or attending a funeral—as a *chesed shel emmet,* a true act of charity, for there is no way for the dead to repay the kindness.

Funeral rites in Judaism were standardized in the first century by the head of the community in ancient Israel, Rabban Gamaliel, who decreed that all, both rich and poor, "be buried in plain linen instead of expensive garments." The Talmud (Mo'ed Katan, 27a–27b) says that the rabbi was reacting to excessively elaborate funeral rites among the wealthy class. The rich would bring out their dead on "a tall bed, ornamented with rich covers." The poor brought out their dead in "a plain box." The pressure to hold elaborate funerals, the Talmud says, "was harder for a family to bear than the death itself, so that sometimes family members fled to escape the expense."

The simple rites outlined by Rabban Gamaliel established an equality of the rich and poor in death that extended even to their living relatives. They form the basis for the Jewish funeral today.

WHEN DEATH COMES

When death comes, the body is treated with the utmost respect as the vehicle for the soul while the deceased was alive. Normal conversation among those present must cease; the only talk permitted is that concerning the care for the corpse. The eyes of the deceased are closed, preferably by a son or daughter, as Jacob is promised in Genesis 46 that his favorite son Joseph would close his eyes. The body is covered and is placed on the floor, head to the door, until it can be removed to the funeral home. As an added sign of respect, the deceased is not to be left alone. Family members will often take turns reciting psalms at the bier day and night until the moment of the funeral.

To prepare the body for burial, it is washed from head to foot by members of the burial society, known as the *chevra kadisha*. The procedure is known as the *tahara,* or purification. The corpse is then dressed in a simple white shroud made of cotton, linen, or muslin. The shroud, known as *tachrichim,* is made up of seven pieces that wrap around the body and are secured with attached drawstrings. Some people who live into old age acquire their shroud, just as they might buy a burial plot; they want to be sure they have everything in order. My cousin David had a grandmother named Sara who was very well organized. After she died at the age of ninety-six, her children found a hatbox that contained her *tachrichim.* Inside, she had left a note: "For my final journey."

In addition to being placed in a shroud, the corpse of a man is also wrapped in a *tallit,* or prayer shawl, although one of the four corner fringes is removed to indicate that the *tallit* is no longer fit for religious use. Traditional Judaism forbids any cosmetic procedures on the body, such as embalming or dressing the body for public viewing. Wakes and viewing are not allowed in Judaism. Autopsies and medical research are also not permitted, except in rare cases in which the procedures would directly save another life. Decisions in this realm should be discussed on a case-by-case basis with a rabbi. Cremation is also forbidden in Judaism. It, too, is seen as a desecration of the dead.

A simple pine casket constructed with wooden pegs rather than nails is preferred. In Israel, the shrouded bodies are put directly into the ground without a casket. The simplicity of these rites ensures that all, both rich and poor, are treated equally. The objective is to return the body to the earth quickly and naturally.

THE FUNERAL AND BURIAL

Burial is supposed to follow death quickly. Most families try to have a funeral the day after the death, although if someone dies too late on Friday the burial cannot be held until Sunday. Funerals are not allowed on the Sabbath or on festivals. In Israel, funerals are sometimes held on the same day or even in the evening.

In the hours between the death and the funeral, the immediate relatives are to concern themselves above all else with funeral arrangements. In some ways it would be easier to leave these details to others, but the tradition sees this engagement as the first of many steps of coming to terms with the loss. The official mourners, defined very narrowly by Jewish law, are those who have one of seven relationships with the deceased: father, mother, son, daughter, sister, brother, or spouse. Others—such as grandchildren, cousins, and friends—may also acutely feel the loss, but they are technically not mourners. As in other aspects of the laws of mourning, the law puts a limit on the circle of grief.

Between the time of death and the burial, the official mourner is called an *onen* and is absolved of positive religious obligations such as daily prayer. Before the funeral, the mourner rends his or her garment (usually the lapel of a jacket) and accepts God's judgment with the one

funeral-related prayer: "Blessed art thou, Lord our God, King of the universe, the true and righteous judge." One modern custom is to attach a black ribbon to the mourner's jacket. The mourner tears the ribbon without ruining the jacket. The innovation may fulfill the law, but it lacks the impact of ripping one's garment. For a parent, the jacket is torn on the left side, over the heart, as a sign of greater grief. For other relatives (sibling, spouse, child), it is torn on the right side.

No music is played at Orthodox and Conservative funerals, although the Reform branch does permit it; sometimes the favorite music of the deceased is played. Psalms are read, especially Psalm 23, "The Lord is my shepherd, I shall not want," and Psalm 144, "O Lord, what is man that thou shouldst notice him? . . . Man is like a breath; his days are like a passing shadow." The centerpiece of the service is formed by the eulogies. A generation ago, eulogies were often left to the rabbis who performed the service. Sometimes these rabbis had intimate knowledge of the deceased, but at other times they were unfamiliar with the person they were talking about. In recent years, it has become more popular for the mourners and other relatives to offer tributes to the deceased. Their words may not be as polished, but they are often more stirring and heartfelt than those of the professionals.

Funerals can be held at the graveside or at a synagogue or funeral chapel. Cemetery groundskeepers can take over after the service, but it is considered an honor to the dead to be handled by those who knew and loved the deceased. Mourners, friends, and relatives carry the casket to the grave and help lower it into place. An additional sign of respect is for the immediate relatives to shovel the earth onto the casket themselves. It is a powerful and tangible sign of the finality of death.

After the burial, those who attend the funeral customarily form two lines facing each other on a cemetery path. At this point, the focus shifts from the dead to the mourners. The immediate family members walk between the lines as the others chant the traditional words of consolation: "May the Holy One comfort you among the mourners for Zion and Jerusalem."

SHIVA

After the funeral, the mourners return home or to the home of the deceased for a week-long period of mourning called *shiva*. At the door, they wash their hands to symbolize that they are finished with the task of burial. Upon entrance into the home, a meal of consolation, known as *seudat havra'ah*, is served to the mourners as a reminder that although their hearts are heavy, life must go on. Eggs and other round foods are served at the start of the meal to symbolize the circle of life. If possible, this meal should be served to the mourners by friends. This is a time when they should be waited on and not feel under any obligation to act as hosts to friends who may be visiting for the funeral. Synagogues or friends often prepare and send this *seudat havra'ah* to the mourners' home.

Traditionally, in the week that follows, the mourners stay home, cease their normal routines of work, and accept the consolation of friends who come to visit. Many find it difficult to take that much time off from work; some will sit *shiva* for only a day or two or three. But the psychological benefits of taking time off to mourn are many. People need to make time to process their loss. In every death, mourners have to come to terms with the unresolved areas of the relationship. Some feel guilt that they did not do more for their loved one. Others harbor anger at the deceased for abandoning them and feel guilty about these feelings. Judaism sets the *shiva* period as a time of introspection, but it does not encourage an excessive amount of mourning or self-flagellation. Mourning has its finite time.

The restrictions on mourners are many. In the first week after a death, mourners are not supposed to shave, listen to music, wear cosmetics, get a haircut, have sexual relations, go outdoors, wear leather shoes, or bathe. Mirrors in the house are covered to discourage vanity. Even the study of Torah is prohibited because it is seen as one of life's great pleasures.

During the week, visitors arrive unannounced. The mourners are, again, not supposed to feel that they are hosts. Traditionally, they do not even get up to greet their guests. The custom is not even to say hello or make introductions, although this is hard to observe. The mood is subdued. The mourners sit on low stools (hence the expression "sitting *shiva*"), an ancient gesture of being struck low by grief. The mourners should be allowed to set the agenda for conversation. At times they will need to talk about the deceased, recalling both good times and sad; at other times they will need to be reminded that life goes on by talking about their work, politics, or sports. It is an honor to the dead and part of the healing process for the mourners to recall moments and incidents in the life of the deceased.

Every effort should be made to visit friends and relatives in mourning during the *shiva* period. The point is not to cheer them up but to share their grief; sometimes this is done just by being present. Making a *shiva* visit is not easy. It means walking into someone's home and confronting his or her most difficult reality. I have to admit that I've felt at least a bit of discomfort each time I've made a *shiva* call. Walking in the door is hard. But I have never regretted going. It is a small act of kindness that is long remembered. I have my own rules about *shiva*, learned

SAYING GOOD-BYE

 In the Bible, the patriarchs take stock at the end of their lives. Jacob, sick and approaching death, calls to his beloved son Joseph. With his family before him, Jacob rallies to bid his sons and grandsons a final farewell. He provides a short summary of his life before blessing his progeny one by one. At the end, in the words of Genesis, Jacob "is gathered to his people."

I had always thought of this scene as the stuff of legend until I saw it reenacted at the end of my mother's life. After months and months of trying everything that modern medicine could offer to hold back the cancer spreading through my mother's body, the doctors said that there was nothing else they could do. "She is in the hands of God," one told us. The doctors suggested my mother be transferred from the cancer hospital where she was being aggressively treated with chemotherapy and surgery to a hospice where the prime objective would be to keep her comfortable until the end.

The best hospice for the level of care my mother needed was a Catholic one, Calvary, run by the Archdiocese of New York. When we arrived at the hospice with my mother in the ambulance, I ran ahead to the room and checked for Christian symbols. I took down the crucifix above the bed and instead affixed a *mezuzah* to the door.

After we got her settled, she told us that she wanted us to gather the family to say good-bye. That night, my brothers and I stood around her bed with our aunts and uncles, my mother's siblings, and her husband, my stepfather, Jack. Her body was deteriorating and she was tired, but her mind and emotions were sharp. As we stood by in silence, she looked around the dimly lit room at the people she loved the most in the world. She spoke in barely a whisper, so quietly that my younger brother had to repeat every word so all could hear. My mother, ever vigilant, listened to his words to make sure he got everything right.

"I love you," she said. "I've had a good life. Now I have to leave. I hope I go quickly and without pain. I have been blessed with sons and a wonderful husband. I mention them not to the exclusion of everyone else but because they need me most."

My mother, a former schoolteacher and librarian who had put words together so magnificently all her life, had to stop every few words to catch her breath. She was both exhausted and energized by the challenge. She looked at each of us and said a few words about what she wanted for us and what we meant in her life. When she finished the last one, she closed her eyes and smiled peacefully. One of my uncles, a rabbi, then led her in the final deathbed confession. She said the sh'ma, the Jewish creed declaring the oneness of God, and then repeated seven times: "Adonai, hu haElohim" (the Lord alone is God).

My mother lingered for another four months, but within days of saying good-bye to us, she lost the power of speech. I would sit next to her and talk and sometimes pray. When my mother heard a familiar prayer, like the sh'ma or the prayer over the Sabbath candles, she would momentarily regain her speech and pray along with me. Then she would fall sadly silent.

As my mother deteriorated further, the doctors suggested that we move her closer to the nurses' station. Before the move, I checked for crucifixes in her new room and hung up the Jewish art she loved and arranged it amid the get-well cards, flowers, and grandchildren's draw-ings that cheered the room. Finally, we moved my mother into the new room and closed the door. A few minutes later there was a knock. I opened the door and found one of the hospice's nuns, Sister John St. Claire, holding a mezuzah. "You forgot this," she said with a smile. The irony of a nun bringing me a mezuzah was lost on my mother, but she still knew what it was. I showed the mezuzah to my mother and put it to her lips. She kissed it—an act, like prayer, that was beyond conscious-ness.

Death came on a Saturday morning. My mother was at peace.

from experience. My visits are short; I never stay more than twenty minutes. And I never eat anything. As far as I'm concerned, food at a *shiva* home is for the mourners only.

It is not always possible to make the visit, especially if friends are sitting *shiva* out of town. In such cases, it is important to call or send a card. It is also appropriate to send a gift of food, such as a fruit basket or a meal for the mourners. Flowers or wreaths are not appropriate at Jewish homes of mourning. A more appropriate gift would be a donation to a charity valued by the deceased.

Since it is traditional for mourners to sit on low stools or benches, the end of the week of mourning is known as "getting up" from *shiva*. I visited an older friend, Maks Rothstein, while he sat *shiva* for his wife of fifty-two years. "She was the love of my life," he told me again and again. Before leaving, I asked Maks, "When are you getting up?" He looked at me sadly and said, "I will never get up."

But one cannot mourn forever. *Shiva* ends with a touching custom. One person, a rabbi or a friend, takes the hand of each mourner and lifts the mourner to a standing position. For the last time, the rabbi says the traditional words of mourning: "May God console you together with the mourners of Zion and Jerusalem," and adds, "May you know no more sorrow." The mourners then take a walk around the block to symbolize their reentry into society after a week of looking inward.

KADDISH

When possible, a *minyan*, the quorum of ten necessary for communal prayer, gathers in the *shiva* house in the morning and again around sunset for the afternoon and evening prayers. The mourner rises to say *kaddish*, one of the most famous but most misunderstood prayers in the Jewish liturgy. It is sometimes known as the prayer for the dead, but death is not mentioned. Instead, *kaddish* extols the greatness of God. "Glorified and sanctified be God's great name throughout the world," the prayer begins. The reason that this of all prayers is said is that it is a strong and public reaffirmation of faith at a time when people could justifiably feel anger at God. I may not understand God's ways, the mourner is saying, but I still have faith in God and I will praise God. The early twentieth-century Hebrew writer S. Y. Agnon imagined that *kaddish* was first recited to comfort God, who is also said to grieve over the deaths of men and women.

Leon Wieseltier's book *Kaddish* relates a chilling story that illustrates the power traditionally associated with this prayer. In this tale, Rabbi Akiva, an outstanding scholar from the first century, tells of passing a graveyard late at night and seeing a man, dirty and naked, running among the tombstones and shouldering a heavy load of wood. "What are you? A man or demon?" he asked the figure. "I am a dead man, who has to gather wood every day to prepare the funeral pyre for myself," came the answer. "What was your occupation while you were alive?" Akiva demanded. The man replied, "I was a tax collector who favored the wealthy and oppressed the poor, and committed acts of despicable immorality."

"Have you heard from your superiors whether there is any means of saving you?" Rabbi Akiva called after the man.

"There is no way to redeem me," came the answer, "unless my wife, who I left pregnant, should bear a son, and he should recite the *kaddish* in public. But, who would teach him?"

Rabbi Akiva did not rest until he found the woman and her son. With great effort, he succeeded in teaching him to pray and recite the *kaddish*. Soon afterward, the father appeared to Akiva in a dream and said: "You have redeemed me from the punishment of *Gehinnom*. May your spirit, therefore, rest in Heaven."

Wieseltier finds the story and variations on it repeated in various traditions. It dramatically illustrates the belief that when *kaddish* is said by a child, the parents receive a measure of solace.

Kaddish, is first said at the graveside after the burial and repeated at least three times a day for eleven months for departed parents and for thirty days for siblings, spouse, or children. If no immediate relative is able to say *kaddish,* the obligation can be assumed by a nephew, niece, cousin, or even friend.

For those who accept the discipline of *kaddish* beyond the week of *shiva,* it can be a source of comfort. Since it must be said with a *minyan,* it forces the mourner back into contact with people and does not allow a retreat from society. Every morning and late afternoon, the mourner goes to the synagogue to say the prayer in the company of other worshipers. It is a demanding discipline, but one that I found a solace after my mother died in 1995 and again after my father's death four years later. My parents were both great believers in the value and power of prayer and tried to convince me of it too. When I was young, and even as I grew into adulthood, my mother would never serve me breakfast without inquiring, "So, did you *daven?*" My father taught by example; he *davened* every day, in the morning and at night. I knew it would be a tribute to their memories to *daven* each day, especially in the year following their passing. *Kaddish* was in some ways the excuse for going to synagogue to pray the way my parents hoped I would.

The Basics

BIBLICAL ORIGINS "And Sarah died at Kiryat-arba, that is Hebron, in the land of Canaan; and Abraham went in to mourn for Sarah and to weep for her" (Genesis 23:2).

FIRST FUNERAL "After this, Abraham buried Sarah his wife in the cave of the field of Machpela facing Mamre, that is Hebron, in the land of Canaan" (Genesis 23:19).

TREATMENT OF THE DECEASED The body is washed and dressed in white garments in preparation for burial. The deceased is not left alone from the time of death until the burial, which is supposed to follow quickly, preferably within a day. Embalming and cremation are forbidden practices.

TREATMENT OF THE MOURNER There is an obligation to visit and comfort the mourner. The mourner receives visitors at home for seven days in a rite known as *shiva.*

IMMEDIATE OBLIGATIONS OF THE MOURNER The mourner is pri-

marily responsible for the care and burial of the deceased. This obligation is so serious that he or she is exempt from performing all positive religious commandments, such as daily prayer. At the burial, the mourner rends his or her garment as a sign of grief. After the burial, the mourner observes a seven-day period during which the mourner stays at home and receives the consolation of visitors. During these seven days, the mourner is forbidden to work, get a haircut, shave, wear cosmetics, have sexual relations, wear leather shoes, wash clothes, or bathe. Even the study of Torah is prohibited during this period.

VOCABULARY Between the time of death and the burial, the mourner is known as an *onen*. The seven-day *shiva* period begins after burial. A modified thirty-day mourning period follows known as *sheloshim*. It is followed by a year of *aveylut*, during which the mourner is known as an *avel*. The major obligation on the mourner is to daily recite the *kaddish*, a prayer of praise to God, with a quorum of ten Jews. *Kaddish* is said for eleven months for one who is mourning parents and thirty days for one who mourns for other immediate relatives, such as a spouse, a child, or a sibling.

BLESSING Upon hearing the news of the death, the mourner accepts God's judgment with a prayer: "Blessed art thou, Lord our God, King of the universe, the true and righteous judge."

REGIONAL CUSTOMS The men of Sephardic burial societies break an earthenware jar in front of the house of the deceased. In some Sephardic communities, the mourners walk around the bier seven times, chanting dirges and lamentations.

MODERN INNOVATIONS Instead of tearing one's garment at the funeral, some tear a black swatch of cloth attached to their lapel. Reform Judaism allows such practices as embalming and cremation. It also allows for music at the funeral and in the home. Some mourners find it especially appropriate to play music beloved by the deceased. Some observe three days of mourning instead of seven. Others just hold a brief service after returning from the cemetery.

BOOK TWO

The Jewish Year

INTRODUCTION

To be sensitive to the Jewish year means being just a bit out of step with the prevailing Christian culture. Jewish festivals arrive with the seasons—from Rosh Hashanah in the fall to Passover in the spring—but not always on the same dates as on the secular calendar. And they can fall on virtually any day of the week, including the Sabbath.

One modern American Jewish quirk is to adjust the Jewish holidays to fit into the Christian calendar—or, at last, the rhythm of the week. I know several families who will celebrate the Passover seder on the nearest Saturday night to the festival because that is the day when the extended family can most easily gather. Strictly speaking, that's not kosher. It would be like having fireworks on the third of July because it's a Saturday night. You can have the rockets' red glare, but it's still not Independence Day.

The Hebrew calendar has 354 days over twelve lunar months. Left unadjusted, the Jewish calendar would fall 11 days behind the solar calendar, with its 365 days, and become out of sync with the seasons. For that reason, a thirteenth month is added seven out of every nineteen years. With that added month, the holidays fall each year roughly in the same solar months. The first month is Tishrei (usually commencing in September), which starts with a period of self-examination known as the Ten Days of Repentance. The Ten Days begin with **Rosh Hashanah,** the Jewish New Year, and end with the holiest day of the year, **Yom Kippur,** the Day of Atonement, also called the Sabbath of Sabbaths.

ADD A DAY IF YOU ARE OUTSIDE ISRAEL

The three pilgrimage festivals—Passover, Shavuot, and Sukkot—are observed differently in Israel than in Jewish communities outside Israel. In the Diaspora, each of the major holidays (other than Yom Kippur) is a day longer than in Israel. This came about because of a historical anomaly that no longer pertains but has become part of the tradition. In ancient times, the three pilgrimage festivals were set by rabbinical courts in Israel based on the sightings of the moon. Those who lived in the Diaspora did not know exactly when each holiday had been declared and therefore had to estimate its time. To guard against missing the festival, they added an extra day. Today, with a set calendar and modern communications, the reason for the extra day technically no longer exists. However, because it was an established tradition, the practice continued and became known as *yom tov sheini shel galuyot*, literally the second day of the holiday in exile. The practice was abolished by the Reform and Reconstructionist branches of Judaism, which keep as many days in the Diaspora as in Israel. But the Orthodox and Conservative movements continue with the old practice. For some, the extra days serve as a penalty and a reminder that the festivals are not complete unless observed in the Holy Land.

This extra-day phenomenon applies only to the three festivals mentioned above. It does not apply to Rosh Hashanah or Yom Kippur, which are celebrated for two days and one day, respectively, both in Israel and in the Diaspora. It also does not apply to minor festivals like Hanukkah and Purim or to fast days.

As with virtually all Jewish observances, each festival starts the night before the calendar day. This is true of the weekly Sabbath, which begins Friday night at sundown, and so with all the festivals (but not with most of the fasts, which are observed during the day only).

Rosh Hashanah and Yom Kippur are referred to collectively as the High Holy Days or, in Hebrew, as the *Yamim Nora'im,* literally "Days of Awe." On the next level of importance are the three pilgrimage holidays known as **Sukkot, Shavuot,** and **Passover,** all three of which are mentioned in the Torah. On the next tier are the rest of the holidays and fasts, which were set by the rabbis.

Yom Kippur is quickly followed by the harvest festival known as **Sukkot,** during which Jews construct booths as a reminder of the ancient journey of the Israelites through the desert. The next major holiday on the calendar is **Hanukkah,** which falls in the Hebrew month of Kislev (invariably in December). It commemorates an ancient Jewish military victory and is celebrated with the kindling of lights, one for each night of the eight-day festival.

Purim comes next, in the month of Adar (usually March). It is a sort of Jewish Mardi Gras, with revelers dressing up in costume and even drinking booze. Purim celebrates the foiling of an evil decree against the Jews of Persia.

Passover, the ultimate Jewish festival of freedom, comes next, in the month of Nisan (usually April). It celebrates the Exodus from Egypt, when the Israelites moved from being a slave people to a nation. A few days after Passover comes **Yom HaShoah,** a national commemoration and memorial for the six million Jews killed in the Nazi Holocaust during World War II. About a week later, in the month of Iyar (April or May), is **Yom Ha'atzmaut,** which marks the founding in 1948 of the modern state of Israel. A month later in the month of Sivan (usually May) is **Shavuot,** the festival that marks revelation: the giving of the Torah on Sinai.

The last notable date on the calendar before the close of the year is **Tisha B'av,** the ninth day of the Hebrew month of Av (usually August). **Tisha B'av** is a day of sadness and fasting in commemoration of the destructions of the two Temples: the first by the Babylonians, in 586 B.C.E.; and the second by the Romans, in 70 C.E.

These are the months of the Hebrew calendar and the festivals and fasts that fall within them:

Tishrei	Rosh Hashanah
	Fast of Gedaliah
	Yom Kippur
	Sukkot
Cheshvan	
Kislev	Hanukkah
Tevet	The Fast of the Tenth of Tevet
Shevat	
Adar	Fast of Esther
	Purim
Adar II	Occurs only in a leap year, in which case the Fast of Ester and Purim are celebrated in Adar II
Nisan	Fast of the Firstborn
	Passover
	Yom HaShoah
Iyar	Yom Ha'atzmaut
Sivan	Shavout
Tammuz	Fast of the Seventeenth of Tammuz
Av	Fast of the Ninth of Av
Elul	

CHAPTER FIVE

Rosh Hashanah

In one of my favorite *Saturday Night Live* sketches, Jane Curtin plays a television news reporter who is out on location in Times Square squawking about the excitement of New Year's Eve: the crowds, the confetti, the minutes ticking away before the ball drops to announce the New Year. The announcer in the studio interrupts her and asks why Times Square appears to be empty. "It is the New Year," she insists, and then she looks with surprise to the empty streets. "Oh," she stutters with embarrassment. "It's Rosh Hashanah."

On Rosh Hashanah you won't find Jews partying out in the streets. There is no champagne, no kissing at midnight, no confetti, and no fireworks. The Jewish New Year starts with solemn reflections in the synagogue over the year that has passed, and festive holiday dinners at home that feature sweet foods.

The New Year brings opportunities for personal renewal in Judaism that hearken back to the story of the creation of the world. The message is clear: On Rosh Hashanah we can create ourselves anew. The Talmud links these two concepts—creation and personal renewal—by saying that humankind was created on Rosh Hashanah and that every year on this day God reviews the deeds of men and women to decide their fate for the coming year. These themes are repeated again and again in the Rosh Hashanah prayers, in the Torah reading for the festi-

val, and in the sound of the shofar, the ram's horn that is a kind of spiritual alarm clock for the soul.

While it marks the start of a new calendar year, Rosh Hashanah is as much about looking back as looking ahead. The past and the future are linked; our fortune in the new year depends on our behavior in the year that has passed. Rosh Hashanah is a time to ask, How did I do? Did I live up to my obligations? Did I observe the *mitzvot*? Was I good to those around me? Did I give to charity? Was I honest in business? We ask ourselves these questions, and God watches. God, the creator of heaven and earth, cares about every individual and his or her behavior. God knows our actions and our thoughts. In the image of the prayer book, God writes it all down; weighs our actions, our intentions, and our repentance; and decides our fate.

"On Rosh Hashanah, God inscribes," according to the prayers. "And on the Fast of Yom Kippur, God seals." What's at stake is nothing less than our lives.

On Rosh Hashanah, one has to be reconciled both with God and with one's fellow human beings. We pray for God's forgiveness, but God cannot pardon us for the sins we have committed against others. In the days before Rosh Hashanah, it is customary to call or visit friends and family members and apologize for any offenses committed against them. Many also make an effort to pay off their debts before Rosh Hashanah. They want to go into the holiday without obligations to others.

HISTORY

The Torah prescribes one day of "holy convocation" based on the sighting of the new moon, but because of confusion over the exact day when the moon is sighted over Jerusalem, Rosh Hashanah is celebrated over two days. This is the case in both Israel and the Diaspora. (The procedure for other festivals is different; Shavuot, for example, is celebrated for one day in Israel and two days in the Diaspora.) The Talmud records that the tradition of two days for Rosh Hashanah goes back to the time of the early prophets, which would mean that even in ancient Israel, two days of the festival were kept. In a bit of rabbinic sleight of hand, the two days are referred to by the rabbis as *yoma arichta:* one long day, a forty-eight-hour New Year's observance. Reform Judaism, reasoning that the justification for two days is no longer applicable, observes only one day of Rosh Hashanah. But for other Jews, the power of the tradition of two days is unquestioned.

The festival is not called Rosh Hashanah in the Bible. The terms used instead are *yom teruah* (the day of sounding the shofar) and *yom hazikoron* (the day of remembering). The idea that this is the beginning of the year apparently developed later. The Talmud, in fact, says that there are four Rosh Hashanahs, enumerating a new year for kings (in the month of Nisan), another for trees (Shevat), a third for the tithing of animals (Elul) and, finally, a new year marking the creation of the world (Tishrei). Tishrei earns the ultimate Rosh Hashanah crown, although others are still marked, especially the new year for trees, which in recent years has become a cause for celebration among Jewish environmentalists.

SYNAGOGUE

Many Jews who do not go to synagogue all year do so on Rosh Hashanah. The festival has one of the longest prayer services of the year, exceeded only by Yom Kippur. The Rosh Hashanah service can run from three to five hours. As always, synagogue is also a social occasion. People exchange wishes for a good year with the words "*l'shanah tova ti-ka-tey-vu*," literally, "May you be inscribed [in the Book of Life] for a good year." To demonstrate our confidence that forgiveness will come, it is customary to wear white, a symbol of purity, on the High Holy Days. A white velvet or silk mantle is also used to cover the ark and the Torahs within.

For many rabbis, the Rosh Hashanah and Yom Kippur sermons are the most important they deliver all year. Gathered before them are their biggest and often most receptive audience. The music program of the synagogue will also be polished, and many synagogues organize choirs. Among Reform and some Conservative and Reconstructionist congregations, the singing may be accompanied in the synagogue by an organ or other instrument. The Orthodox do not allow instruments to be played on the Sabbath or festivals. But among all branches, the finest and most inspiring cantors will be engaged to lead the services on these days. They lead the congregation in special High Holy Day melodies, which set a solemn yet hopeful tone for the day.

The liturgy is based on classic texts. God's sovereignty is declared by invoking ten verses from the Bible, including this verse from Isaiah:

"I am first and I am the last and aside from me there is no other God." The secondary theme of the day, is about judgment and repentance. Perhaps the most stirring prayer on this theme is the hymn *unetaneh tokef*, written about a thousand years ago and attributed to Rabbi Amnon of Mainz, Germany. The prayer shows God's concern with each individual. "You alone are the One who judges, proves, knows and bears witness; who writes and sees, counts and calculates, who remembers all that was forgotten. . . . All mankind will pass before You like members of the flock."

The legend behind the prayer gives it added power. As the story goes, the bishop of Mainz ordered Rabbi Amnon to renounce Judaism and embrace Christianity. When the rabbi refused, the bishop ordered that his limbs be severed one by one. In his agony, Rabbi Amnon was brought to the synagogue and placed before the ark, where, with his final breaths, he recited *unetaneh tokef*. "Who will live and who will die?" the prayer asks. "Who by water and who by fire, who by sword, who by beast, who by famine, who by storm, who by plague, who by strangulation?"

It is a gruesome list. (The folk singer Leonard Cohen put a rhyming version to mischievously dirgeful music years ago.) It continues: "Who will rest and who will wander, who will live in harmony and who will be harried, who will enjoy tranquility and who will suffer, who will be impoverished and who will be enriched, who will be degraded and who will be exalted?" The prayer ends with a formula for salvation: "And Repentance, and Prayer, and the Giving of Charity avert the evil decree."

My friend Rabbi Michael Paley, a teacher who cannot easily be tied down to any one modern movement in Judaism (he has both Reconstructionist and Orthodox ordinations), says that averting the "evil decree" is not an effort to avoid death, for, indeed, death is an inevitability that we all face. "The evil decree," he says, "is to have a life without meaning. As he chanted *unetaneh tokef*, Rabbi Amnon had no illusion that he would avoid death. On his deathbed, he said, in effect, 'I made it.' It's living a meaningful life that's important." The formula for meaning, as the prayer says, is to reach in three directions: repentance (*inward*), charity (*outward*), and prayer (*upward*).

THE SHOFAR

The sounding of the shofar is at the heart of the Rosh Hashanah service. Befitting the themes of the day, it is a sound that at once inspires us to God's greatness and humbles us before our own limitations. In the Torah, the image of the shofar is often evoked: at Sinai, in the admonitions of the prophets, at the binding of Isaac, at a time of military victory, at the coronation of a king, and ultimately, at the coming of the Messiah and on the final judgment day. All these symbols are remembered on Rosh Hashanah. But perhaps the greatest message of the shofar is its primitive sound, one that goes beyond words—a sound that takes off where our words fail us. After volumes and volumes of spoken prayer, it is the sound of the shofar that finally pierces our hearts and the heavens.

The rabbis of the Talmud debate how the shofar should be sounded. Some say it is the sound of a wailing *(teru'ah)*, other says it is the sound of a sigh *(shevarim)*, and still others maintain that it is a combination of both—sighing and wailing *(shevarim, teru'ah)*. In order to satisfy all three opinions, all three blasts are sounded, each preceded by the standard blast known as a *tekiyah*. Each sound has its own character. While the *tekiyah* is one long blast, the *teru'ah* is broken into nine shorter parts and the *shevarim* into three. Before the sounding of the shofar, a blessing is made praising God for giving us the commandment "to hear the shofar." The Biblical requirement is that the shofar is heard; there is no obligation for each person to sound his or her own horn. Before each blast of the shofar, the rabbi calls out the name of the sound: for example, *tekiyah, shevarim, tekiyah*. Long, three short, and long again. In some congregations, it is not the

rabbi alone who announces the blasts but the whole congregation, giving the shofar blowing a rhythmic and participatory quality. Sets of these blasts are sounded at intervals during the Rosh Hashanah service. In many synagogues, one hundred blasts in all are sounded. The one hundredth blast, known as the *tekiyah gedolah,* is the longest, testing the endurance of the shofar blower.

In the literature of Jewish mysticism, the blasts of the shofar serve one other purpose: to frighten and confuse Satan, the accuser of Israel. With the blasts of the shofar, Satan hears that Jews still declare their obedience to God, and cherish the *mitzvot,* and so Satan loses his argument. He hears the sound of the shofar and worries that it is the sound that heralds the coming of the Messiah and the day of judgment.

Even those who can't make it to synagogue are supposed to hear the shofar. Jewish chaplains at hospitals will often go from room to room to make sure that Jewish patients hear the sounds. Others will visit the homebound elderly or sick to sound the shofar in their homes. The sound of the shofar inspires not only awe and forgiveness among mankind, but compassion by God. One of the psalms read before the sounding of the shofar is from the book of Lamentations: "You have heard my voice. Do not shut your ear from my prayer for my relief."

TASHLICH

Another symbol of ridding ourselves of our sins comes on the second day of Rosh Hashanah in a ceremony known as *tashlich*. The custom is to walk to the edge of a river or lake and symbolically throw away one's sins. Some Jewish scholars opposed the practice, fearing it was being taken too literally by believers; it's not that simple, these scholars said. But *tashlich* has become a widely accepted practice and something of a social event. In large Jewish communities near lakes and rivers (New York, Cleveland, Miami, Chicago, and Los Angeles, for example), police are often on hand to control the crowds. As children, my brothers and I enhanced the symbolism by putting bread in our pockets when we went for *tashlich*, declaring that these were the sins we were throwing away. Nothing of the sort is required, but the fish must have been happy. As adults, we all carry our burdens with us, and it is good to leave them by the river, even if it is only a symbolic act.

I used to sit next to a stooped-over elderly man named Joseph at Lincoln Square Synagogue in Manhattan. He came to synagogue virtually every Sabbath and every holiday. "I don't do *tashlich*," he confided in me one day when the High Holy Days were drawing near.

"Never?" I asked.

"Never," he said emphatically. I asked him why, and he told me this story: "When I was little, we lived in Far Rockaway, right near the water. On Rosh Hashanah afternoon, we, and all the other religious families, would walk down to the beach. One year, I hung back and watched all the men in their dark suits and the women in their long

No Ticket Required

Don't be put off by the fact that most synagogues sell seats for the High Holy Days. It has become an economic necessity, but it certainly does not mean that you won't be admitted if you do not have a ticket. Nearly all synagogues will set aside some seats for those without tickets. Some synagogues will even have a special service, at which time seating is open and free.

The seating charge is in some ways linked to the fact that commerce is forbidden on the Sabbath and holidays. It is a violation of the Sabbath rules and spirit to pass a collection plate in the *shul*, as is done in a church. Since few people voluntarily send money to the synagogue during the week, many synagogues have to wait for the High Holy Days for an infusion of money. The membership year often begins with the High Holy Days, and seats may be included in the price of synagogue membership. You may hear that someone spent $1,000 on seats for the High Holy Days. This is probably the cost not just of the seat, but of a year's membership for a family, which comes to about $20 a week. Many synagogues also have membership fees on a sliding scale, depending on income. And all synagogues welcome non-members. You just might not get the best seats.

dresses standing on the shore, saying their prayers and casting their sins on the water. The waters glistened before them. Suddenly, the winds changed and a great wave came up on shore, splashing them all—the men, the women, and the children. A great cry rose up from the crowd, and they ran, in wet shoes, to higher ground.

"It was then I realized that God does not want our sins."

"Was your faith shaken?" I asked him.

"No, no, not at all," he said. "I just decided never to go to *tashlich*."

The Basics

BIBLICAL ORIGINS "On the first day of the seventh month, you shall have a holy convocation; you shall not work at your occupations. It is a day for you to blow the trumpets, and you shall offer a burnt offering, a pleasing odor to the Lord" (Numbers 29:1–2).

TALMUD Rosh Hashanah, the day God first created man, is also the day each year when God judges every individual man and woman.

CODE OF LAW No work or commerce is to be done on the holiday. In lieu of the "burnt offering" mentioned in the Bible, an extra *musaf* prayer is added to the regular three prayers said daily in the synagogue.

CALENDAR The festival is celebrated over two days, the first and second of the Hebrew month of Tishrei, except by Reform Jewry, which marks only one day of Rosh Hashanah.

RITUAL The sounding of the ram's horn, known as the shofar. In the synagogue, one hundred blasts of the shofar are sounded.

GREETING "May you be inscribed [in the Book of Life] for a good year" (*L'shanah tova ti-ka-tey-vu*).

CUSTOMS At this time of the year, prior to the commencement of the holiday, it is customary to visit the graves of loved ones, especially parents. On the first day of the festival, Jews gather at lakes and rivers to perform a symbolic casting off of their sins into the water in a ritual known as *tashlich*. There is a custom *not* to take a nap on either day of the festival. The Jerusalem Talmud warns: "If one sleeps at the beginning of the year, his good fortune also sleeps." As if to show confidence in God's willingness to forgive, many people wear white clothes on Rosh Hashanah and Yom Kippur. The colorful velvet covers on the ark and on the Torahs within are often changed to white.

FOODS Apples and honey, symbolic of a sweet year to come. Eating a pomegranate and saying, "May our merits be as plentiful as the seeds of a pomegranate." Eating round challah, symbolic of the cycle of life. *Not* eating nuts, because the numerical value of the Hebrew word for nuts *(egoz)*—seventeen—is the same as the value of the word for sin *(chet)*.

CHAPTER SIX

Yom Kippur

A rabbinic tale: Adam meets Cain outside the locked gates of the Garden of Eden. Much has transpired since the first family was banished from Paradise. Most traumatically, Cain killed his brother Abel in a jealous rage. "So what is your punishment?" Adam asks his son anxiously. Cain answers, "I showed remorse, and God annulled half my sentence." Cain, who had been cursed by God to be a wanderer, has nonetheless found a home in the land of Nod, as the Bible says, "east of Eden." Adam is dumbfounded. He looks at his son and then longingly toward the gates of Eden and says, "So this is the power of repentance. If only I had known!"

Yom Kippur is very much about the power of repentance. In the imagery of the Yom Kippur prayers, God weighs our deeds, looks at our remorse and our resolve, and, with mercy, determines our fate for the next year. But believing in a supernatural God is not necessary to make it through Yom Kippur. Sometimes it is within our own hands to change our destiny.

Yom Kippur is a fast day—a day of denial, in the words of the Bible—but it is not considered a sad day. There are five disciplines of the day: no eating or drinking, washing, anointing, wearing leather, or having sexual relations.

Several years ago, I heard Rabbi Norman Lamm, now president of

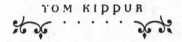

Yeshiva University but once a prominent Orthodox pulpit rabbi, explain that the five forms of self-denial sensitize the Jew to the suffering of fellow human beings. "We refrain from food and drink to teach us sympathy with the hungry," he said in a sermon on Yom Kippur. "We abstain from sex and thus learn sensitivity to those who have no families. We wear no leather shoes and so identify with the poor who are unshod. We do not anoint our bodies with oil or lotions to better understand those deprived of luxury all year long."

The day is centered on the synagogue. In many American synagogues, the prayers go from morning until night, with only an hour or so of a break in the late afternoon. In Israel, where there tends to be less ceremony in the synagogue and greater familiarity with the service, the service does not run as long but always ends with nightfall. Five prayer services are offered on Yom Kippur, one more than on the Sabbath and other festivals. They are:

Ma'ariv, the evening service, which begin with *Kol Nidrei*, perhaps the most famous of the High Holy Day prayers.

Schacharit, the morning service, which precedes the morning Torah reading.

Musaf, the additional service, which is also said on the Sabbath and festivals. On Yom Kippur it also includes the *avodah*, which recalls the words and drama of the Temple service of old.

Mincha, the afternoon service, which includes the reading of the book of Jonah.

Ne'ila, the special Yom Kippur addition, which ends with the blast of the shofar, concluding Yom Kippur.

THE EVE OF YOM KIPPUR

The eve of Yom Kippur is given special importance. It is regarded as not merely a preparation for, but an inseparable part of, the Day of Atonement. The Talmud states: "Everyone who eats and drinks on the

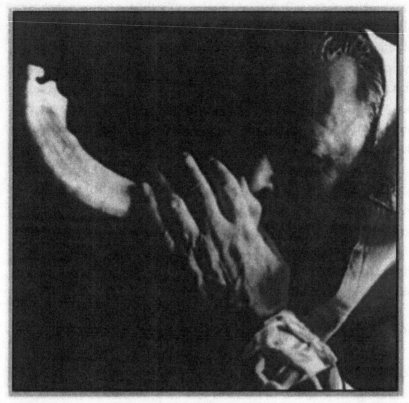

ninth [of Tishrei] is considered by Scripture as having fasted on the ninth and tenth." Marking the eve of Yom Kippur with eating and drinking is not only a preparation for the fast but an observance of the holy day itself. Today, the fact that Yom Kippur is a festival, "a holy convocation" in the words of the Bible, has largely been overlooked. But I've often felt that if only Yom Kippur could be marketed better as a time for rejoicing *and* fasting, it would draw even more adherents. The eve of Yom Kippur is a day to eat without guilt. First, it is encouraged by the sages; second, whatever you gain you can take off by fasting the next day.

In the late afternoon on the eve of Yom Kippur, a festive holiday meal is served. The table is set with a white tablecloth, as it is for the Sabbath. Traditional foods are prepared: fish and soup and chicken and beef. At the table of my grandparents when I was a child, I remember how serene that meal was. There was no warning that a major day of introspection and denial would soon be upon us. We'd all be dressed in our holiday clothes. Family members would pass the food, eat heartily, and talk leisurely and comfortably. But then the mood would shift. One by one we would line up in front of my father and grandfather to receive a special Yom Kippur blessing. My grandfather would hold my head in his hand and offer a tearful prayer, as much, I'm sure, for me as for him. During the grace after meals, the floodgates would open. My grandparents would be crying like children. It was as if this was our last meal not just for Yom Kippur, but forever.

We would walk to the synagogue quietly together, where the men—my father and grandfather—would each put on a white gown, known as a *kittel*. Even as a child, I knew of its dual symbolism. The *kittel* was a sign of purity; we were approaching God with a clean slate. But it was also a sign of death. A Jew is buried in a white shroud. On Yom Kippur, life and death hang in the balance.

The story is told of one great rabbi who looked out on his congregation, all dressed in white, and said: "Take heart that it is in white garments like these that we shall ascend to the World to Come to be judged and give our accounting before the King of all kings, the Holy One, blessed is He. Let us then imagine on this Yom Kippur that we are standing before the very Throne of Glory."

IN THE SYNAGOGUE

Just before sunset, the ark is opened, and all the Torahs are taken out and handed to congregants, who carry them in a great circle throughout the synagogue. Worshipers reach out and kiss the scrolls with their hands or the fringes of their prayer shawls. All but two of the Torahs are then put back in the ark. Two remain in the arms of two wor-

KAPPAROT

To put it bluntly, *kapparot* is the act of substituting an animal—usually a chicken—for oneself on the eve of Yom Kippur. The instructions are as follows: Lift the chicken (live!) over your head, move it in a clockwise motion, and say, "This is my exchange, this is my substitute, this is my atonement. This rooster/hen will go to its death while I will enter and proceed to a good long life, and to peace."

A woman uses a hen; a man uses a rooster. And a pregnant woman uses both a hen and a rooster (in case she is carrying a boy). The preferred color of these chickens is white.

Scholars are quick to point out that this is not a sacrifice. (No Jewish animal sacrifice has been permitted since the destruction of the Temple.) Rather, *kapparot* is another symbolic act of atonement. In keeping with the theme of charitable giving as another kind of atonement, the chicken is slaughtered and given to a needy family.

Kapparot is widely practiced in Hasidic neighborhoods. In Brooklyn's Crown Heights, for example, Hasidic Jews line up by the hundreds for *kapparot* at the headquarters of the Lubavitch Hasidim. There are two lines: the rooster line for men, and the hen line for women. Pregnant women don't have to wait in line; hen and rooster are brought right out to them.

Kapparot was a part of my own childhood. On the eve of Yom Kippur, my grandfather—not a scholar or a rabbi but a businessman who dabbled in Connecticut politics—brought live chickens home in a burlap sack. I remember watching the sacks squawking and tumbling on the back porch. Many years later, when I was a reporter at *The New York Times*, I shared my memory with a friend. "I'd like to do that again someday," I said. But one has to be careful what one wishes for. A day

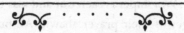

before Yom Kippur, the *Times* security guard called me from the lobby: "Mr. Goldman, there's a chicken waiting for you downstairs." Amazed (and, as I recall, on deadline), I told the guard to send it up. "Not allowed," he said. "No livestock in the building." The guard held the chicken until the end of the day, when I took it home on the commuter railroad. My children were delighted. My wife gave me a less than loving look. We performed the ritual out on the back porch, but Shira insisted that we give the poor animal a reprieve. We donated the chicken to a nearby day care center that had a coop. As for the needy family this was supposed to benefit, we made a special contribution to a local charity. It was all in the spirit of the day.

VARIATION ON A THEME: YOM KIPPUR AT THE BEACH

My friend Arthur, a writer and book editor, was sitting with his wife and teenage daughters in their synagogue in suburban Baltimore, bored silly. "This is meaningless," he announced. "Next year, we're spending Yom Kippur on the beach. We'll read Abraham Joshua Heschel. We'll contemplate God's creation. We'll review our lives together as a family." Everyone was overjoyed. As the year progressed they even looked forward to Yom Kippur, all the while wondering whether Arthur would keep his word.

And he did. A year later, Arthur drove the family to the Maryland coast. It was a bit chilly, but they spread out a blanket. The sun came out. The kids ran to the water. They walked and they waded. They got hungry. Someone threw a ball. Then a Frisbee. They ran out for Chinese food. They never read Heschel. They never contemplated God's creation. They never did the year in review.

"Next year," Arthur announced, "we're going back to Temple."

shipers, an honor guard of sorts, who stand next to the cantor as he or she chants the *Kol Nidrei* prayer. On the face of it, *Kol Nidrei* has nothing to do with the theme of repentance. It literally means "all vows" and is a formula for the nullification of vows made in the last year. "All vows, prohibitions, oaths . . . will be abandoned, canceled, null and void, without power and without standing." The prayer, sung in a haunting but hopeful melody, is repeated in Hebrew three times, the first time quietly and then each subsequent time with greater force and resolve. The traditional *Kol Nidrei* melody was adapted for the cello by the nineteenth-century composer Max Bruch. In some Reform congregations, the piece is played by a cellist, but the Orthodox and Conservative leave it to the cantor.

The significance of beginning the service with a prayer about vows is open to various interpretations. Some explain that it is yet another attempt to start the year with a clean slate. But others explain that the message is one that we want to turn on God. With this prayer about vows, we want to remind God of His promises that the people of Israel will forever be under God's protective wing.

The rest of the evening prayer is much like the standard festival service, except for two important differences that are repeated in all the Yom Kippur prayers. Every evening, one recites the *sh'ma*, the Jewish declaration of the oneness of God, and then silently adds, "*Baruch shem kvod malchuto le'olam va'ed*" (Blessed is the name of His glorious kingdom for all eternity). The verse is traditionally whispered on ordinary evenings because it is said to belong not to mankind but to the angels. According to legend, Moses heard the angels singing this verse when he went to the top of Sinai to get the Torah from God. On Yom Kippur, however, the verse is chanted out loud; for it is a day when all of Israel aspire to be ministering angels.

The other change in the liturgy is the addition of a section called *vidduy,* which are special confessional prayers. The list of sins that one confesses on Yom Kippur go on for pages. It is an alphabetically arranged laundry list of every sin imaginable—from not honoring one's parents to committing adultery. They are said not for the individual ("I sinned") but for the community ("We sinned"). You say them whether you knowingly transgressed or not, on the theory that all Jews are responsible one for the others.

The *vidduy* is said ten times over the festival (including the afternoon prayer on the eve of Yom Kippur), corresponding, according to one interpretation, to the Ten Commandments. This is our opportunity to embrace them anew.

FASTING AND DANCING

Nowhere have I experienced the joy of Yom Kippur more than at the synagogue of the late Rabbi Shlomo Carlebach, the most influential Jewish songwriter of the twentieth century. Rabbi Carlebach, who maintained a small synagogue on West Seventy-ninth Street in Manhattan, as well as one in Los Angeles and a religious settlement in Israel, joyously sang his way through Yom Kippur.

On Yom Kippur 1994, the last Yom Kippur before Carlebach's death, at the age of seventy, I joined the rabbi at his congregation in Manhattan for the *ne'ila* prayer. *Ne'ila* is the final prayer of the day and is said right before sunset on Yom Kippur evening. Literally, it means "closing the gates"; in this case the gates of heaven. Rabbi Carlebach implored us to "pierce the heavens" with our prayers so that we—"and all Israel and all the world"—would be inscribed for a good year.

Anyone who knows a Carlebach tune (and there are hundreds) knows that they are songs without endings. Carlebach never ended his songs; they just keep going and going until the singer and the song are exhausted. On the night of his last Yom Kippur, the crowd at the Carlebach *shul* was hungry and exhausted but energized by the songs. The singing kept us going well beyond the hour when Yom Kippur was over. No one wanted to stop; no one—least of all Carlebach—knew how to stop. We sang and swayed and sang until finally the rabbi cried out the final prayer seven times: "God is our God!" Next to him stood a young man swathed in a *tallit* who held a long and winding shofar.

"*Tekiyah gedolah,*" Rabbi Carlebach demanded with vigor. The sound of the shofar cut through the air, and it was as if we could see its notes dancing through the synagogue in slow motion, pew by pew, touching each man and each woman with holiness and forgiveness.

The Basics

BIBLICAL ORIGINS "Now, the tenth day of this seventh month is the day of atonement; it shall be a holy convocation for you: you shall deny yourselves and present the Lord's offering by fire; and you shall do no work during that entire day; for it is a day of atonement, to make atonement on your behalf before the Lord your God. . . . It shall be to you a sabbath of complete rest, and you shall deny yourselves; on the ninth day of the month at evening, from evening to evening you shall keep your sabbath" (Leviticus 23:27–32).

TALMUD What does the Torah mean when it speaks of denial? There are five areas of prohibition: eating or drinking, washing (for pleasure), anointing the body (with oil), wearing of leather, and sexual intercourse.

CODE OF LAW No work or commerce is performed. In lieu of Temple sacrifices, a special *musaf* prayer is added in which the sacrifices are recalled. In addition, a fifth prayer, *ne'ila,* is added at the end of the day.

CALENDAR the festival is marked on the tenth day of Tishrei, concluding the Ten Days of Repentance.

RITUALS The prayers in the synagogue take up most of the day. They involve confession—complete with breast beating—and a detailed recollection of the Temple service of old known as the *avodah.* In a departure from Jewish prayer the rest of the year, worshipers get down on their knees at special points during prayers in the synagogue. The day ends with a long blast of the shofar, known as a *tekiyah gedolah.*

GREETING "May you be inscribed and sealed [in the Book of Life] for a good year" (*L'shanah tova ti-ka-tey-vu vetechateymu*).

CUSTOMS Eating a festive meal *before* the fast is meritorious. Also before the fast, one lights special long-burning candles, known as *yahrtzeit* lights, in memory of relatives who have died. These candles burn throughout the festival. It is also customary to wear white clothing, a symbol of purity.

FOODS None. Minors and those who are ill, pregnant, or elderly may, upon consulting a rabbi, eat, but they are to do so in moderation and refrain from meat and wine.

CHAPTER SEVEN

Sukkot and Simchat Torah

Just five days after Yom Kippur comes the festival of Sukkot. And in that short span of time, our image of God evolves from stern judge to sheltering mother. God's maternal side is manifest in the *sukkah,* the hut where, according to the Bible, God provided for the Israelites as they journeyed through the desert after the Exodus from Egypt.

The festival of Sukkot has numerous identities:

First, it closes the New Year festivities that begin on Rosh Hashanah. Echoes of the New Year season can be heard in the greetings (it is still appropriate to wish one another *l'shanah tova*) and in the foods (we continue to dip bread in honey and eat other sweet dishes to symbolize a year of sweetness).

Second, Sukkot is linked to the Exodus, as are other holidays that occur later in the calendar year. Passover represents leaving Egypt, Shavuot, the receiving of the Torah on Sinai, and Sukkot, the wandering in the desert.

Third, Sukkot is a harvest festival, known in the Torah as *chag ha'asif,* the festival of the ingathering.

The holiday huts built on Sukkot are associated both with the Exodus and with the harvest. The Torah tells us that God sheltered the Israelites in huts. The huts that Jews traditionally build to mark the holiday resemble agricultural booths more than desert dwellings. In the agrarian society where these customs originated, workers moved out of their homes and into thatched huts closer to the fields during the harvest season so they could work from morning until night. One authority in the Talmud, Rabbi Eliezer, says that the huts built for Sukkot are merely symbolic; they represent the "clouds of glory" that sheltered the Jews. Another Talmudic authority, Rabbi Akiva, takes the Scripture literally; the *sukkah* huts, he says, symbolize the booths built for protection in the desert.

BUILDING THE BOOTH

Regardless of the origin of the custom, the Talmud goes to great lengths to describe the dimensions and materials that are to be used in the holiday booths. The *sukkah* must have a minimum of three walls and must be of a certain height. But the most important characteristic of the *sukkah* is the *schach*, the agricultural material used to cover the *sukkah*. While there is a covering, it is supposed to be porous, allowing air and light to flow in. The preferred coverings are branches from a tree or bamboo poles. The requirement is that there be more shade than light. At night, one is supposed to be able to see the stars through the roof of the *sukkah*.

While the *sukkah* is a temporary dwelling, it is also supposed to have a festive feel. Decorative household items are brought outside to give it a sense of home. One is supposed to "dwell" in the *sukkah*, in the words of the Torah, but comfort is also key. The experience is supposed to be a pleasant one; the requirement is that the *sukkah* be habitable. If it is raining or exceedingly cold, for example, one is not obligated to sit in the *sukkah*. Today, the *sukkah* is used mostly for eating, although the tradition also encourages people to sleep, study, and relax in the *sukkah*. Eating is the most communal of these activities, and there is joy in celebrating the holiday together with others.

Observant Jews go to great lengths to observe this holiday. *Sukkot* can be found in backyards and driveways and on terraces. I once visited a *sukkah* on a houseboat in the Hudson River, and another on the back of a flatbed truck on a Manhattan thoroughfare.

There is a famous New York story about an apartment house dweller who builds his *sukkah* on the fire escape outside his kitchen window.

When mealtime comes, he climbs out the window to eat in the *sukkah*. His landlord is furious and hauls him into housing court to demand that the obstruction be removed immediately. The judge, a fellow named Shapiro, is stern with the tenant but issues his ruling with a wink: "You've got seven days to get this down," he orders.

For seven days, Jews eat and drink in the *sukkah*. While the Orthodox tend to make a greater effort to build their own family *sukkah*, the non-Orthodox put a great emphasis on building communal *sukkot* that all can share. Everyone gets involved. Children are called upon to decorate the booths with their artwork. Members bring their Jewish New Year cards and pin them to the walls. It is also customary to hang produce from the rooftop—I've seen everything from popcorn and cranberries strung on a thread to ears of Indian corn.

THE FOUR SPECIES

The *sukkah* is the main symbol of the holiday; it gives the holiday its name. But there are others, also ordained by the Torah. These are known as the "four species," or *arba minim* in Hebrew. They are the citron (*etrog*), palm branch (*lulav*), myrtle (*hadasim*), and willow (*aravot*), which likewise represent the harvest. In ancient times, the four species were used for Temple worship.

The ritual of the four species is merely to take these items in hand and say a blessing. One then waves them to the four corners of the earth—north, south, east, and west—and then to the heavens above and the earth below. In the synagogue, the four species are held during a special hymn of praise known as *hallel* and shaken in the prescribed manner. During another prayer, *hakafot*, they are held as worshipers walk in a great circle around the sanctuary.

For someone who grows up in a synagogue, the four species are familiar items. Looked at from the outside, waving around of agricultural products might seem like a decidedly strange custom. I first saw this with the eyes of an outsider when I was in graduate school at Co-

VARIATION ON A THEME: THE INDOOR *SUKKAH*

Manhattan's Temple Emanu-El has a beautiful *sukkah*, richly decorated on the walls and the ceiling with evergreens. It is a kosher *sukkah* in every way except that it is located indoors. For the Orthodox, this *sukkah* is invalid; by law its top must be open to the sky. But to the Reform, the symbol is what is important, and the symbol is preserved.

lumbia and took a course with the great religion anthropologist Theodor Gaster, a curmudgeonly professor who enjoyed riling his students by shaking their most basic assumptions. "Who here is Orthodox?" he asked at the beginning of one class on the origins of myth. I stupidly raised my hand. "What is it that you do on the Feast of Booths?" Gaster, the son of the Sephardic chief rabbi of London, purposely used an outdated English name for Sukkot. I proceeded to explain to my classmates about the citron, the palm, etc. Gaster cut me off. "And what do you do with them?" he demanded. "You wave them to the four corners of the earth," I said timidly.

Gaster dramatically picked up an ancient text and began to read about how the early Hittites of Asia Minor did the same thing. "It's all about the fertility of the earth," he said. "You know that, don't you?" He didn't have to point out that the rite was pagan.

While it was a shocking revelation to me at the time (and somewhat rudely delivered), the ritual is not diminished for me by its origins. The ancient Israelites obviously took a fertility ritual and transformed it into a religious rite that has endured and taken on new meaning. The waving of the items in all directions expresses a most unpagan belief—that God is everywhere.

Sukkot has the power to connect even the most urban Jew—the guy

---

VARIATION ON A THEME: A KOSHER *SUKKAH*

A family in Philadelphia takes great pains each year to build a *sukkah* open to the sky. Sukkot is one of the family's favorite festivals. But they don't keep kosher. So they eat non-kosher food each night in the *sukkah*, keeping the *mitzvah* that is meaningful to them and ignoring the one that, for them, has lost its meaning.

---

sitting on his fire escape—with the miracles of nature: the planting, the rainfall, and the harvest. It reminds us that the environment is a Jewish issue. We both inherit the earth and are its custodians for future generations. Some Jewish communities and synagogues organize neighborhood cleanup and recycling efforts at this time.

The rabbis offer symbolic meanings for the four species. While the *sukkah* represents impermanence and wandering, the four species represent rootedness and fertility. Another interpretation is that the shapes of the four species symbolize a person. The palm is the spine, the myrtle the eyes, the willow the mouth, and the citron the heart. We praise God with all our essential parts. A more mystical interpretation ascribes symbolism to only two of the four species: the palm is the phallus and the citron is the breast—appropriate fertility symbols for the time of harvest.

The citron has other associations. According to some commentaries, the story of Eve and the apple in the Garden of Eden was not about apples at all but about a citron (*etrog*). The Bible (Genesis 3:6) notes that both the tree itself and the fruit were "good for food," a characteristic of the citron tree. Everyone knows of Eve's punishment for succumbing to its temptations: God tells her that she and all the women after her will experience great pains and other difficulties in childbirth. It is perhaps for this reason that the *etrog* became a popular item of folk medicine among Sephardic Jews. At the end of the Sukkot holiday, it is customary for a woman who has trouble conceiving to bite off the tip of the *etrog*, known as the *pittom*. If pregnancy ensues, the woman places the *pittom* under her pillow to ensure an easy labor.

COMMUNITY IMPACT

The sheltering motif of Sukkot is also used to make homelessness a Jewish issue. If God provided for us in the desert, don't we have a responsibility to provide for those without shelter today? Many synagogues use the holiday as a chance to support a local homeless shelter or to collect food and clothing for the needy.

There is a leveling effect to the *sukkot*. Rich and poor dwell in the modest huts, reminiscent of a time when all Jews were still emerging from slavery. Rich and poor dwell in the huts that also evoke the homes of the workers during the harvest. The rich family may fill its storehouses, but they too must remember the needy by living modestly.

A related theme is the custom of inviting guests to the *sukkah* for a meal. Since not everyone can build a *sukkah*, often those who can open it up to others. No one expects the *sukkah* to be very roomy; the important thing is that it be filled with people enjoying the holiday. Some Jewish communities organize "*sukkah* walks," in which groups of people visit different *sukkot* for a progressive meal. They have drinks in one *sukkah*, appetizers in a second, entrées in a third, and coffee and dessert in a fourth.

USHPIZIN

The tradition of inviting guests on Sukkot is so strong that we even invite into the *sukkah* the spirits of those who have passed on. Upon entrance into the *sukkah* each night, there is a brief mystical prayer, called *ushpizin*, which invokes the spirits of the three patriarchs (Abraham, Isaac, and Jacob) and the four major Torah personalities (Joseph,

Moses, Aaron, and David). Each of the seven nights, another is invited to be a spiritual guest at the table. In some communities, an extra chair and place setting are put on the table for the imagined guest. It is customary to tell the stories of each of the personalities—stories that are linked to the themes of Sukkot. All the seven personalities were exiles: Abraham left his father's house, Isaac dwelled in Philistia, Jacob fled to Aram and then went to Egypt, Joseph was exiled from his family, Moses and Aaron wandered for forty years in the desert, and David fled from Saul. Each of them has a lot to teach us about exile.

A modern variation on the *ushpizin* is to invite women as well as men. One new custom is to invite seven women along with (or instead of) the seven men. The women usually chosen are the four matriarchs—Sarah, Rebecca, Rachel, and Leah—and three others who spoke with God: Miriam, Hannah, and Deborah. God knows, they too have much to teach us about wandering and exile.

Remembering more recent ancestors is also appropriate. I cannot sit down to a meal in the *sukkah* without thinking of my grandfather, Samuel H. L. Goldman, a small-businessman who rose to be the first (and possibly only) Jewish police commissioner of Hartford, Connecticut. My Grandpa was a worldly man, but he took great pains to observe the Sukkot holiday properly. The back porch of his home had a roof that could be lifted by a pulley from a second-floor bedroom closet. All year long, the porch was just a porch. But then, on Sukkot, it was transformed into an agricultural delight, with hanging fruit and Indian corn. Grandpa would literally raise the roof and leave it up for the whole week so that we could see the stars through the evergreen branches above. Sukkot provides us with a link to nature, to agriculture, to the history of the Jewish people, and to our ancestors.

SHEMINI ATZERET–SIMCHAT TORAH

In Israel, the holiday of Sukkot begins with a single festival day during which no work is permitted and special prayers are said in the synagogue. Outside Israel, two days are observed, originally because of confusion over the calendar but, according to some commentators, as a means of remembering the exile from the land. (Reform Judaism observes only one day, both in Israel and in the Diaspora.)

The days after the opening of Sukkot are known as the Intermediate Days, during which work is permitted (except, of course, on the Sabbath). But the rituals of the holiday—the *sukkah* and the four species— are still observed. Special prayers are said on these days as well.

The festival closes with what is in some ways an independent holiday period, known as Shemini Atzeret–Simchat Torah. In Israel (and among Reform Jews), this is a one-day celebration known by the two names linked together (Shemini Atzeret–Simchat Torah). In the Diaspora, it is celebrated over two days, with each day taking one name. Work is not permitted on these days.

Shemini Atzeret–Simchat Torah has its own biblical passage: "On the eighth day you shall hold a solemn gathering; you shall not work at your occupations" (Numbers 29:35). But the holiday has no distinctive ritual, so it is generally associated with Sukkot. Its origins have to do with the fact that Sukkot was a pilgrimage festival, during which Jews came to Jerusalem. According to the Talmud, God is like a king whose children return home to the palace for a visit from their own lands; He begs them to tarry another day. "It is difficult for me to separate from you," God says in establishing this holiday. Shemini Atzeret–Simchat Torah is a day to linger.

The Simchat Torah part of the holiday (either combined with it in Israel or observed as a separate day in the Diaspora) is when the annual cycle of Torah reading officially ends and begins anew. Each week in synagogues all over the world, the same portion of the Five Books of Moses is read. Centuries ago, the Scripture was divided into sections so that there is a continuous reading on each of the fifty-two Sabbaths of the year (with occasional exceptions for holidays and leap years). Each weekly portion is divided into smaller sections, known as *aliyot*. Worshipers are called with the honor of an *aliyah* and say a blessing on the section.

On Simchat Torah eve, as on the eve of Yom Kippur, all the Torah scrolls are taken from the ark and paraded around the synagogue. But instead of the somber mood of Yom Kippur, Simchat Torah is a time of joy. People sing and kiss the Torah and dance with it in great circles around the synagogue. The Torah is personified as the bride of Israel, and it is an honor to dance with the bride. There are seven of these circumambulations around the synagogue, known as *hakafot*, reminiscent of the seven circuits a bride makes around her groom. After the *hakafot*, the Torah is opened, and some of the Scripture (but not the final verses) is read.

The last verses are not read until the next morning, when the Torah is officially concluded—and begun again. There is an effort to include everyone in the festivities. On Simchat Torah, many synagogues aim to give everyone who attends an *aliyah*. This necessitates reading the portion over and over again or doing group *aliyot*, where several people recite the verse together. Even children under the age of thirteen, who normally are not called to the Torah, are given a special *aliyah* on Simchat Torah, usually accompanied by a shower of sweets from the congregation. After the children's *aliyah*, the congregation recites Genesis 48:16: "The angel who has redeemed me from all evil, bless the youths; and let my name be named on them . . . and let them grow into a multitude in the midst of the earth."

After everyone is called to the Torah, the final verses are read. They are rich in drama. They record the death of Moses, who, as the Scripture says, was the only mortal to know God "face to face." No sooner are the final words—"in the sight of all Israel"—read than the reading of the Torah starts again, from the "In the Beginning." It is a special honor to have both the last and the first *aliyot* of the Torah. The person who gets the last *aliyah* is called the *chatan Torah*, the groom of the Torah. The person honored with the first is the *chatan B'reshit*, the groom of Genesis. For the Orthodox, the honored are men, since it is only men who can get an *aliyah*. In the non-Orthodox movements, women are called to the Torah, but if they get these special honors they are known as the *kallat Torah*, the bride of the Torah.

In the space of a few weeks, then, the Jewish holidays move from the solemnity of Rosh Hashanah and Yom Kippur, when life hangs in the balance, to the joyous wedding imagery of Simchat Torah.

The Basics

BIBLICAL ORIGINS "Now, the fifteenth day of the seventh month, when you have gathered in the produce of the land, you shall keep the festival of the Lord, lasting seven days; a complete rest on the first day, and a complete rest on the eighth day. On the first day you shall take the fruit of majestic trees, branches of palm trees, boughs of leafy trees, and willows of the brook; and you shall rejoice before the Lord your God for seven days. . . . You shall live in booths for seven days . . . so that your generations may know that I made the people of Israel live in booths when I brought them out of the land of Egypt. I am the Lord your God" (Leviticus 23:39–43).

TALMUD An entire tractate deals with the complex laws of Sukkot. There is a debate between two Talmudic scholars over whether the Israelites actually sat in booths or whether these are symbolic of the "clouds of glory" that protected them in the desert. Regardless of whether they are real or symbolic, the authorities agree that there is an obligation to "live" in these booths over the holiday. For most, that means eating the main meals there; for others, that means sleeping in the booths as well. The Talmud goes on at some length about the construction of the booth. Among the requirements is that the roof top be made of natural agricultural material and that it should provide shading but not a complete cover. Also discussed in detail are the "four species."

VOCABULARY The festival booth is known as a *sukkah;* the plural is *sukkot,* like the holiday. The "four species" are known as the *arba minim* and consist of the *etrog* ("majestic fruit"), *lulav* ("branches of palm trees"), *hadasim* ("boughs of leafy trees"), and *aravot* (willows of the brook).

CALENDAR The holiday begins on the fifteenth of Tishrei. The first and last days are considered festivals; the days in the middle are the Intermediate Days, known as *Chol Ha'moed*. In Israel Sukkot is celebrated for seven days, and then an eighth day is added, known as Shemini Atzeret–Simchat Torah. It is also celebrated in this way by Reform Jews. Conservative and Orthodox Jews living outside of Israel, however, separate out the two holidays at the end, making each one a separate day, for a total of nine days. While the entire holiday is supposed to involve joy, special festivities are reserved for Simchat Torah. On that day the annual cycle of the Torah reading is completed.

FOODS It is not so much *what* you eat on Sukkot, but *where* you eat it. The major meals are taken in the *sukkah*. One customary food is honey, which is eaten in the same spirit as it is eaten on Rosh Hashanah—to symbolize a sweet year. The problem with eating it in the *sukkah* is that it often attracts bees. Visiting bees have become part of the holiday experience.

CHAPTER EIGHT

Hanukkah

Because of its proximity on the calendar to Christmas, Hanukkah may be the best known of Jewish holidays, but it is not among the most important. In the Jewish liturgical calendar, Hanukkah is of far lesser significance than, say, Sukkot or Shavuot, two holidays most Americans have never heard of. While Sukkot and Shavuot are biblical holidays, Hanukkah is not even mentioned in the Hebrew Bible (although it is found in the apocryphal works of the first and second books of the Maccabees). No doubt the festival owes its popularity to Christmas. Hanukkah arrives on the twenty-fifth day of the month of Kislev, which usually falls in mid to late December.

In a sense, Hanukkah has become the Jewish answer to Christmas, an occasion for holiday symbols, family gatherings, and gift-giving in a Jewish way. But while the holiday is ancient, some of these observances—like the giving of gifts—are of recent vintage.

Like Christmas, Hanukkah is a festival of lights. Both holidays are rooted in primitive fears that come in the dead of winter, when the days are short and the hours of natural light few. We kindle lights to stave off the darkness and to urge God literally to lengthen our days. Apparently it works.

HISTORY

The story of Hanukkah is stitched together from several historical texts: from the first and second books of Maccabees; from the Jewish historian of the first century, Josephus; and from a brief discussion in the Talmud. The apocryphal books, which are not included in the Hebrew Bible, tell the story of the victory of the Hasmonean dynasty over the forces of the Greek-Syrians in the second century B.C.E. The Greek-Syrian King Antiochus outlawed such Jewish rituals as Sabbath observance and circumcision and introduced the sacrifice of pigs to replace the Jewish Temple rites. The Hasmoneans, headed by Mattathias and, later, his son, Judah Maccabee, mounted a three-year revolt against the larger and better-armed Greek-Syrian armies. Eventually, the Maccabees and their followers prevailed, recaptured Jerusalem, and saved the temple from its defilement.

Hanukkah means "dedication," and that is just what the Maccabees set out to do in the Temple by lighting its great menorah. As the story goes, only one cruse of suitably pure oil could be found. It was only enough for one day, but miraculously it burned for eight. The story of the oil is not in the historical accounts from the Apocrypha but can be found in the Talmudic story, which appears to minimize the military victory and elevate the miracle of the oil. At different times in Jewish history, one or the other aspect of the Hanukkah story was emphasized, usually to make a point. In the era when the Talmudic passage was written, Jews were under the thumb of conquerors who might have been threatened by a holiday celebrating rebellion. A holiday celebrating light seemed more palatable.

The story of the little-oil-that-could does not rank up there with other biblical miracles, like the parting of the Red Sea or the revelation on Mount Sinai, but the miracle of the oil has clearly captured the Jewish imagination for reasons that go beyond the menorah. In the natural order, the Jewish people, like other persecuted minorities, should have been extinguished long ago. But Jewish spiritual power, like the oil that burns miraculously, has kept Jews alive and still burns bright.

"ADVERTISING" THE MIRACLE

The main *mitzvah* of Hanukkah is to "advertise" the miracle. Jews set up the eight-branched candelabrum known as the menorah, or, in Hebrew, *hanukkiah,* in the windows of their homes so that passersby can see the light burning. Oil is the preferred agent, but most people light candles. One light is kindled on the first night, and another is added each night until there are eight lights burning. An additional light also sits on the menorah (usually to the side or raised above the other candles). It is known as the *shamash,* or helper candle, and it is used to kindle the others. Since the Jewish days begin the night before the day of the holiday dawns, the candles are lit on the evening of Hanukkah, right after sundown. The *shamash* is lit first, and then the others are lit from its flame. Two blessings are sung, one praising God who commanded us to kindle the Hanukkah lights, and the other praising God "who performed miracles for our ancestors in those days, in this season."

In some Hasidic communities, the menorahs are not placed simply in the windows of Jewish homes, but in the streets. To walk through the religious neighborhoods of Brooklyn or Jerusalem is to see virtually every windowsill and stoop occupied by a candelabrum with flickering lights. Some build ventilated Plexiglas cases to protect the menorah and its fragile flame.

Among some Hasidic groups, followers gather in the synagogue to see their rebbe, or grand rabbi, perform the *mitzvah.* One Hanukkah night several years ago, I joined a hundred Bobover Hasidim who went to see their rebbe, Rabbi Shmuel Halberstam, light the Hanukkah menorah. Men were on one side of the room and women on the other. The synagogue set up bleachers so that the Hasidim could watch their leader, a diminutive man in his nineties, prepare for this *mitzvah.* It was the sixth night of Hanukkah, and the rebbe poured the oil and prepared the wicks with intense concentration. He shook back and forth as he pulled off a piece of cotton and gently rolled it in his hands to make the wick. He meditated over each wick and then poured the oil. The Hasidim in the bleachers sang a doleful tune, shaking back and forth with their rebbe. After some thirty minutes of preparation, Rabbi Halberstam abruptly stood up and began to recite the blessings over the lighting of the menorah.

His Hasidim fell silent. The rebbe sat down in his leather chair facing the menorah and stared into the light. This went on for another half hour. The rebbe stared into the lights with intense fascination; it was almost as if he had never seen light before. I asked a Hasid what the rebbe was staring at. "He's gathering the power of the rays of the miracle," the Hasid told me.

His meditation over, the rebbe rose from his chair and, walking slowly with a pronounced stoop, gradually made his way to the head of a waiting U-shaped table. His Hasidim came down from the bleacher seats and greeted him one by one. To each congregant, he gave a blessing, reflecting the light of the miracle he had just witnessed.

HANUKKAH IN MONTANA

A long way from Brooklyn, in Billings, Montana, another Hanukkah story unfolded. During Hanukkah 1993, a brick was thrown through the menorah-lit window of the home of a Jewish family in Billings. Inside the room slept a five-year-old boy, Isaac Schnitzer. His family was one of fifty Jewish families in the town. The attack came in a season when there had been several hate crimes against both Jews and blacks in Billings. But this incident, complete with the poignancy of a window smashed near the bed of a little boy, had a special impact. Isaac's kindergarten classmate Teresa Hanley told her family about the incident, and the family came up with a plan: they would put a menorah in their window as a sign of solidarity with the Schnitzers.

The idea caught on. Just as one little cruse of oil burned for eight days, so did the menorah idea spread throughout Billings. The local

newspaper printed drawings of menorahs suitable for clipping and pasting, and within days, ten thousand menorahs went up in windows all over Billings. Priests and ministers preached about tolerance from their pulpits and urged people to join the menorah campaign.

GIVING GIFTS—AND OTHER CUSTOMS

The Hanukkah liturgy is minimal. There are a few additional prayers, but the synagogue service is relatively short. Even the most observant Jews go to work and children go to school. There is, however, an old custom that women should not perform any work (even cooking and sewing) while the Hanukkah lights burn—which might give some women an excuse not to clear the dinner dishes—but it is not widely observed.

The gift-giving tradition is rooted in the old East European concept of Hanukkah gelt, which means Hanukkah money. One night during the holiday—by tradition, on the fifth night—the children of the family would gather around the menorah and receive small gifts of money, never more than a few coins. The reason probably has to do with the fact that Hanukkah is one of the few Jewish holidays when one is permitted to handle money (on the Sabbath and festivals, money represents commerce, and both are forbidden). Coming after Rosh Hashanah, Yom Kippur, and Sukkot, finally there's a holiday when the children's pockets can jingle. Even in my youth, I remember getting handfuls of dimes and quarters for Hanukkah. But don't try that on kids today. Hanukkah gelt is a thing of the past. Kids today expect presents—eight of them, one for each night.

Judaism has always borrowed from the surrounding culture, so it is not necessarily bad that Hanukkah has followed the example of Christmas. Gift-giving doesn't have to mean following the throngs at the mall looking for the latest gizmo. There are, of course, many Christian clergy who decry the commercialization of the holiday and talk about getting back to simpler and more meaningful observances. What some Jewish families do is set aside special themes for giving gifts. For example, one night is set aside for handcrafted rather than store-bought items. These items, like a wall hanging or a home-knitted sweater, demonstrate another level of caring and devotion. Another theme may be a night when everyone gets a book or a music CD. Giving to others is also a feature of the holiday. Some families set aside one night when the youngsters forgo their presents for the night and donate them to children at a homeless shelter.

Another holiday custom is the dreidel, a four-sided top, with which children play a game of chance. On each side of the dreidel are Hebrew letters that together form the acronym for the phrase *Nes gadol hayah sham:* "A great miracle happened there." (In Israel, the acronym stands for "A great miracle happened *here.*") The rules of the game are simple and are apparently a variation on a German gambling game called *trendle:* Each player puts a coin, a candy, or a nut into the pot, and the players then take turns spinning the dreidel. Depending on the letter of the acronym the top falls on, they either take, add to, or divide the pot. Many a young yeshiva student has blown all his Hanukkah gelt in this pursuit.

Another Hanukkah custom is to eat foods fried in oil as a way of commemorating the miracle of the holiday. Among Jews of Eastern European descent, the custom is to eat latkes, heavily fried potato pancakes. Among Jews from Spain and northern Africa, the custom is to eat special fried doughnuts called *sufganiyot.* Another European tradition is to eat a goose on Hanukkah because its fatty nature seems to fit into the Hanukkah cholesterol-fest.

Another food custom is to eat salty cheese; some also make latkes with cheese. The custom derives from the legend of Judith told in the apocryphal book of the same name. (Like the book of the Maccabees, the book of Judith was not included in the Hebrew Bible.) Judith, also a member of the Hasmonean dynasty, is described as a wise, beautiful, and wealthy widow who lived at the time the Israelites were about to surrender to the Assyrian forces that were at the gates of Jerusalem. Judith stole into the enemy camp and was taken to the military commander, Holofernes, who was struck by her beauty. In his bedchamber, Judith fed Holofernes wine, together with cheese to increase his thirst. As the story goes, he drank and drank until he was overcome by sleep. Judith took a sword, beheaded the commander, and lifted his head atop a pole. Seeing that their commander was dead, the Assyrians were filled with dread. Emboldened, the Israelites rallied their ragtag army and defeated the enemy. "Woe to the nations that rise up against my people," Judith exclaims.

Hanukkah is about the heroism of Judith and Judah Maccabee. And about a people, small in number but great in spirit, who manage to survive against the odds.

The Basics

BIBLICAL ORIGINS None.

OTHER SOURCES The Apocrypha, ancient texts that were not accepted into the Hebrew Bible, recount the story of the Hasmonean Dynasty, the heroes of the Hanukkah story. In the second century B.C.E., the Hasmoneans purified the Temple from the Greek-Syrian armies.

TALMUD The Talmud introduces the notion that upon rededication of the Temple, only one vessel of pure oil was found to rekindle the Temple's great candelabra. It was enough to burn for one night, but it somehow burned for eight. The miracle became a symbol for the victory and the dedication. The word *hanukkah* means "dedication."

CODE OF LAW The primary observance is to light the Hanukkah menorah. One candle is added each night of the eight-day holiday.

FOODS In honor of the miracle of the oil, foods fried in oil are especially popular. These are latkes (potato pancakes), a dish prepared by Ashkenazic Jews; and *sufganiyot* (fried doughnuts with jelly filling) among Sephardim. Two other traditions are to eat salty cheese and to cook a fatty goose.

CUSTOMS Spinning a four-sided top called a dreidel and giving gifts of money, known as Hanukkah gelt.

SONGS *Ma'oz Tzur*, "Rock of Ages" and, for the kids, "I Had a Little Dreidel."

CHAPTER NINE

Purim

"When Adar comes in, we increase in joy," the Talmud states. The cause of this joy is the spring holiday that falls on the fourteenth of Adar, Purim—without a doubt the most unbridled and raucous festival on the Jewish calendar. Something of a mix between Mardi Gras and St. Patrick's Day, Purim is a time when Jews dress in costume and heartily imbibe alcoholic beverages. Wine and liquor, usually used sparingly in Jewish ceremonies, flow freely on Purim. It's a rabbinic injunction. One is supposed to drink, the Talmud says, until he does not know the difference between "blessed be Mordecai" and "cursed be Haman."

Haman and Mordecai are the protagonists of the Purim story. The two are set against each other in the book of Esther. Haman, the prime minister of Persia, is enraged by Mordecai, a Jew, because he will not bow down before him. Haman convinces his king, Ahasuerus, to destroy Mordecai and all the Jews, for they are "a certain people scattered and separated among the peoples . . . their laws are different from those of every other people and they do not keep the king's laws." The heroine of the story is Esther, Mordecai's stepdaughter, who wins a beauty contest to become the new bride of Ahasuerus and then risks her life to save the Jews. Haman, his ten sons, and their followers are sent to the gallows, and Mordecai becomes the new prime minister.

HISTORY

It is a great story, and, for many Orthodox, believing it is an article of faith. But many historians say that it probably never happened. Ahasuerus may be King Xerxes I, who reigned in the fifth century B.C.E., but there is no record of the Esther story during his reign. In any event, historians say that it is unlikely he would have taken a wife who was not Persian royalty, and there is no record that he had a Jewish prime minister. While the book of Esther is taken literally by some, many modern scholars see it as a Jewish fantasy based on pagan legends. They note that the names Mordecai and Esther bear a striking resemblance to the pagan gods Marduk and Ishtar. It could well be that Jews, long victimized by others, dreamed up a story in which they were ultimately victorious. Biblical scholars date the writing of the book of Esther to the second century B.C.E., a time when antagonism to Gentiles ran high among Jews.

Some suggest that the rabbis' directive that Purim revelers be unable to distinguish between Mordecai and Haman on Purim indicates that they too knew the story of Esther to be a flight of fancy. Others find an important lesson in the interchangeable rolls of the hero and the villain; after all, there's something of the hero and the villain in all of us. Whether metaphor or history, the story of Purim has power and resonance, largely because just as Jews were a minority in Persia, Jews continue to be a minority around the world today (except in Israel). A story of a small remnant that continues to survive—and maybe even succeed—is one that Jews need to hear every year.

THE WHOLE *MEGILLAH*

Purim is among the minor holidays, somewhat more important than Hanukkah but less important than Passover. The principal obligation on Purim is to hear the story read. In the synagogue on Purim night

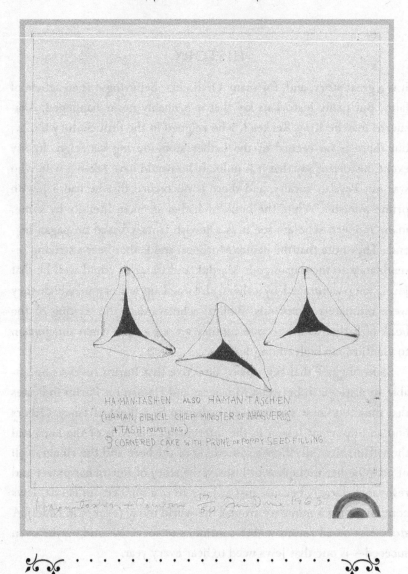

HA·MAN·TASH·EN ALSO HAMAN·TASCH·EN
(HAMAN, BIBLICAL CHIEF MINISTER OF AHASUERUS
+ TASH: POCKET, BAG) :
3 CORNERED CAKE WITH PRUNE OR POPPY SEED FILLING

and again in the morning, the book of Esther is read in Hebrew from a handwritten scroll known as the *megillah*.

Whenever the name of Haman is mentioned, synagogue-goers stamp out the sound of his name. Children armed with noisemakers (known as *graggers*) and horns, drums, and even cap guns wait eagerly for the name of Haman to be uttered. In the lighthearted mood of the holiday, one synagogue I know uses a traffic stoplight to help put an end to the noise so the reading of the *megillah* can resume.

Holiday revelers, especially children, come to synagogue in masks and costumes, sometimes as characters from the *megillah* (Haman and Esther are favorites), and also as contemporary characters: Saddam Hussein, Bill Clinton, Monica Lewinsky, or Darth Vader. Gorilla costumes are also popular, not because they have any meaning associated with Purim but just because they're readily available and make a big impression on the kids.

HAMANTASHEN

Two other laws of the holiday, both of them enumerated in the *megillah*, are: *mishloach manot*, the exchange of food gifts with a neighbor; and *matanot l'evyonim*, gifts to the poor. The traditional food of the holiday is *hamantashen*, a three-cornered pastry, said to resemble the hat worn by Haman. The *hamantashen* are stuffed with sweet fillings like prune or apricot and raspberry jam. Another, less appetizing name for these pastries is *aznei haman*, which means Haman's ears. (In ancient times, a prisoner's ears were apparently cut off before execution.)

Other food customs are associated with the holiday. Sephardic Jews eat sweet and sour dishes at the same meal to demonstrate that the Purim story had its bitter and triumphant moments. The other custom is to eat beans and peas, apparently to commemorate what Esther ate in the Persian palace (they were the only kosher items she could find, the story goes).

One reason that the Purim story has endured has to do with the position of Jews during our long Diaspora among the nations. Except in the modern state of Israel, where Jews are a majority, Jews continue to be a "certain people" set aside from society, with their own calendar, laws, and customs. Purim demonstrates that Jews can be set aside and yet at the same time be loyal to their country. Esther and Mordecai, the champions of the Jews, ultimately serve their king and their people.

SPECIAL PURIMS

Purim is not just for Persia. That is, miracles of salvation happened to the Jews in other places as well. And while the whole Jewish world celebrates the original Purim story set in ancient Persia, many Jewish communities established the custom of annually celebrating their own deliverance from peril. These became known as Special Purims.

To look over a list of these—more than one hundred are listed in the *Encyclopaedia Judaica*—is to get a sense of how Jews were persecuted and how they suffered over the centuries. Most of those recorded are from the sixteenth, seventeenth, and eighteenth centuries in communities that no longer exist. But at a certain time in history, someone had cause to celebrate. For example, the Jews of Sarajevo marked the special day in 1819 when ten community leaders were spared execution. The Jews of Sermide, Italy, commemorated the day in 1809 when they were saved from an earthquake. The Jews of Verona marked the day in 1607 when they were given permission to lock the

THE HIDDEN GOD

The book of Esther is the only book in the Hebrew Bible in which God's name is not mentioned. Some say the reason is that the book was written as a letter to Jewish communities abroad, and therefore God's name was not included (in case the letter was lost or defiled). Other scholars say that God's name was not mentioned so as not to offend King Ahasuerus and the religions of pagan Persia. These opinions about the book of Esther led to a debate among the rabbis as to whether the book should be included in the canon of the Hebrew Bible at all. But in the end, the lessons of the Purim story seemed to be more important

ghetto gates from the inside instead of from the outside. One of the most recently listed Special Purims commemorates the day in 1943 when the Jews of Casablanca escaped the threat of Nazi persecution. It is called the Purim of Hitler.

There are also Special Purims celebrated by families to remember the deliverance of their ancestors. The Altschul family of Prague marks the day in 1623 when the head of the family was saved from death. The Brandeis family remembers the day in 1731 when its patriarch was saved from accusations of having killed Gentiles by poisoning plum jam. And the Segal family of Kracòw celebrates the day in 1657 when the family was saved from drowning in the river while escaping a pogrom.

The observance of Special Purims follows the pattern of Purim. Families or whole communities gather to hear the salvation story read from a book or scroll. Special hymns of praise are sung, and a family meal is shared. Celebrants exchange gifts and make a contribution to the needy.

than its historicity. It was included in the canon, and the holiday was embraced wholeheartedly.

As to God's hiddenness in the text, the book of Esther is an example of how God often works behind the scenes. God's hand in history is not always clearly evident, as it was in the earlier books of the Hebrew Bible. God spoke to Moses from the burning bush; God made water flow from the rock; God revealed the Torah to the Jews on Mount Sinai. In some ways the Purim story summons us to dig even more deeply into our reserves of faith. God's hand cannot be seen, but the Jews believe God is always there.

The Basics

BIBLICAL ORIGIN The book of Esther.

TALMUD An entire tractate describes in great detail the rules for reading the *megillah*, the scroll that contains the book of Esther.

CALENDAR The holiday falls on the fourteenth day of the month of Adar, except in walled cities, such as Jerusalem, where it is celebrated on the fifteenth day of the month. It is a spring holiday, usually falling in March.

RITUALS Reading the *megillah*, the book of Esther written on a scroll, is the major observance. The *megillah* mentions two other rituals for the holiday: gifts for the poor and sharing foods with others.

VOCABULARY The special Purim gifts for the poor are known as *matanot l'evyonim*. Sharing food packages is called *mishloach manot*. Among the foods people send to one another are *hamantashen*, three-cornered pastries with sweet fillings. When the name of Haman is read in the synagogue, children blot out his name by sounding noisemakers called *graggers*.

CUSTOMS Dressing up in costume, drinking alcoholic beverages, and making a racket with *graggers*.

FOODS Sweet and sour dishes at the same meal, to symbolize the interplay of good and bad in the Purim story.

CHAPTER TEN

Passover

It was a concept unheard of in the ancient world.

People born into slavery remained that way—no one, let alone an entire people, could rise above their class. Their children were slaves, and they all died as slaves. But the Israelites broke the mold when they left Egypt more than three thousand years ago. In so doing, the Exodus became the first recorded liberation story. As a result, Passover became the paradigm for freedom movements throughout history. The Pilgrims who left a hostile Europe to find religious freedom in the New World likened themselves to the Israelites fleeing Pharaoh. (They even had a vast body of water to cross—the Atlantic Ocean—just as the Jews had their Red Sea.) American blacks fighting for equality also used the language and imagery of the Exodus in their struggle. "When Israel was in Egypt land," they sang in churches and on the freedom marches. "Let my people go."

The Exodus is the seminal moment in Jewish history; it is when the Israelite tribes, enslaved for four hundred years by the Egyptians, become a people. At the Red Sea, the Torah says, the people see the hand of God at work. "Israel saw the great work that the Lord did against the Egyptians. So the people feared the Lord and believed in the Lord and in His servant Moses" (Exodus 14:31).

But God is operating in the story from the very beginning, when

Moses is rescued from Pharaoh's decree against the Israelite firstborn.
His mother can hide him no longer and places him in a basket among
the reeds of the Nile. Miraculously, he is found by none other than the
daughter of Pharaoh, who raises him in the palace. Along the way,
Moses learns of his heritage, sees the oppression of his people, and,
after standing up for them against an Egyptian slavemaster, flees to

Midian. There, God calls to him from a burning bush "that is not consumed" and tells him to return to Egypt to lead the Israelites to freedom. He reluctantly returns and begins a negotiation with Pharaoh that—after many miracles and ten plagues—leads to the Exodus.

THE SEDER

The story is well known and has been told in many formats, including the movies, from Cecil B. DeMille's *Ten Commandments* (1956) to Dreamworks' *Prince of Egypt* (1999).

But what has really kept the story alive for three thousand years is the annual ritual of telling the story on Passover at a meal called the seder. Studies of the Jewish community in America have found again and again that the Passover seder is the single most observed ritual among Jews. Jews who do not go to synagogue on Yom Kippur, the holiest day of the year, wouldn't miss a seder. Jews who do not keep any of the dietary laws, or keep the Sabbath, observe a seder. The reason is simple: Passover is marked around the family dinner table rather than in the synagogue. And while there are prescribed songs, readings, and rituals, no two homes have the same kind of seder. For some, it is just a family gathering—a time for people to come together for a holiday meal. For others, it is an occasion to reenact a moment in history through rituals and readings. Some seders last an hour; others go on for four or five. But for all, the very fact that they gather makes it a way of commemorating the Passover story.

The Torah doesn't want the story forgotten: "And you shall tell your child on that day, 'This is what God did for me when I came out of Egypt'" (Exodus 13:8). The manner in which the story is told is through the reading of the haggadah, the seder guide that dates to the fourth century B.C.E. The word *haggadah* is from the Hebrew root "to tell," but the guide does more than that; it provides the words as well as the stage directions for the Passover drama. "In every generation, we are commanded to see ourselves as if we were taken out of Egypt," the haggadah says. Follow its words closely, and you will know when to drink the wine, when to wash your hands, when to open the door, when to hold up the matzah, when to call on the children, when to eat the bitter herbs, and when to break for the meal. The meal comes in the middle of the seder, so that there are activities before and after the participants dine.

The haggadah uses some basic symbols to tell the story. Matzah, the "bread of affliction," represents the sudden flight from Egypt; the Israelites left in such a hurry that there was no time for the bread to rise. Additional symbols are arrayed on a dish called the seder plate. These include the shank bone, which evokes the memory of the paschal lamb and the offerings brought during the time of the Temple; the *maror,* bitter herbs that represent the hardship the Israelites suffered under the lash of the Egyptians; and the sweet concoction known as *haroset,* made of apples, dates, and wine, which is supposed to look like the mortar the Israelites used to build the pyramids.

THE FOUR CUPS

Central to the seder is the wine. Four cups are drunk at intervals throughout the seder, representing the four expressions of redemption used in the Scripture. God promises the Israelites: (1) I will take you out of Egypt, (2) I will save you, (3) I will redeem you, and (4) I will take you to the land I have promised. In the ancient world, wine represented freedom, for it was only a free man who could drink without fear. There are also other symbols of freedom at the seder, such as leaning to the side, in the manner of nobility. In many families, participants bring pillows to the table for this purpose.

The seder is filled with contrasting images of denial and indulgence. There is both matzah, called in the Torah the "bread of affliction," and wine, a symbol of freedom. But before the second cup of wine is drunk, a few drops of wine are removed as the participants recite the ten plagues that God brought on the Egyptians: blood, frogs, lice, wild

beasts, cattle, boils, hail, locusts, darkness, death of the firstborn. The wine (and the concurrent joy) is diminished as a recognition of the human suffering that accompanied the plagues.

Given the injunction to "tell your child" about the Exodus, youngsters are a central part of the seder. The tradition is that the youngest person at the table gets the story rolling with the haggadah's Four Questions, beginning with the most famous: "Why is this night different from all other nights?" The rest of the haggadah is the answer, beginning with a verse: "We were slaves to Pharaoh in Egypt." There are numerous moments throughout the evening designed to keep young children awake and engaged. But beyond all the stories and the songs, the greatest incentive to kids is the *afikomen*. The *afikomen* is the last thing eaten at the meal, and with it comes a surprise for the children. Depending on the family tradition, the children either hide or have to

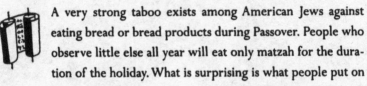

Variations on a Theme: Matzah à la Mode

A very strong taboo exists among American Jews against eating bread or bread products during Passover. People who observe little else all year will eat only matzah for the duration of the holiday. What is surprising is what people put on their matzah. At a spring party at the journalism school, the dean's office was good enough to provide matzah on the buffet table. One adjunct professor carefully scraped the shrimp salad off the bread and transferred it to the matzah. "Oh, I love Passover," he was overheard saying. An old friend from Tucson, Emily, goes one step further. She makes sure to order the most expensive and most carefully supervised matzah, known as *matzah schmurah,* but she puts all sorts of unkosher toppings on it.

Another story comes from my friend David, who is Orthodox and careful about what he eats all year round. He was at a business meeting with some colleagues during the intermediate days of Passover, and he took a break for lunch. While others went out to local restaurants, David remained at the conference table and took out his matzah and hard-boiled egg. As he unwrapped it, a colleague joined him and unwrapped his lunch. It was ham and cheese—on matzah. The colleague looked at David and smiled. "Boy, I'm glad I'm not the only one. It's hard to explain Passover, isn't it?"

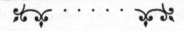

find (or both) the *afikomen.* As a reward for its retrieval, special gifts are distributed.

The *afikomen* is also seen by some as an amulet with protective properties. Each year at the seder, my great-aunt Minnie would take out a special velvet *afikomen* bag. Inside, she had a piece of the *afikomen* from the previous year's seder. She would replace the old *afikomen* with the new, which she would save for another year. It was one of her secrets of longevity, she insisted. It must work. When Aunt Minnie passed away in 1999, she was 105.

Perhaps even more magical than the *afikomen* are the things that cannot be seen but only imagined. During the second half of the seder, one participant (again, usually a child) is dispatched to open the front door of the house to welcome Elijah the Prophet. Elijah, the herald of the Messiah, is said to visit every seder on Passover night. A cup full of wine, "Elijah's cup," is set on the table to greet him. As a child, my brothers and I would stare intently at the wine, looking for any evidence that Elijah indeed took a sip.

A feminist addition to the seder is "Miriam's cup," a vessel filled with spring water rather than wine and also placed on the seder table. In rabbinic interpretations of Exodus, it is Miriam who watches her brother Moses as he floats down the Nile, and it is she who suggests to the daughter of Pharaoh that a Hebrew nurse be summoned for the child. Miriam's cup on the seder table recalls her merits and her leadership at the miracle of the parting of the Red Sea. The Scripture relates that it was Miriam who "took a timbrel in her hand" and led the people in a song of praise: "Sing ye to the Lord, for He hath triumphed gloriously; the horse and his rider hath he thrown into the sea" (Exodus 15:21).

PREPARING FOR PASSOVER

Putting on a traditional seder requires a great deal of work and preparation that can start weeks before the actual holiday. The laws of Passover involve not only eating matzah but getting rid of *chametz*: all bread or bread products, including cereals, pastas, cookies, crackers, and even beer (because it is made of hops). The house is thoroughly cleaned, couches are vacuumed, rugs are shaken—all in an effort to find that last crumb of *chametz*. Kitchen cabinets are cleared; food is either given away or "sold" in a bit of religious sleight-of-hand that allows it to remain in the house. (All *chametz* items are put in a sealed cabinet.

By arrangement with a rabbi, a non-Jew officially takes legal possession of the items even as they remain in the house of a Jew.) New food is brought into the house, all of it certified "kosher for Passover."

A kosher home normally has two sets of dishes, cutlery, and pots and pans—one for dairy and the other for meat. On Passover, these are put aside and Passover dishes are hauled out—again, one set for dairy and one for meat. Four sets of dishes in all. Silverware and pots and pans that are used all year round can be made kosher for Passover through a system called *kashering* in which the utensils are placed in scalding-hot water.

The task of preparing a house for Passover is Herculean. But with the cleaning and the preparation, there is a sense of starting anew. Passover does not come in the spring by accident. With the change in the seasons, from winter to spring, we see that the human being, too, has incredible potential for transformation. We can overcome the things that enslave us. We can change our lives in dramatic ways.

The Basics

BIBLICAL ORIGINS "For the Lord will pass through to strike down the Egyptians; when he sees the blood on the lintel and on the two door posts, the Lord will pass over that door and will not allow the destroyer to enter your houses to strike you down" (Exodus 12:23). "And on the fifteenth day of the same month is the festival of unleavened bread to the Lord; seven days you shall eat unleavened bread. On the first day you shall have a holy convocation; you shall not work at your occupations. For seven days you shall present the Lord's offerings by fire; on the seventh day there shall be a holy convocation: you shall not work at your occupations" (Leviticus 23:6–8).

TALMUD The laws of Passover are the most complicated of the Jewish holidays. First, there is an obligation to eat unleavened bread, called matzah. Second, one is not supposed to eat leavened bread or bread products, including cookies, cereals, pasta, or rice. Third, one has to

rid the home of all such products; every crumb must be removed prior to the beginning of the holiday.

CALENDAR The holiday begins on the fifteenth day of Nisan and lasts for seven days in Israel and eight in the Diaspora. (Reform Jews keep seven days in the Diaspora.) The first and last days are holy days during which work is prohibited. The intermediate days are known as *Chol Ha'moed*. The holiday usually begins in April and sometimes stretches into May.

RITUALS The seder, a family meal in which the story of the Exodus is retold using symbols of the holiday: the matzah, the shank bone, and the bitter herbs.

VOCABULARY Any leavened bread or bread product is called *chametz*. This includes flour of five grains—wheat, spelt, oats, barley, and rye—that is mixed with water and allowed to ferment before being baked. *Seder* means "order," and in the Passover context it means the order of the meal and its associated stories, songs, and symbols. *Haggadah* (literally "to tell") is the name of the book used at the seder.

CUSTOMS On the night before the seder, the house is searched by the light of a candle to be sure all *chametz* has been removed. The next morning, the *chametz* is burned.

SONGS The seder is filled with hymns and songs, the most famous of which is *dayenu*.

OTHER NAMES *Zeman herutanyu* (the season of our liberation), *hag-ha'aviv* (the holiday of spring), and *hag hamatzot* (the holiday of the unleavened bread).

MODERN INNOVATIONS Feminist seder, environmental seder, gay and lesbian seder.

CHAPTER ELEVEN

Yom HaShoah
and Yom Ha'atzmaut

YOM HASHOAH

At 10 A.M. on the morning of Yom HaShoah, the sound of a siren can be heard throughout Israel. For two minutes, virtually everything ceases—pedestrians stop their conversations, teachers stop teaching, chefs stop cooking, children stop dribbling their ball in the yard. Cars, trucks, and buses pull over to the side of the road. The country stands at silent attention in memory of the six million Jews who were killed by the Nazis during World War II.

Yom HaShoah, a Holocaust commemoration officially known as the Day of Remembrance for the Martyrs and Heroes of the Holocaust, was established by the Israeli Parliament in 1950. It is observed in the spring, a week after Passover, on the twenty-seventh day of the Hebrew month of Nisan, both in Israel and in Jewish communities around the world. *Shoah* is the Hebrew term for Holocaust; it is a term that has gained wide acceptance, and not only from the Claude Lanzmann film of the same name. Even recent Vatican documents have used *Shoah* rather than *Holocaust*.

Out of a period of misery and tragedy that stretched from 1933 to 1945, there were numerous dates to choose from to hold a commemoration: the day Hitler rose to power in 1933, or Kristallnacht in 1938, or the days at the end of the war when the camps were liberated. Nearly all the dates are associated with tragedy—decrees, deportations, massacres, and the discovery of the full horror of the Nazi murder machine. But the Yom HaShoah date is linked to a brief period of resistance—the uprising in the Warsaw Ghetto in 1943, when the sixty thousand Jews remaining in the ghetto made a heroic but futile attempt to defeat the Nazis.

There is no developed liturgy or elaborate observances for Yom

DISSENTERS

While it is fair to say that Israel comes to a standstill for the two-minute siren on Yom HaShoah, not everyone joins in. Arabs don't. For them, the establishment of the state is the *Nakbh*, the tragedy. And neither do the Haredim, the rigorously Orthodox who do not acknowledge the modern state of Israel (although most of them take money from it in terms of stipends and social services). The Haredim argue that it is against Jewish law to establish a secular state; the only government that can rule Israel, they say, is a religious one established by a Messiah who will rebuild the Temple. The Haredim regard the moment of silence as a secular observance that denigrates rather than honors the fallen. "We are not entitled to innovate anything on our own," Yisrael Speigel wrote in a column in *Yated Ne'eman*, the Haredi paper. It is arrogance, he insisted, to add to the existing ceremonies for the dead. The national day of mourning, he argues, is Tisha B'av, the day that marks the destruction of the Temple and other Jewish tragedies, not modern innovations such as Yom HaShoah.

The opposition to Yom HaShoah is curious, especially since entire communities of Haredim in Europe were wiped out by the Nazis. One Haredi man explained it this way: "How dare the secular tell me how to behave! My grandmother has a number on her arm from Auschwitz. I've got five children named after relatives who perished in the Holocaust. I think about the Shoah all the time, not just for two minutes one day a year."

HaShoah as there are for the ancient Jewish holidays. While some lament this and urge that more formal prayers and practices be instituted, the lack of a set liturgy has allowed for more creativity and cooperation among the various branches of Judaism. In many American communities, Yom HaShoah presents an opportunity for synagogues of different affiliations to hold joint services—something that would be difficult at other times of the year because of liturgical differences. The symbolism of this unity is important and is not lost on the participants, since the Nazis were intent on killing all Jews regardless of whether they were Orthodox, Conservative, Reform, or secular.

Yom HaShoah commemorations usually include the public reading of Psalms and the recitation of *kaddish* and *El Moleh Rachamim* (God, Full of Mercy), both prayers for the dead. Many congregations or Jewish community centers will show Holocaust films or sponsor talks by Holocaust survivors or their children. The centerpiece of the service comes when survivors rise to light six candles or torches, one for each million Jews annihilated. In some communities, day-long marathons are held in which people take turns reading the names of those who died. The reading is sometimes referred to as "To Every Person There Is a Name." The reading of the names, one after another in monotonous rhythm, helps us in some small way to begin to understand the magnitude of the catastrophe that was the Holocaust.

Israel rose from the ashes of the Shoah. About 250,000 survivors, some from the concentration camps and others who had been in hiding, made their way to what was then Palestine after the war. Sick, tired, and torn from home and family, they often had to dodge British blockades for the chance of a new beginning in Israel. They were conscripted into Israel's new army or worked long hours on the kibbutzim and in industry. In a popular song of the time, they sang: "We have come to the land to build and be rebuilt by it." By the time statehood was declared in 1948, survivors represented one half of the new nation's population.

After nineteen centuries of the dream of a return to Zion, the

Holocaust convinced the Jews, and apparently much of the world, that the Jews needed a state. Only in a country of their own, it seemed, could Jews live without fear.

MARCH OF THE LIVING

One annual event that vividly demonstrates the link between the Shoah and Israel is the March of the Living. The march, which in fact is done by bus and airplane as well as on foot, takes its name from the infamous Death March that Jews endured during the Holocaust. The March of the Living begins around Yom HaShoah in Poland, the site of the six major death camps, and concludes in Israel about a week later on Yom Ha'atzmaut, Israel Independence Day. Several thousand young Jews, most of them from North America and Israel, have gone on the March of the Living. The tour begins in Warsaw, Kraków, Lublin, and other Polish cities, where the participants learn about Jewish life before the war. They visit the deportation centers where families were rent asunder and human beings were herded into cattle cars. Some groups also go to the factory where Oskar Schindler saved more than one thousand Jews in an elaborate and dangerous deception of the Nazis. The marchers go to the concentration camps at Majdanek, Treblinka, and Auschwitz-Birkenau, where 2.5 million Jews and others were murdered. They see monuments and museums, such as the one at Auschwitz, where there are 1.6 million shoes and mounds of human hair, some of it braided and tied with faded ribbons. There are human bones that were used for medical experimentation and huge piles of human ashes from the crematoria. The visitors can walk into the gas chambers, see the holes where the deadly Zyklon-B pellets were dropped, and view the tiny windows through which the Nazi executioners watched the Jews die.

After visiting the camps, the marchers board airplanes for Israel to witness the redemption that followed the Holocaust. They learn about Israel's wars for survival; about its religious, educational, and agri-

cultural institutions; and about the quest for peace. The march concludes with the Israel Independence Day celebrations in Tel Aviv and
Jerusalem.

YOM HA'ATZMAUT

Israel Independence Day, which is known as Yom Ha'atzmaut, is a holiday of the Jewish present. It is observed two weeks after Passover, on
the fifth day of the month of Iyar, and marks the day in 1948 when
Jews achieved sovereignty over their ancestral land after nineteen cen-

RIGHTEOUS GENTILES

German atrocities are recalled on Yom HaShoah. But so, too, should the rare acts of kindness shown to Jews by people who chose to stand up against their governments and show compassion to the Jews of Europe.

In November 1997, soon after we arrived in Israel, I went to Poland to give a paper at an academic conference near Warsaw. I had one day free for touring before I had to catch a plane to Israel. I asked a friend, Rabbi Michael Schudrich, who then worked in Poland for a Jewish foundation, to recommend a death camp that I could visit. He proposed an alternative itinerary: a visit with him to the home of an eighty-nine-year-old rescuer. I reasoned that the death camps would still be there if I ever returned to Poland but that the rescuer might well not be.

No one knows exactly how many rescuers there were. Thousands never lived to tell their stories, let alone be recognized for their deeds. Yad Vashem has documented the cases of fifteen thousand of what it calls "righteous among the nations," of whom roughly one third were from Poland.

Rabbi Schudrich and I visited Genowefa Mazurkiewicz, a Polish peasant woman, in her drafty two-room cottage in the town of Kielce. In 1941, as a young mother, she opened her door to find a

turies of dreaming of a return. The achievements of Israel over its half century of existence have been breathtaking. Israel was born a struggling and impoverished nation of immigrants and refugees living in a hostile political environment. Its pioneers built a new country on hardscrabble land and arid desert, and they succeeded in ways no one ever dreamed possible: Israel today is a prosperous and technologically

hungry ten-year-old Jewish girl, Monique Bronstein, whose parents and brother had been shot to death in a Nazi roundup. Genowefa Mazurkiewicz simply told her children that they had a new sibling in the house, and for four years she raised the girl as her own. After the war, the girl was reunited with relatives in Paris, where she still lives.

Like other rescuers, the old woman did not see her actions as anything heroic. When I asked her why she had risked her life for the youngster, she said simply, "It was the right thing to do." Her daughter, Maria, who sat close by and held her mother's hand, said, "My mother always taught us, if you share bread with a stranger, you'll never go hungry."

Not everyone, of course, can visit a rescuer or a concentration camp. But Yom HaShoah provides us with an opportunity to reflect on what Jews endured during the Holocaust and to think about the proper moral response to other injustices around the world. While millions of others perished during World War II, the Holocaust is a uniquely Jewish event. As Elie Wiesel has said, "Not all the victims were Jews, but all Jews were victims." Hitler wanted to exterminate all the Jewish people and would have succeeded if not stopped by the Allied armies. But to see Yom HaShoah as only a Jewish event is to miss its message. Yom HaShoah is about both remembering the past and resolving to take a stand against the suffering of all humankind.

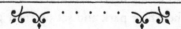

advanced country. Its high-tech industry is one of the most sophisticated in the world. The standard of living is more like that of a Western European country and nothing at all like a stereotypical Middle Eastern country. Its population has multiplied from its founding to nearly six million residents, five million of them Jews.

But in some ways the Zionist dream that gave birth to Israel has not succeeded. Fewer than half the world's population of Jews have chosen to live in Israel; the ingathering of all Jews, the dream of its founders, has not been achieved. And within the country itself, there are deep divisions among different factions—Orthodox and secular, Ashkenazi and Sephardi, hawks and doves. The final evidence that the dream remains unfulfilled is that Israel is still not at peace with most of its Arab neighbors. Still, it has achieved treaties—uneasy though they may be—with Egypt and Jordan. And it has begun to take major steps toward peace with the Palestinians and Syria.

In many American cities, parades are held to mark the Israeli holiday, and schoolchildren gather to sing Israeli songs and eat falafel, the popular Middle-Eastern dish of fried chickpeas. In Israel, where they eat falafel all year, the major Yom Ha'atzmaut custom is the *manghal*, the outdoor barbecue. Concerts featuring Israeli music and dance are held all day, and a military parade marches down the main streets of Tel Aviv while the Israeli Air Force flies overhead. As evening falls, fireworks light up the skies over many Israeli cities.

On the surface, it is a very American-sounding Fourth of July–like celebration, with barbecues and fireworks, but Israelis try to infuse both activities with a bit of the spiritual. The tradition of the barbecue began decades ago with a desire to demonstrate on this day in particular the Jew's connection to the land. Families organized tours and hikes through different neighborhoods. They began to bring along steaks, and portable grills to cook them on. With time, the walks became shorter and the barbecues more elaborate. On Yom Ha'atzmaut, Israelis drive to the beach or park and set up their grills for the holiday meal.

For religious Zionists, the establishment of the state represents the *at'halta degeula*, the beginning of the messianic redemption. Religious Zionists add a special prayer of thanksgiving, *hallel*, said on major festivals.

Fireworks have been part of the Yom Ha'atzmaut celebration since 1950, when a government committee recommended them for creat-

Variations on a Theme: "I'll Never Drive a Volkswagen"

 For some Jews, the Shoah looms large. They may do little else Jewishly, but they wouldn't think of driving a Volkswagen because it was the prototype car of the Third Reich.

They wouldn't go to a Wagner opera, visit Berlin, or buy a German clock. They wouldn't want to honor the American poet Ezra Pound because of his anti-Semitic broadcasts while Jews were being murdered by the Nazis in Europe.

In Manhattan recently, the Episcopal Cathedral of St. John the Divine put forward—and then reconsidered—a proposal to honor Pound alongside other distinguished poets in the cathedral's Poets' Corner. An author's committee voted to bestow the honor on Pound, but the committee was reversed by the dean of the cathedral after an uproar from several members of the congregation. In broadcasts and writings from Fascist Italy from 1941 to 1943, Pound blamed Jews and other groups for the world's economic problems.

One of the leaders of the anti-Pound movement at the cathedral was Marsha Ra, a convert to Christianity who was born a Jew. Fifteen of her cousins died in the Holocaust. In an interview with *The New York Times*, Ra said: "He was giving anti-Semitic radio broadcasts while my relatives were being gassed."

Marsha Ra was no longer Jewish, but clearly something Jewish remained part of her.

ing a festive and joyous atmosphere. In some ways, fireworks are like a modern-day shofar: they inspire awe and get our attention.

The Basics

YOM HASHOAH (HOLOCAUST REMEMBRANCE DAY)

ORIGINS Declared the official day of commemoration for the Shoah by the Israeli Knesset in 1950.

CALENDAR Twenty-seventh day of Nisan, a week after the end of Passover, usually in April.

CUSTOMS Solemn assemblies with candle lighting but little liturgical content.

OTHER NAMES Day of Remembrance for the Martyrs and Heroes of the Holocaust.

YOM HA'ATZMAUT (ISRAEL INDEPENDENCE DAY)

ORIGINS May 14, 1948, when Israel was declared a state. It is celebrated on the equivalent Hebrew day, the fifth of Iyar, usually in late April or May.

CUSTOMS Parades, barbecues, and fireworks; special synagogue services.

CHAPTER TWELVE

Shavuot

The festival of Shavuot operates on several different levels. In the Torah, it is described as an agricultural festival during which the first fruits were brought to the Temple in thanksgiving. At the time of the destruction of the Temple, the rabbis gave new meaning to the holiday by saying that it was on Shavuot that the Torah was given to the Israelites.

The Jewish mystical tradition puts it another way: Shavuot is the time when God and Israel are wed. But no Jewish wedding is complete without a marriage contract, known as a *ketubah*. The mystics explain that the contract binding God and Israel is the Torah. It records the duties of Israel to God—to follow God's law by being a holy people—and the duties of God to Israel—to maintain Israel as a Chosen People. The marriage imagery starts with the festival of Passover and continues through Shavuot and to Sukkot. Passover is the courtship of the Jews, Shavuot is the wedding, and Sukkot, the festival of booths, is the setting-up of a home together where both—God and Israel—can live.

Several of the Shavuot traditions fit into this mystical teaching. On Shavuot, the synagogue and the home are adorned with flowers and foliage in an image reminiscent of the *chuppah*, the marriage canopy. In addition, there is a tradition of Jews going without sleep the first night of the festival, like a groom standing vigil before his wedding day.

HISTORY

Shavuot started as an early summer agricultural festival. The Torah calls it *chag ha'katzir*, a festival of the harvest, and describes it as a time when the first fruits of the season were brought to the Temple as a gesture of thanksgiving. Around the time of the destruction of the Temple, however, Shavuot took on another significance: the time of Revelation on Sinai.

Making the connection was easy for the rabbis—and in some ways necessary. It was easy because there is a natural link between the Exodus, celebrated on Passover, and the Giving of the Torah. "You shall count until seven full weeks have elapsed: you shall count fifty days, until the day after the seventh week; then you shall bring an offering of new grain to the Lord" (Leviticus 23:15–16). This counting, called the *omer*, is the link between the grain offerings brought for Passover and the breads brought to the altar in the Temple on Shavuot. In the Temple rites, these were seen as essential for ensuring a bountiful harvest. With the destruction of the Temple, however, the rabbis had to find a new focus for Shavuot, so the tradition arose that it was the time of the Giving of the Law on Sinai.

REVELATION

According to the Torah, six hundred thousand Israelite men stood at Sinai to receive the Torah together with their wives and children—perhaps two million people in all. But the rabbinic tradition adds that the Israelites of that time were joined by the souls of all the Jews who would be born in the future—as well as future righteous converts to the faith. When the Israelites responded at Mount Sinai with the call

"We will do and we will listen," it was the voice of Jews from all time. At Sinai, all Jews entered into an everlasting covenant with God.

Jews make much of this public revelation. While other faiths also have moments when God speaks to human beings, the moment is usually a private one, like the dreams of the Prophet Muhammad in which the Koran was revealed, or the Holy Spirit descending upon the twelve apostles of Jesus. But here, recorded in the Scripture, there is a public revelation, complete with "thunder and lightning and a heavy cloud," the piercing sound of a ram's horn, and a people who "tremble" before the Lord.

The Torah portion read in the synagogue on Shavuot describes the

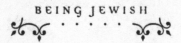

THE EARTHLY TORAH

 A story from the Kabbalah says that if the heavenly angels had their way, the Torah would never have been given to the Israelites. "They will squander its riches," the angels warned God. "Give it to us instead. We will keep it holy."

But Moses intervened. "The Torah says: 'Honor your mother and father.' Do you have a mother and father? It says: 'Eat only the food of clean animals.' Do you eat food? It says: 'Do not covet another man's wife.' Do you have wives?"

The angels fell silent.

Moses concluded: "The Torah does not belong with you. It belongs with the people of Israel."

revelation at Sinai, culminating with the reading of the Ten Commandments. Afterward, the book of Ruth is also read in the synagogue. Ruth is a young Moabite widow whose story of love for her Israelite mother-in-law, Naomi, leads her to declare one of the most poignant verses in the Bible: "For where you go I will go, where you lodge I will lodge. Your people shall be my people and your God my God" (Ruth 1:16). Ruth follows Naomi to Bethlehem, where she looks for food in the fields of a well-to-do merchant. The merchant falls in love with her and takes her for a wife. The book of Ruth ends with the record of her progeny. She gives birth to Oded, who gives birth to Jesse, who gives birth to David, the king of Israel. Thus, this poor convert to the faith becomes the progenitor of its greatest king.

Ruth's act of faith, set in the harvest season, echoes the embrace of the Torah by the Israelites at Sinai. But the Torah is not only for those

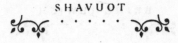

born Jewish. The Shavuot festival is one that speaks with special power to those who choose Judaism.

RECEIVING THE TORAH

The tradition of staying up all or part of the first night of Shavuot is a custom that dates to the Jewish mystics of the northern Israeli town of Safed in the sixteenth century. Still today, many synagogues organize study programs and lectures, and others just open their doors to people who want to study, alone or in pairs. Since the Torah describes God coming down to meet Moses at "the peak of the mountain," there is a folk tale that the heavens still open up on this night. Prayers go straight, unimpeded to God. It is considered a meritorious time to be engaged in study and prayer. The faithful who stay in the synagogue and study all night hold a sunrise service at 5 or 6 A.M. before going home to catch some sleep. Most synagogues have a separate service later in the morning, about 9 A.M., for those who didn't stay up all night.

Shavuot was also associated with the education of the young. Reform congregations often use Shavuot as an occasion to hold the graduation for a confirmation class. Unlike bar and bat mitzvah, an individual rite of passage when a youngster reaches twelve or thirteen, confirmation represents the coming of age with a group of one's peers. Some synagogues hold these rites when youngsters are older and better suited to assume the full duties of Jewish adulthood. In some Reform congregations, confirmation is performed when a young person is sixteen. On Shavuot, the confirmation class might plan the service by preparing the Torah readings or performing a play or cantata based on the readings.

OTHER TRADITIONS

Meat is the usual fare for Jewish festivals. But on Shavuot, there is a strong tradition to eat dairy foods. One reason is that the Torah is likened to milk and honey. "Honey and milk are under your tongue," the verse in Song of Solomon (4:11) states. Another explanation of the dairy foods has to do with the speculation that the ancient Israelites were unprepared for the intricate kosher laws given at Sinai. When they heard all the laws about clean and forbidden animals, they decided to take the easy way out and adhere to a simpler dairy diet.

Whatever the reason, Shavuot is a time when Jewish cholesterol readings soar. I remember my Grandma Tillie making cheese blintzes by the score, wrapping them in tinfoil, and distributing them like little treasures among her five children and fifteen grandchildren. My Aunt Bracha's cheesecake never tasted as good as it did on Shavuot.

The Basics

BIBLICAL ORIGINS "You shall observe the Festival of Weeks, the first fruits of wheat harvest, and the festival of ingathering at the turn of the year (Exodus 34:22). "You shall count seven weeks; begin to count the seven weeks from the time the sickle is first put to the standing grain. Then you shall keep the Festival of Weeks for the Lord your God (Deuteronomy 16:9–10).

TALMUD Shavuot is not only an agricultural festival, as stated in the Torah, but also marks God's revelation to the Jews on Sinai.

CALENDAR Shavuot is marked on the sixth day of the month of Sivan and also on the seventh outside Israel. It usually falls in May.

CODE OF LAW No work or commerce is permitted. Special prayers are added, calling Shavuot *zeman matan torateynu*, the time our Torah was revealed. In the synagogue, the book of Ruth is read.

CUSTOMS Eating dairy foods, decorating the synagogue with plants and flowers, staying up and learning Torah the whole first night of the holiday in anticipation of the giving of the Law.

OTHER NAMES The Festival of Weeks, Pentecost.

CHAPTER THIRTEEN

Fast Days

Aside from Yom Kippur, the holiest day of the year, there are six Jewish fast days, all of them linked to events in Jewish history. Whereas Yom Kippur is intended to inspire repentance and self-examination, the other fasts commemorate ancient Jewish tragedies. In the messianic age, the Talmud says in a joyous twist, all the fasts will become festivals.

Jewish fasts are serious affairs. When Catholics talk about fasting in the period of Lent, leading up to Easter, they mean going without chocolate or cigarettes or meat. When Jews fast, it means going without anything—all food and beverages (even water) are forbidden. In that sense, these fasts are more like the Muslim fast during Ramadan than like Christian fasts.

Of the six fasts, only one, Tisha B'av, involves fasting for twenty-five hours, from sundown to sundown, like the practice on Yom Kippur. The others are daytime fasts that begin at sunrise and end at sundown.

Four of the fasts—Tisha B'av, the tenth of Tevet, the seventeenth of Tammuz, and the Fast of Gedaliah—revolve around the destruction of the Temple. Among the other fasts, one comes right before Passover and another immediately before Purim.

TISHA B'AV
AND THE OTHER TEMPLE FASTS

The Temple in Jerusalem was destroyed once by the Babylonians, in 586 B.C.E., and once by the Romans, in 70 C.E. Both events were said to have taken place on the same day: the ninth of Av, known as Tisha B'av. The day the siege began is also marked: the Babylonian siege began on the tenth of Tevet (which usually falls in January), and the Roman siege began on the seventeenth of Tammuz (usually in July).

There are three weeks between the seventeenth of Tammuz and Tisha B'av, a period that usually stretches from mid-July to mid-August. It is a time set aside for public mourning for the Temple. During this period, observant Jews do not cut their hair, attend live music events, or hold weddings. The last nine days of the countdown, from the first of Av and on, there are additional restrictions. Observant Jews do not shave, swim for pleasure, eat meat, or drink wine.

The most significant of the Jewish fasts is Tisha B'av, which occurs in the late summer, when the days are long and the weather is often hot. Tisha B'av comes with several Yom Kippur—like restrictions. On Tisha B'av, it is forbidden to wear leather shoes (a sign of luxury in Judaism), have sexual intercourse, or bathe. And, like Yom Kippur, it is a twenty-five-hour period of refraining from food and drink.

On Tisha B'av, the synagogue is transformed into a house of mourning. The lights are often turned low, the silver and decorative velvet are removed from view, and low benches are used instead of the regular pews. At the Spanish and Portuguese Synagogue, the oldest synagogue in Manhattan, there was a long-standing custom to give everyone a candle to follow the reading of the book of Lamentations. However, because of fire regulations, the congregation had to stop distributing candles but began instead to give out small flashlights. In the darkened sanctuary, the lights flicker like a city on a distant hill. In sad and low tones, members of the congregation take turns reading the biblical book of Lamentations.

Alas!
Lonely sits the city
Once great with people
She that was great among the nations
Is become like a widow.

.   .   .   .

Zion spreads out her hands,
She has no one to comfort her.

While the destruction of the Temple is the official theme of Tisha B'av, other national tragedies have also become associated with the day. By tradition, the expulsion of the Jews from England in 1290 and from Spain in 1492 also occurred on that day. It is so closely associated with Jewish tragedy that some people wanted to commemorate those who died in the Holocaust on Tisha B'av, but a separate day of mourning, Yom HaShoah, was eventually established. (Yom HaShoah is not observed by most Hasidic Jews, however, who see it as an innovation of the secular state. Hasidic Jews mark the martyrs of the Holocaust on Tisha B'av.)

At the end of the Tisha B'av evening service, the congregation sings mournful dirges called *kinot*, the best known of them *"Eli Zion V'areha,"* which begins, "Wail, Zion, and its cities, like a woman in labor pains, and like a maiden dressed in sackcloth to mourn the betrothed of her youth."

At the synagogue the next morning, worshipers do not put on *tefillin*, which are a sign of Israel's pride. These are put on instead at the afternoon prayer, at a time when the mourning restrictions are eased and a note of comfort enters the day. Because the study of Torah is considered a joyous activity, study is also limited during Tisha B'av to doleful topics, like the book of Lamentations itself.

Implicit in the observance of Tisha B'av is that someday the tragedy of losing the Temple will be reversed through the rebuilding of the Third Temple in a messianic era yet to come. According to Jewish tra-

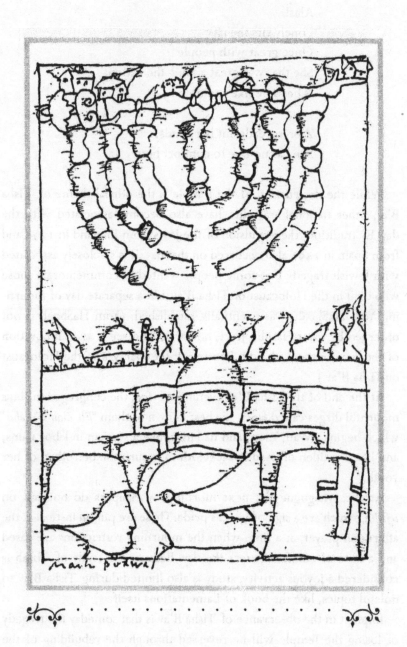

dition, the seeds of the redemption are contained within Tisha B'av. The Talmud says that the Messiah will be born on this day.

Some argue that Tisha B'av is an anachronism. There is no need to mourn for Jerusalem in a time when Jews have sovereignty over the city, they say—a time when its buildings are not in ruin as described in Lamentations but have been lovingly restored. Reform Judaism, for example, does not observe this fast day.

But others argue that there is merit in continuing the observance of Tisha B'av. Clearly, the redemption is far from complete. For some this might mean that the Temple is not rebuilt. For some others it might mean that most Jews have neglected to return to the Holy Land despite the opportunities that modern Israel offers. For still others it might mean that Jews have yet to learn how to share power with their Arab neighbors. In any event, Tisha B'av gives us a chance to focus on the hardships of the past and to dream of a better Jewish future.

THE FAST OF GEDALIAH
AND THE MEMORY OF YITZHAK RABIN

The fourth temple-related fast is the Fast of Gedaliah, which marks the sixth-century B.C.E. murder of a great leader of Israel, Gedaliah ben Akhikam. The fast took on new meaning for many with the 1995 assassination of Israeli Prime Minister Yitzhak Rabin. Rabin was killed on November 4 of that year by a religious nationalist who was opposed to the peace process with the Arabs that Rabin and his government had pursued with great vigor.

There are sad parallels between Rabin's death and that of Gedaliah. Soon after Jerusalem was sacked in 586 B.C.E., the Babylonian rulers appointed Gedaliah to rule over the Jews. Jewish zealots, seeing Gedaliah as a collaborator, invited him to a meeting, where they killed him. While over the course of Jewish history many rulers had been slain, the legacy of Gedaliah was preserved for all time by the prophet Jeremiah, who had put great hope into what Gedaliah represented.

Jeremiah hoped that someday the Babylonians would allow Gedaliah to rebuild the Temple. When he was slain, a Babylonian ruler was installed and Jeremiah lost hope.

For many Jews, Rabin represented a hope of peace in a Middle East that for so long had known war and strife. His death also brought to a crescendo the divisions between secular and religious people in Israel over the peace process.

THE FAST OF ESTHER

In the book of Esther, Queen Esther prepares to approach her husband, the king, to ask him to avert Haman's decree to kill all the Jews. She tells Mordecai to instruct all the Jews to "hold a fast on my behalf, and neither eat nor drink for three days, day and night." She adds: "I and my maids will also fast as you do. After that I will go to the king, though it is against the law; and if I perish, I perish."

In the end, the Jews are redeemed. To commemorate that obviously effective plea to God, the rabbis instituted a fast on the eve of Purim, known as the Fast of Esther.

THE FAST OF THE FIRSTBORN

The Fast of the Firstborn, which comes on the day before Passover, is technically for firstborn males only. It commemorates the tenth plague, in which the firstborn of the Egyptians were slain. Out of gratitude that the firstborn of the Israelites were spared, the fast was instituted.

However, the rabbis were lenient about this fast by excusing the firstborns if they attend a *siyyum*, a party to mark the completion of learning a book of the Talmud. The joy of the *siyyum* in this case overtakes the fasting. Instead of fasting, the firstborns have a small party and are able to eat the rest of the day.

Perhaps because this is a fast-turned-party, even those who are not firstborn males are known to mark the event. Since religious obligations do not begin until a boy reaches the age of thirteen, the father of firstborn minors who are not themselves firstborn (like myself) also mark the day by attending a *siyyum*. And I also know at least one girl who does. Her name is Eliza, and her father, a firstborn, has very fond memories of going to synagogue with his father on Passover eve for the *siyyum*. Even though his eldest is a daughter and technically is not required to observe the day, he takes her along as a sign of both tradition and innovation.

The Basics

Aside from Yom Kippur, there are six fast days in the Jewish calendar.

1. The ninth day of Av, known as Tisha B'av, is the fast that marks the destruction of the First and Second Temples. The First was destroyed by the Babylonians in 586 B.C.E; the Second, by the Romans in 70 C.E. In the synagogue, the book of Lamentations is publicly read.
2. The tenth day of Tevet marks the beginning of the Babylonian siege that led to the destruction of the First Temple.
3. The seventeenth day of Tammuz marks the beginning of the Roman siege that led to the destruction of the Second Temple.
4. The Fast of Gedaliah marks the assassination in 586 B.C.E. of Gedaliah ben Akhikam.
5. The Fast of Esther is held the day before Purim, as noted in the Book of Esther.
6. The Fast of the Firstborn is held the day before Passover. As told in Exodus, the Angel of Death passed over the houses of Israelites during the tenth plague, the death of the firstborn. In commemoration, the firstborn fast on Passover eve.

CHAPTER FOURTEEN

Sabbath

The ultimate Jewish holiday is not Passover or Hanukkah or even Yom Kippur. It is the Sabbath, known in modern Hebrew as Shabbat. And while some might quibble that Shabbat is not technically a holiday, I can think of it in no other way. Shabbat is both a celebration and a vacation, and it serves as a reminder that peak religious experiences can be a regular part of life. You don't have to wait all year for the lighting of the menorah or for the camaraderie of the seder or for the spiritual high of Yom Kippur. You can have it every Friday night—candles, a warm family meal, and a process of cleansing and renewal. Within Shabbat, you can find the themes of all the other holidays. There are the lights of Hanukkah, the joy of Sukkot, the revelation of Shavuot, the redemption of Passover, the creation themes of Rosh Hashanah, the renewal of Yom Kippur, and a touch of the messianic promise of Yom Ha'atzmaut.

Shabbat is one of Judaism's great gifts to humankind. The concept that there is a day when you stop your labors, when you turn inward instead of out, is a Jewish innovation. Shabbat, with its ties to the story of creation, also provides an environmental lesson. Humankind is given "dominion" over the earth in the Genesis account, but Shabbat places limits on our authority over nature. On the Sabbath, we do not work the soil, so that both people and the earth take a break. Like humans, the natural world needs downtime.

The lessons of Shabbat need to be heard in the competitive culture of modern America, where work has become such an obsession. For many, rich and poor, work often substitutes for family and the inner life. Shabbat isn't suggested in the Torah as a nice option to take a breather; it is a command. It is the only Jewish holy day mentioned in the Ten Commandments. "Six days shall you labor and do all your work," God says in Exodus 20:9. "But the seventh day is a Sabbath to the Lord your God." And it is not just a day off for the chosen few. God enumerates: "You, your son or your daughter, your male or female slave, your livestock, or the alien resident in your town."

The Ten Commandments are repeated in Deuteronomy, with small variations, especially with regard to Shabbat. "*Remember* the Sabbath day," the Exodus account begins. "*Observe* the sabbath day," Deuteronomy says. The reasons given for Shabbat also differ in the two accounts. Exodus says that man and woman must rest because God "rested on the seventh day." But the Deuteronomy account sounds the theme of the exodus from Egypt: "You were slaves . . . therefore, the Lord your God commanded you to keep the Sabbath day."

Rather than seeing contradictions in the two renditions of the Ten Commandments, the rabbis of the Talmud extracted theme on top of theme here, describing Shabbat as a richly layered time that calls on us to both observe and remember, to rest as God rested, and to reflect on the lessons of the Exodus.

In rabbinic literature, the Sabbath occupies a unique place. In one commentary on Exodus, the Sabbath is seen as equal in weight to "all the other precepts of the Torah." The legend goes that if all of Israel keeps the Sabbath as it should be kept, even just once, the Messiah will come. In one of the songs sung around the Sabbath table, Shabbat is said to be a "taste of the World to Come."

While the Sabbath laws are meticulously codified, they all go out the window if a life is in danger. Life takes precedence. "You shall live by them," the Torah says of the commandments. The rabbis add, "Live by them and not die by them."

There is a long list of things one is not supposed to do, all centered on avoiding normal activities that constitute work. The different branches of Judaism differ on how many of these restrictions are still binding. But there is broad agreement on what *should* be done on Sabbath, in realms reaching from prayer to sex. All the denominations favor prayer on the Sabbath, in synagogue if possible. All agree that one should also eat three meals, drink wine, and, under the right circumstances, have sex. (The right circumstances begin with having sex with one's spouse.)

The intention of these commandments is to set the Sabbath day apart from all other days of the week. Sabbath stands alone as a day when you are fully aware that something special is going on. If you allow yourself to open up to it, it can be, in the words of the late Rabbi Abraham Joshua Heschel, a true "oasis in time." Or, as Rabbi Irving Greenberg puts it, "a day to spend being, not doing."

ANTICIPATING SHABBAT

One prepares for the Sabbath all week. In Hebrew, the days of the week do not have names. They are all a launch pad for Shabbat—Sunday is the first day, Monday the second, and so on until Friday, which is both the sixth day and "the eve of Shabbat."

In anticipation of the Friday-night meal, observant Jews tend to eat lighter meals during the daytime on Friday. There is also much to do. In fact, the more observant you are of the details of Shabbat, the more you have to prepare before it arrives. The late eminent rabbinic scholar Rabbi Joseph B. Soloveitchik used to say that the true mark of a pious Jew is not that he or she is *shomer Shabbat* (a Sabbath observer) but is *shomer erev Shabbat* (one who properly prepares on the eve of the Sabbath). By traditional Jewish law, one cannot shop on the Sabbath, so marketing is usually done during the day on Friday. Cooking is prohib-

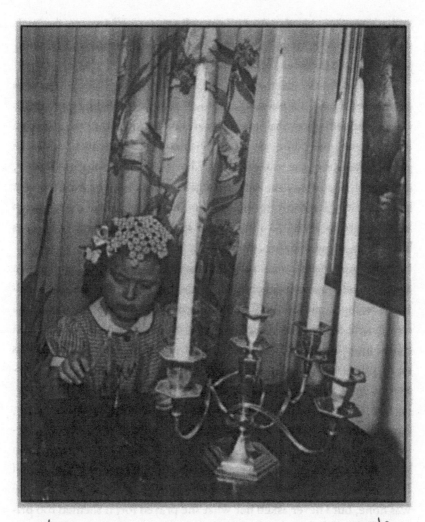

ited on the Sabbath, so that must be done in advance, too. Foods prepared beforehand can be kept warm on a hot plate or on the stove—a
condition that has led to a preference for certain hearty dishes like a
meat-bean-and-potato stew called *cholent*.

In our home, we try to give our children special Sabbath eve responsibilities. Of course, there's cleaning up their own rooms, but we
also divide up family responsibilities like sweeping, or setting up the

Sabbath candles. My daughter, Emma, loves art projects, so she is always willing to write and decorate place cards if we are having company for Shabbat dinner. My son Adam vacuums.

Shabbat officially begins with the lighting of the Sabbath candles eighteen minutes before sundown on Friday eve, a time that varies widely depending on the time of year and the place on the globe. In winter, when the days are short, Sabbath arrives early—in some places, like Boston, as early as 4 P.M. For the strict Sabbath observer, this might necessitate an early exodus from school or work to get home in time for the mini-holiday. In summer, Shabbat starts hours later, as late as 8 P.M. In either case, it is finished twenty-five hours later, or forty-two minutes after sunset.

In the home at the start of the Sabbath, two candles at a minimum are lit, usually by the woman of the house. In many families, the tradition is to light one candle for each member of the family; so when a new child is born, a new candle is added. In our house, we added a fifth candle after Judah, our third child, was born. And while Shira oversees the lighting, she shares the honors with the children, who are encouraged to light their own candles: one for each. The ritual involves waving the hands in front of candles as if to gather in their holy light, covering the eyes, pausing for a moment of meditation, and then reciting a special blessing. My late mother always spent several minutes in silent contemplation before the candles with her hands over her eyes. I remember that her eyes were always a bit red and watery when she was done, but I never asked her what she prayed for; it seemed too private and sacred a moment. When my mother lit the Sabbath candles, I always felt that she was closest to God. To watch her, eyes covered before the flickering candles, was to see sparks of the divine.

The reasons for the candles are many. Lighting the candles echoes God's act on Day One of Creation of separating light from darkness and commanding: "Let there be light." As the sun goes down we do conquer the darkness by creating light. Another reason has to do with the Sabbath aspiration for *shalom bayit,* peace in the house. Before the days of electricity, candles were often scarce; poor Jews would save their candles for the Sabbath, thus ensuring that the house would be lighted and joyous. There is an old tradition, in fact, also to place candles throughout the house, one in each room on the Sabbath, although the main Shabbat candles are on the table where dinner is served. Today, when artificial light is plentiful, there is something special about the glow of a candle. In our house, we turn the lights down to bask in the Sabbath candlelight.

FRIDAY-NIGHT SERVICE

Friday-night services in Orthodox synagogues begin minutes after the time the candles are lit in the home. Starting time depends on the calendar. Many Conservative and Reform congregations, however, have Friday-night services that are set for later in the evening, around 8 P.M., although many Conservative synagogues are now abandoning the late service in favor of ones timed to the start of Shabbat.

As synagogue services go, the Friday-night one is short and is made up mostly of songs of praise. There is no Torah reading and no elaborate preaching. The highlight of the Friday-night service is *l'cho dodi*, a rhyming Hebrew poem written in the middle of the sixteenth century by a Jewish mystic, Solomon Alkabez. The hymn is sung, and some congregations even break out into dance for *l'cho dodi*, which personifies Shabbat as a bride. In the last verse of *l'cho dodi*, the worshipers rise, the dancers stop, and everyone turns and faces the door of the synagogue. With a bow, the worshipers symbolically welcome the Sabbath: "*Bo'e kalah, bo'e kalah.*"—Welcome bride, welcome bride.

After the service, people greet and wish one another "*Shabbat Shalom*" or, in Yiddish, "*Gut Shabbos.*"

According to legend, at the end of the Friday-night service, two Sabbath angels, one good and one not so good, accompany the worshiper home. If, when a worshiper reaches home, the table is prepared, the meal is ready, and a Sabbath calm has settled over the house, the good angels says, "May Shabbat always be greeted this way in this house." To which the not-so-good angel must respond, "Amen." If, however, the table is not prepared and the tensions of the week persist, the not-so-good angel gets to make a wish that it always be so. The good angel must answer "Amen." The initial hymn sung at the Sabbath table is *Shalom Aleichem,* which welcomes the accompanying angels.

SHABBAT TABLE

A family's best household items are used on Shabbat: the candles and candlesticks, the best china, the whitest tablecloth, the best food, the sweetest wine. Over the course of history, the Sabbath preserved a sense of Jewish nobility, and even royalty. All week, you may be a common laborer, but on the Sabbath the Jew takes on a princely air. In the darkest days of Jewish history, Shabbat kept the dream of Jewish redemption alive. Perhaps that is one meaning of the famous saying of the nineteenth-century poet Ahad Ha'am: "As much as the Jews kept the Sabbath, the Sabbath kept the Jews."

The Sabbath provides a vivid lesson in Jewish history. If you wonder what happened to Judaism after the destruction of the Second Temple, almost two thousand years ago, you can find the answer at the Sabbath table. Where was Judaism centered and preserved? Most people answer that the rituals were transformed into rites in the synagogue, such as communal prayers and Torah reading. In fact, they were preserved most faithfully in the home. In the ancient Temple there was a menorah with lights, priests who gave blessings and made water libations, Levites who sang psalms, and an altar that had meat, bread, salt, and wine upon it. All these acts continue to be practiced, but in the home, not the synagogue. After the candles are lit, the man or woman of the house says *kiddush,* a prayer that sanctifies the day over wine. The wine is shared by all those gathered around the table.

Next the children are blessed, with the same blessing that the

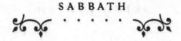

SHABBAT ENDURES

On January 1, 2000, in honor of the millennium, *The New York Times* tried to imagine what its edition of January 1, 2100, would look like by running an imaginary front page. There were articles about robots demanding equal rights and statehood for Cuba. In business news, Mc-Donald's, "the struggling restaurant chain," was taken over by "99-Plus, the nursing home company." It was a portrait of a totally changed world—except for one item. At the bottom of the 2100 front page was a small four-line advertisement:

JEWISH WOMEN/GIRLS LIGHT SHABBAT candles today 18 minutes before sunset. In New York City 4:39 P.M. Elsewhere touch for local time and for information.—ADVT.

priests spoke in the Temple: "May the Lord bless you and keep you. . . ." Then all ritually wash their hands by filling a cup and pouring water from one hand over the other. The tradition is not to speak between the time of the hand washing and eating the bread. This is a great challenge, especially in our house, where the children outnumber the adults. No one talks until Shira makes the blessing on the bread, and, in accordance with a Sephardic custom we adopted, she rips off a piece of bread and tosses it across the table, first to me and then to each child, in birth order. The tradition of throwing the bread comes from an obscure law regarding mourning on the Sabbath that is not nearly as interesting as the act of throwing the bread itself. (The details: there is no mourning on Shabbat, and since handing bread is a sign of mourning, it is tossed, not handed off.)

Traditionally, the meal includes fish and meat, although vegetarian options are becoming more popular. It is not only the best meal of the week, it is often the only meal at which family members gather, talk, and eat together. On Friday night, traditional Jews do not work late or go to movies or parties. Being at home is the priority. The children do not have homework and do not rush through the meal to catch their favorite television show or play a video game. The telephone never interrupts the meal. According to the Orthodox interpretation of Jewish law, it is forbidden to use all these modern conveniences on the Sabbath. One is not even allowed to touch them. The legalistic reason for not using these appliances has to do with the prohibition of completing an electrical circuit or causing a fiery spark—activities that violate the letter of the law. But, more important, these gadgets are distractions that rob Shabbat of its essential spirit. In our house, Shabbat is a time for reading. While turning machines on and off is a forbidden act, there is nothing wrong with enjoying what is already on. We leave on plenty of lights. Children who find every excuse all week not to read happily pick up a book on Friday night. The simple pleasure of reading is alive at least one night a week in our house. We also try to read out loud around the Shabbat table. Shira or I will often clip a newspaper article that we have liked to share with the children at the Shabbat table.

There is no doubt about it, Shabbat is made for families and—once the children are put to bed—for couples. There is a Talmudic tradition that says that it is especially meritorious to have sex with one's spouse on the Sabbath. Through the union of man and woman we model the union of God with Israel. The Sabbath is a time of joy, and Judaism recognizes and celebrates the joy of sex.

Celebrating Shabbat alone is just not the same. The solution for many single men and women who are observant is to find a community with which to celebrate Shabbat. Many synagogues have communal Shabbat dinners. These dinners may lack the intimacy and intensity of family meals, but they are a good place to learn the songs, prayers, and traditions of the Shabbat. They are also a good place to connect with others who might want to inaugurate a series of "round robin"

Shabbat dinners at private homes where people bring dishes and share a meal. Synagogue is also a place to find families who would welcome Shabbat guests. (Some synagogues even have an organized hospitality committee to make the introductions.) At our house, we never feel that our Sabbath table is complete without guests, married or single.

MANY WAYS TO CELEBRATE

Technically, the laws of Shabbat are draconian. There are thirty-nine official "don'ts," and they each have subcategories that add hundreds more. One cannot mow the lawn, hunt for food, light a fire, plant a seed, cook food, boil water, sew on a button, erect a tent, use a hammer, bake a cake, or gather kindling. Derived from these ancient laws, a host of modern restrictions has been added by scholars, so now it is forbidden to turn on a computer, drive a car, flick on a light switch, talk on the phone, replace a battery, or watch television. The list is a long one. Conservative rabbis prohibit many of these same activities, but the level of observance among the Conservative laity is not as widespread as it is among the Orthodox. Reform rabbis, for the most part, say that these ancient restrictions are no longer binding, but they increasingly add that if people find meaning in the restrictions, they should incorporate them into their religious lives.

There are, of course, many ways to celebrate Shabbat. Some people light candles at the appointed hour, and others do it later in the evening when everyone arrives home and gathers around the table. Some remain for a family meal, and others say a blessing and scatter. Some relax by watching a family movie on HBO, and others catch up on their reading. Some unplug the phone, and others use it to connect with relatives they've been missing all week. Some won't touch a car; others will use it to go to synagogue. Some will drive to synagogue but not to the mall. Some will drive to the beach but not the mall. And there are those who go to the mall but not to the office.

The important thing about Sabbath observance is that you make the

VARIATIONS ON A THEME: SHABBAT HIGHS AND LOWS

 People observe Shabbat in the strangest, sometimes most inconsistent ways. Here is some of what I found in my interviews.

David, a stockbroker, uses the telephone to make outgoing calls on the Sabbath but never takes incoming calls. One day a week, he wants to set the telephone agenda. Syd, a college professor whose mother is in a nursing home, answers the telephone but does not call out. "What if she's trying to reach me?" he wonders.

Gloria, our grandmotherly neighbor at our summer bungalow in upstate New York, doesn't observe the Sabbath, except for one thing: she won't knit or crochet. I have met others of her generation who also single out one activity that they refrain from doing: cooking, laundry, cleaning, and putting on makeup. One thing they choose; everything else is okay.

Sandy, an executive of the Jewish Federation in Los Angeles, drives his car on Shabbat, but not on the freeways. Streets are okay, he explains, but "the freeways remind me of work."

Leslie, a Reconstructionist rabbi in Detroit, told me that she drives but doesn't carry money. This became a problem one Saturday when she encountered a toll on her way to visit her mother. She began to explain to the toll taker that she was a Sabbath observer and didn't carry money, but he quickly cut her off. "Lady, then why are you driving?" She convinced the toll taker to let her through.

Ilan, an Orthodox college student who sleeps with his girlfriend on Friday nights, tears open his condom packages early in the day so that he does not violate the Sabbath by tearing unnecessarily.

In one Orthodox home I know, the television stays off on Shabbat, as do the CD player, the radio, and the computer. No one answers the telephone, and all the men wear yarmulkes. But on Saturday afternoons, the family's fifteen-year-old son sits down to play the piano for an hour. He plays Chopin and Mozart and his own compositions. "He needs to express himself," the father explains. "And this is how he does it."

Fred, a Jewish educator in Providence, Rhode Island, observes Shabbat but takes the summers off. His wife, he explains, simply can't resist the beach in July and August. That's the only time of the year they drive on Saturdays.

Traditionally, one doesn't smoke on Shabbat, but Jerome, a retired corporate executive from Westport, Connecticut, honors the day with a Havana. "I can't think of a better time to smoke my favorite cigar," he explained.

In his youth, my Orthodox friend Lenny was a Deadhead, one of those devotees who followed the Grateful Dead around the country getting high as a kite. But Lenny couldn't bring himself to smoke pot on Shabbat. His solution: He baked hash brownies on Friday and ate them on Saturday for a special Shabbat high.

day different in big ways and in small ways. For example, I was brought up not to carry my wallet on the Sabbath, which is a good idea because it keeps me from carrying money and therefore from spending money. Shabbat is not a day for commerce. But everyone around me wore watches. Several years ago, when I was a reporter who lived by the watch, I stopped wearing my watch on the Sabbath. By the strict laws of Shabbat, there is nothing wrong with wearing a watch, but not wearing one liberated me from my enslavement to time. Shabbat gives us the opportunity one day a week to live for ourselves and not for the clock.

SYNAGOGUE

The secret about Saturday-morning services is to get there late. Most Orthodox and Conservative synagogues begin their services at about 9 A.M. and drag on until noon. Reform temples, which have an abbreviated service, tend to start a bit later. But being prompt to synagogue is not important. No one will look askance if you show up late. The beginning of the service is, in fact, rather quiet and reflective (and a little boring). It picks up as a public event around the midpoint with the reading of the Torah, when the scroll is taken out of the ark and paraded around the congregation. The Torah is placed on a central table, known as the *bimah,* and the week's portion is read. Depending on the denomination, as many as seven people are called to the Torah for the *aliyah* blessing. The Torah portion is followed by the Haftorah, a selection from the prophetic writings. A sermon by the rabbi or a Torah discussion led by a layman often follows before the additional service of *musaf* is chanted.

For newcomers, the service can be daunting. For one thing, prayer books are usually in Hebrew, which means that they open in the opposite way from how an English book opens. Even the page numbers run the "wrong way." The more traditional the service, the less the newcomer is bound to understand. But even without understanding or following the service, a worshiper can tap into its rhythm. There are times for meditation, times for song, and times for just sitting, listening, and watching.

The best place to check out a congregation is not at the service but at the *kiddush* afterward. (Although the words are similar, there is a big difference between *kiddush* and *kaddish*, the prayer for the dead.) The *kiddush* is like the coffee hour that follows a Protestant church service, except that before the coffee, there's a cup of wine. A blessing is said over the wine, and then cakes or light snacks are served. This is the place where people mingle, catch up with one another, and make connections. For single men and single women, *kiddush* is a great time to meet people. And it's not too late to ask someone out for a movie Saturday night. For parents of young children, it's time to arrange play dates for the kids, especially to fill the long summer Saturday afternoons.

HAVDALAH

Shabbat afternoon is a time for more non-mechanized leisure, like reading and walking in the park or playing board or card games. Scrabble and Monopoly (the old-fashioned varieties, not the ones on the computer) are favorites in our house. A walk in the park is appropriate, although vigorous sports are not permitted. Napping is good, too. Toward evening, the "star hunt" begins. Since the Sabbath is officially over when the stars come out, you don't have to rely on the calendar or your watch but can find the answer in the skies. On summer Saturday nights, I often take my children on a walk toward the end of the day. We keep our eyes peeled on the heavens. We count the stars, and when we find three, we announce to all that Shabbat is over.

The formal farewell to the Shabbat is called *havdalah*. It is a brief ceremony said over wine, fire, and spices that focuses on the separation between the sacred and the profane. We praise God, who "makes a distinction between the sacred and the secular, between Israel and the other nations, between the seventh day and the six working days." Rabbi Chaim Seidler-Feller, the Jewish chaplain at UCLA, calls *havdalah* "*kiddush* for the week." Whereas the Friday night *kiddush* begins, "And God finished making the heaven and the earth," *havdalah* is about beginning the task of creation all over again. Renewed by the Sabbath, we can approach our labors confident in the knowledge that another Shabbat is less than a week away.

The Basics

BIBLE "And He rested on the seventh day from all his work which he had done. And God blessed the seventh day, and sanctified it" (Genesis 2:2–3). "Remember the sabbath day to keep it holy. Six days shall you labor and do all your work: but the seventh day is a sabbath to the Lord your God. In it you shall not do any work. . . . For in six days the Lord made heaven and earth, the sea, and all that is in them, and rested on the seventh day. Therefore the Lord blessed the sabbath day and hallowed it" (Exodus 20:8–11). Deuteronomy has a similar passage, but it concludes differently: "And remember that you were a servant in the land of Egypt . . . therefore the lord your God commanded you to keep the sabbath day."

RABBINIC LITERATURE "If Israel keeps one Sabbath as it should be kept, the Messiah will come. The Sabbath is equal to all the other precepts of the Torah" (Exodus Rabbah 25:12). "God said to Moses: 'Moses, I have a precious gift in my treasury whose name is the Sabbath and I want to give it to Israel. Go and tell them.'" (Bezah 16a).

FORBIDDEN ACTIVITIES The Talmud lists thirty-nine categories of forbidden work, including planting, cooking, baking, lighting a fire, sewing a button, hunting for food, and erecting a tent, to name just a few. Contemporary Orthodox scholars derive a host of contemporary Sabbath restrictions based on these laws that could not have been imagined by the rabbis of the Talmud.

LAWS AND CUSTOMS Lighting candles on Friday night, the eve of the
Sabbath; saying a blessing over wine and braided bread called challah; eating three festive meals; attending synagogue for prayer and
to hear the reading of the Torah. The Sabbath ends with the *havdalah*
service, a prayer over wine, spices, and the light of a candle.

MODERN INNOVATIONS For the last one hundred years, new tech-
nological devices have produced a multitude of questions regarding
Sabbath observance. Can one drive a car, ride a train, turn on an
electric light, answer the telephone, cook in a microwave, surf the
internet, play Nintendo? Orthodox scholars have by and large ruled
against using any of these modern devices on the Sabbath, saying
that they fall under one of the thirty-nine activities outlawed in the
Talmud. Turning on a light, for example, falls under the prohibition
of lighting a fire. If, however, the light is already on (or is turned on
mechanically or by a non-Jew), then it can be used. The other Jewish branches have been more lenient. In the 1950s, for example, the
legal arbiters of Conservative Judaism said that it was proper to
drive a car on the Sabbath—as long as one was going to synagogue.
This ruling coincided with the migration of Jews from the inner city
to the suburbs, where cars were essential to get around. Conservative scholars said that the innovation in the law was necessary to
keep pace with modern times. Reform Judaism has no problem
with driving a car or with using other modern conveniences on the
Sabbath.

BOOK THREE

The Jewish Day

INTRODUCTION

Many Jews encounter their heritage only at times of crisis or celebration: a family wedding or funeral, a Rosh Hashanah or Yom Kippur service, a trip to Israel, a visit to a Holocaust memorial. In Books One and Two, we looked at all these moments by examining life cycle events and holidays. But Judaism is more than these big-ticket items. It is a way of life lived day to day. I can only compare it to physical exercise. Everyone knows that you cannot stay in shape by running on a treadmill two or three times a year. No one wakes up on an April morning and decides to run the Boston Marathon. Physical conditioning takes a commitment on a regular basis.

Yet, people believe that they can have—indeed, should have—a peak religious experience by just occasionally dropping into synagogue. I've found that it takes practice. You've got to do it, as they say, religiously.

Health clubs seem to know this better than synagogues, so they borrow the language of religion in their advertisements. Right across from Saint Patrick's Cathedral in New York, one club's slogan is posted in the windows: "New York Health and Racquet Club: A Way of Life." Over on the West Side, a sports complex describes itself as "A Shrine to Your Health." Yet another new health club claims to address spirit and body through meditation as well as pumping iron; one ad promises a bit of heaven and a bit of hell.

To my mind, Jews have to recapture some of this spirit of daily religious practice. To live a Jewish life is a constant discipline. One Jewish educational program that has picked up this theme is called Aish Ha-Torah. It tries hard to appeal to the young urban professionals and advertises itself as "a Health Club for the Spirit."

I think of this crossover often when I get up early in the morning while my wife and children are still asleep, put my *tallit* and *tefillin* in a bag, and head for the synagogue for morning prayers. Out on the street, I pass all sorts of people with their gym bags on the way to their morning workout. The way I see it, we're all exercising.

In this final section, we will take a look at the daily exercise of Judaism, beginning with prayer and the laws of keeping kosher, known as *kashrut*. While prayer and *kashrut* are ritual observances, strong ethical imperatives underlie these rules. We will explore these, as well as the laws about honoring parents, visiting the sick and bereaved, lending money, giving charity, and being kind to animals. But Judaism does not leave these practices to the individual to do at will; they, too, are *mitzvot*. Just as one must pray, one must honor parents. Many of these precepts are common to all faiths, but there is a distinct Jewish way of ethical practice. In the final chapter, we will look at the Torah, the source of the ethical and ritual observances, and examine the importance of engaging it daily as part of a spiritual and intellectual exercise.

CHAPTER FIFTEEN

Prayer

A Jew starts the day with "Thank you."

That is the essence of the *modeh ani* prayer that is said each morning upon waking. "I render thanks to you, everlasting King, who has mercifully restored my soul within me," the prayer begins. The acknowledgment of thanks upon waking is the first of a hundred times a day that a Jew is supposed to express gratitude to God. Ideally, prayers spring spontaneously from our lips, and sometimes they do:

"God, what a beautiful sunrise!"

"Please, God, heal my mother!"

"Lord, help me!"

But moments of spontaneous prayer are rare and unpredictable; sometimes we might be as ready to curse as to praise. Instead, the Jewish tradition gives us the words to say; we supply the feelings. The routine of Jewish prayer is so central that the tradition asks first that we pray and later that we feel. Going through the motions of prayer helps lead the worshiper to emotional engagement.

I pray daily. I wrap a prayer shawl, known as a *tallit*, over my head; gather its four fringed corners; and bring them to my lips. It lasts only a moment, but under the *tallit* I feel a sense of security and warmth. It is the closest I get to heaven all day. The *tallit* I wear is one that I inherited from my father after he died in 1999. It is a broad woolen blanket-like shawl with a silver brocade that falls on my shoulders.

Under the *tallit*, I feel my father's presence and my mother's presence. They are no longer in this world, but under the *tallit* I feel connected to a different realm where I encounter my parents and even the Almighty Himself. When I take the *tallit* off my head, I am most often in the presence of my children, who are usually finishing their Cheerios and Kix as I go through my daily devotions. At times I am able to meditate seriously on a verse or two, but usually it is hard to concentrate on what I'm praying. I've got to get the kids off to school, and my work lies ahead of me, but I pray, knowing I've started my day attempting to reach the Divine. My hope is that it makes an impression on my God, my ancestors, and my children.

I know it makes an impression on me. I feel fortified by prayer. I am in a relationship with God. I praise, acknowledge, thank, request, express my love, and sometimes even get angry. My connection with the rest of the world—with my children, my wife, my students, my colleagues—flows out of my daily encounter with God.

B'RACHOT

Jewish prayer comes in two forms: blessings, known as *b'rachot;* and set prayer services, *tefilot,* determined by the time of day. *B'rachot* are said all day, from the time of rising to the moment of going to sleep. *B'rachot* follow a formula that begins with the words "Blessed are you, our Lord our God" and end with a mention of the activity at hand, like eating. Different foods require different *b'rachot.* Bread, wine, fruit, vegetables, and drinks all have *b'rachot* of their own. For example, the prayer for bread praises God for "bringing bread from the earth." In the yeshiva of my youth, my rabbi taught us to be sure to say one hundred *b'rachot* a day. Sometimes it seemed that my late mother worked for the rabbi. She was on constant *b'rachot* patrol, making sure that nothing crossed my lips without the proper *b'racha* offered.

A whole other category of *b'rachot* has to do with acknowledging the greatness of God. One says a *b'racha* upon seeing thunder and lightning, a rainbow, the ocean, the beauties of nature—even a king or a person of great genius. One of my favorites praises God for having "imparted from His wisdom to people of flesh and blood."

TEFILOT

B'rachot are also part of the *tefilot* that are the main services of the day. On weekdays, there are three *tefilot:* morning (*schacharit*), afternoon (*mincha*), and evening (*ma'ariv*). (On Shabbat and festivals, a fourth *tefilah,* called *musaf,* is added.) The centerpiece of the three *tefilot* is a cluster of nineteen *b'rachot* known as the *amidah.* Reciting the *amidah* is like engaging in a conversation with God. Before one begins, it is customary to take three steps back and three steps forward, symbolizing entrance into a different, otherworldly domain. The *amidah* is a silent prayer whose intimacy is heightened by the tradition of reciting it so softly that only the worshiper can hear it.

The *amidah* uses the *b'rachot* formula to first establish God's connection with the people of Israel by invoking the forefathers: Abraham, Isaac, and Jacob. The liberal movements add to this formula the names of the matriarchs: Sarah, Rebecca, Rachel, and Leah. The second part of the *amidah* makes a series of requests for, among other things, wisdom, health, and prosperity. The *amidah* closes with additional words of thanksgiving and praise and a final prayer for peace. It ends with a final three steps back and three steps forward, symbolizing a retreat from divine intimacy.

In the morning and evening service, there is one other central prayer, the *sh'ma.* It begins, "Hear O Israel the Lord Our God, the Lord is One" and is the most important Jewish prayer, the declaration of faith. The *sh'ma* is made up of three passages from the Scriptures: Deuteronomy 6:4–9, Deuteronomy 11:13–21, and Numbers 15:37–41. The first two passages include instructions that these verses

be said "when you lie down and when you rise up." From this, the rabbis deduce that it must be said each morning and evening. The third passage is added as a daily reminder of the Exodus.

There are a host of laws and customs regarding the *sh'ma*, especially the first verse. One must concentrate on the meaning of its words; if one fails to have the proper intention, the first verse must be repeated. As an aid to concentration, it is customary to place the right hand over the eyes while reciting the first verse. The opening verse should be said out loud while one is sitting or standing still; one should not walk around while saying the first verse. The *sh'ma* can be recited in any language as long as it is done with the same intention, concentration, and enunciation as when recited in the Hebrew.

In both the morning and the evening *tefilot*, the *sh'ma* is surrounded by *b'rachot*, known as the blessings of *sh'ma*. These blessings thematically serve as a bridge from the *sh'ma* to the *amidah* that follows.

MINYAN

The *b'rachot* and *tefilot* can be said by a person praying alone. But additional prayers are added when the one worshiper joins nine or more others to become part of a *minyan*, the quorum of ten. In a *minyan*, there is a public, audible rendition of the usually silent *amidah*. Also, *kaddish*, the prayer for the dead, can be said only in a *minyan*. *Kaddish* includes a give-and-take recitation between the congregation and the mourner. In addition, the Torah is read on Mondays, Thursdays, and twice on Saturdays only if there is a quorum.

Prayer in a *minyan* generally takes much longer than prayer at home. Everybody prays at an individual pace, but the basic morning prayers can be finished by one person in a quarter hour. In a *minyan*, it can take two, three, or four times as long.

By the traditional definition, a *minyan* is ten males aged thirteen and over. Among Conservative Jews, however, both men and women can be counted in a *minyan*. This was an innovation approved by the movement's rabbis in 1973. Reform Jews do not feel bound by the ancient laws and pray communally even without a *minyan*.

To pray with a *minyan* means to be bound by the clock. Services are posted in synagogues and Jewish schools, and change according to the season. The one exception is among Hasidic Jews, who, in almost every other regard, are strict about the letter of the law. When it comes to the time for prayers, they are unusually flexible. The summer after my mother passed away, I needed a *minyan* to say the *kaddish* prayer in her memory. My wife found a summer community for us near Kiryas Joel, a Satmar community north of New York City. At Kiryas Joel, there was never a problem finding a *minyan*. It seemed that the men were always praying at all times. The morning prayer would spill into the afternoon prayer, which would spill into the nighttime prayer.

Hasidim, who rebelled against what they saw as the overintellectualization of Judaism in the eighteenth century, are spontaneous when it comes to prayer. They see the strict timetable for prayer as working against its true spirit, which requires proper concentration and preparation. The Grand Rabbi of Sandz, who lived in nineteenth-century Galicia, would call his Hasidim together for prayer and then sit and meditate. As it got later and later, even past the time for the prayers, the Hasidim got impatient. "What is the rebbe doing?" they finally asked him.

He responded: "I am praying that I may pray properly."

HISTORY

It seems as if everyone in the Bible is praying. Abraham prays for the salvation of Sodom; Isaac prays for his wife, who is barren; Jacob prays to be delivered from his brother, Esau; the Israelites cry out for their redemption from the bondage of Egypt; Moses prays for his sister, Miriam; Samson prays for the strength to defeat the Philistines; and Hannah prays for a child.

As the Jews receive the Torah and become a people, service to God is centralized in the Temple in Jerusalem. Animal sacrifice is the major form of worship, as detailed at great length in Leviticus. It is a system overseen by the priests and sometimes questioned by the prophets, who warn that sacrifice without the right ethical behavior is without merit. With the destruction of the Temple in 70 C.E., animal sacrifice among the Jews comes to an end. Prayer at home and in the synagogue takes its place. But the link to the Temple is not broken. The major prayers of the day are connected to the times during the day when sacrifices were offered: morning, afternoon, and night. The Talmud links the three daily prayers not only with the Temple but with the Patriarchs, saying that Abraham instituted the morning prayer, Isaac the afternoon, and Jacob the evening prayer.

THE LANGUAGE OF PRAYER

While one can pray in any language, the universal Jewish language of prayer is Hebrew. Orthodox services tend to have the greatest amount of Hebrew, and Reform the least amount. But all the movements will retain some Hebrew, especially in the central prayers, such as the sh'ma, the expression of the oneness of God, and the amidah, the silent meditation that is recited three times a day. The use of Hebrew guarantees a uniformity to Jewish prayer, so that a Jew familiar with Hebrew can feel somewhat at home in Jewish services throughout the world.

For those not familiar with Hebrew, a Jewish service can be daunting. Each year I take a class of journalism students from Columbia to a Friday-night service at a Manhattan synagogue as part of a class on religion coverage. (Later in the semester, we go to a church and a mosque.) I tell them not even to try to follow the service from the book, but just to try to relax and catch the rhythm of the service, and perhaps join along in a melody even if they don't get the words. It can take months and many, many Hebrew lessons to feel comfortable and proficient at most Jewish services.

The traditional Hebrew prayers speak of God as "King" and "Master" and refer to God as "He." The Orthodox preserve this patriarchal language, both in the original Hebrew and in the English translation. The Conservative prayer book, *Sim Shalom,* has done much to rid the male language from the English liturgy but preserves much of it in the Hebrew. Gender-neutral terms like "ruler" or "sovereign" are used.

Other male-centered references, in both Hebrew and English, have been changed by the more liberal branches. For example, the *amidah* prayer begins with these words, "Praised are You, Lord our God and God of our Fathers." The more liberal prayer books either substitute "ancestor" or simply add "mothers" to "fathers," enumerating the matriarchs—Sarah, Rebecca, Rachel, and Leah—along with Abraham, Isaac, and Jacob.

THE WARDROBE OF PRAYER

Tallit

The *tallit,* a prayer shawl with fringes, is worn during prayer seven mornings a week, in accordance with the biblical command to wear a four-cornered garment "so that when you look upon it you will remember to do all the commands of the Lord" (Numbers 15:37–41). One puts on the *tallit* by placing it over the head and shoulders and then gathering together its four corners in an act symbolic of God gathering the dispersed Jews from the four corners of the earth.

One of the most powerful memories of my childhood was standing under the *tallit* of my father. My father's *tallit* was vast, big enough not only for him but for me and my brothers. On festivals, when the priestly blessing is sung, it is customary for men to put their *tallit* over their heads as a sign of concentration. My father would put all of us under his *tallit,* where I felt safe and truly blessed. It is a moment in my past, but I recapture it in the synagogue during the priestly blessing by bringing my sons and my daughter under my *tallit,* hoping that it will be as penetrating a memory for them as it has been for me.

There is a junior version of the *tallit* known as the *tallit katan,* which is a four-cornered fringed undergarment worn all day by Orthodox men and boys. Some who wear the *tallit katan* let the fringes hang out from the sides of their pants in keeping with the requirement that the fringes, known as *tzitzit,* be visible.

Tefillin

Other prayer garments, *tefillin,* are worn six days a week but not on the Sabbath or festivals. *Tefillin* are black boxes containing verses from Scripture that are affixed to the head and arm by leather straps in accordance with another biblical command, also mentioned in the *sh'ma:* "You shall bind them for a sign on your hand, and they shall be for frontlets between your eyes" (Deuteronomy 6:8). While some commentators took the verse figuratively—keep these laws at hand and in sight—the rabbis interpreted the verse literally. The Torah does not specify how the *tefillin* look; they are a product of the tradition. The Talmud says that even God wears *tefillin.* Our *tefillin* serve as a tactile symbol of adherence to Judaism. *Tefillin* are an ancient Jewish accessory, but one rabbi I know gives them a modern twist. Rabbi Seidler-Feller of UCLA suggests that we view the black boxes on the head and arm as a kind of primitive satellite dish that soaks up spiritual energy from God. The straps help the energy travel down to the fingertips and toward the legs so that we may do God's work on earth.

Kippah

The skullcap, known in Hebrew as the *kippah* (and in Yiddish as the *yarmulke*), is also worn during prayer. It is worn as an acknowledgment that there is a God who rules above; one doesn't go bare-headed be-

---

VARIATION ON A THEME: THE JEWISH LORD'S PRAYER

For some, Jewish prayer means not praying Christian.

Josh, who went to a Christian prep school in New England in the 1960s, started the day with his classmates saying the Lord's Prayer. "There was no escape; everybody had to say it," he told me, reciting "Our Father who art in Heaven . . ." from memory. "But they couldn't stop me from adding my own. When we finished, I used to whisper, *'Sh'ma Yisrael Adonai Eloheynu Adonai Echad.'* I don't think I even knew what it meant, but it made me feel Jewish."

At Christmas, when they passed out the caroling booklets, Josh had another solution. With a bit of teenage mischief still in his eyes, he demonstrated how he used to sing: "Oh, come let us adore him mmm-mmmmmmm the Lord."

fore Him. In the classic difference between Jewish and Christian houses of worship, a Christian man takes off his hat when going into a church, and a Jew puts on a hat. Unlike the *tallit* and *tefillin*, both mentioned in the Torah, the *kippah* is not based on any biblical or rabbinic law. It is a custom first recorded in the Talmud by a rabbi who claimed that he never walked more than four cubits (about six feet) without a head covering. The *kippah* did not become normative, however, until the seventeenth century, when one scholar, David Halevy of the Russian city of Ostrog, declared that Jewish men should cover their heads during prayer to differentiate Jewish prayer from Christian worship. However, the practice was challenged as Reform Judaism took hold in the nineteenth century. Reform Judaism abandoned the *kippah* and favored bare-headed prayer instead. With a recent return to tradition among the Reform, however, the *kippah* is back. Today, it is worn in most synagogues and temples.

Many Orthodox Jews also wear the *yarmulke* at home, and, depending on their piety and their jobs, some also wear it in public. In contemporary society, it is worn by some as a sign of Jewish solidarity and pride. It became a popular item of headgear after Israel's lightning victory against its Arab neighbors in the 1967 Arab-Israeli War. The *yarmulke*, a symbol that many felt was an indoor garment, became a way in which Jews expressed their attachment to Israel.

But not all *yarmulkes* are the same. The size and the shape and even the color give a clue to the beliefs and practices of the wearer. Large black felt *kippot* are worn by Hasidic or other ultra-Orthodox Jews, often under their black felt hats. Large knit *kippot*, in muted blues or browns, are worn by the ardent religious Zionists who live in the occupied territories of the West Bank and Gaza and by their ideological supporters. Smaller knit *yarmulkes* with bright colors or small suede ones, some decorated with action heroes, are worn by the modern Orthodox. Telltale creases in the middle of the *yarmulke*, which cause it to peak slightly on the head, are signs that the *yarmulke* spends as much time folded in the owner's pocket as on his head.

Women's Head Covering

It is considered an act of respect and modesty for married women to cover their hair in an Orthodox synagogue. The head coverings range from a knitted *kippah* and a doily to kerchiefs, wigs, berets, and broad-brimmed hats. Strictly Orthodox women also cover their hair outside the synagogue, following a rabbinic teaching that a woman's hair is sexually alluring. These women reveal their tresses only in the privacy of their homes. In some Hasidic communities, women wear elaborate wigs that look better than their natural hair, seemingly defeating the purpose of the original ban but at least technically in accordance with the law. Unmarried women and single girls are exempt from these hair restrictions; they do not need a hat or a wig, in synagogue or out.

Some women wear hats in Conservative and Reform synagogues out of a sense of modesty and tradition. But it is also becoming increasingly acceptable for women, especially women rabbis, to wear a *kippah* during the service. The impulse is not modesty before men but reflects the same reasons that men cover their heads—to acknowledge God above and to demonstrate Jewish solidarity.

CHOREOGRAPHY OF PRAYER

Jews face Jerusalem during prayer. Many (but not all) American synagogues are built so that worshipers face east. During prayer there are times to sit, times to stand, and times to bow from the waist. There are times to read aloud, times to sing out, and times to whisper or meditate. Silence comes during the *amidah* meditation. Among the fervent, there is a swaying during prayer called *shukling* in Yiddish. The Zohar, the collection of kabbalistic wisdom written at the end of the thirteenth century, explains that the souls of Jews are attached to the Torah as a candle to a great flame. Jews sway like the light of a candle during prayer. The yearning for God is expressed physically. The Talmud (Berachot 6b) suggests that even God prays. And what is God's prayer? God prays, the Talmud says, "that His mercy might overcome his judgment."

PRAYER ON GOING TO BED

The last prayer of the day begins with a blessing:

May it be your will, Lord my God and God of my fathers, to grant that I lie down in peace and that I rise up in peace. Let not my thoughts upset me—nor evil dreams, nor sinful fancies. May

my family ever be perfect in your sight. Grant me light, lest I sleep the sleep of death; for it is you who gives light to the eyes. Blessed are you, O Lord, whose majesty gives light to the whole world.

The first paragraph of the *sh'ma* is then recited, beginning with "Hear O Israel, the Lord our God, the Lord is one."

The prayer concludes with several verses about God's protection. The favorite in our house is one called *b'shem*. We sing it with the children before they go to sleep, and as we do we feel that we are wrapping them in a blanket of angels. "In the name of the Lord God of Israel, may Michael be at my right hand, and Gabriel at my left; before me Uriel, behind me Raphael; and above my head the Divine Presence."

The Basics

BIBLICAL ORIGINS Abraham prays for the salvation of Sodom; Hagar for Ishmael; Isaac for his wife, who is barren; Jacob to be delivered of Esau; Moses for Israel; and Hannah for a child. We pray by example.

RABBINIC LITERATURE Quoting Deuteronomy 11:13: "And serve him with all your heart." The Talmud comments: "What is service of the heart? This is prayer."

EVOLUTION The patriarchs prayed and brought animal sacrifices in thanksgiving. Once the Israelites were freed from Egypt and settled in the Holy Land, the main vehicle for submission to God was animal sacrifice in the Temple. With the destruction of the Temple in 70 C.E., sacrifice ended, and spoken prayer became the main form of religious supplication.

PRAYER SERVICES (*TEFILOT*) There are three each day of the year: morning (*schacharit*), afternoon (*mincha*), and evening (*ma'ariv*). On the Sabbath and holidays, a fourth (*musaf*) is added. On Yom Kippur, there is a fifth prayer (*ne'ila*).

BLESSINGS (*B'RACHOT*) FOR DAILY OCCURRENCES Eating foods (there
are different blessings for bread, wine, pastry, drinks, vegetables,
and fruits), washing hands, going to the toilet.

BLESSINGS (*B'RACHOT*) FOR SPECIAL OCCURRENCES Seeing a rainbow,
hearing thunder, seeing a king, smelling a fragrance, beholding the
beauties of nature, and seeing a person of exceptional intelligence.

CHAPTER SIXTEEN

Kosher

Next to *shalom*, the word *kosher* is probably the best-known Hebrew term in the English-speaking world. It has found its way into our dictionaries, our literature, our sitcoms, our politics, and our culture. When President Clinton, a Southern Baptist, took communion at a Roman Catholic Church in South Africa, the *Washington Post* asked, "Was that kosher?" Technically, kosher means food that is permitted and prepared according to Jewish law, but it has also come to be known as simply the right thing to do. A British rabbi, Shmuley Boteach, recently wrote a book called *Kosher Sex,* in which he extolled the virtues of modesty and abstinence. If Clinton had observed "kosher sex," Rabbi Boteach argued on his book tour, he never would have gotten mixed up in the scandal that almost brought down his presidency.

The kosher laws are highly complex. The higher up the food chain you go—from plants to fish to fowl to mammals—the more complicated the rules. The term *kashrut* refers to the whole system, from raising animals to setting the table and everything in between.

The aim of *kashrut* is to take a mundane act and turn it into a sacred enterprise. That appears to be the intent of the Torah, which three times says "You shall be holy" in connection with *kashrut*.

In Judaism, making something holy often means setting it aside for a

special purpose. For example, a couple is united in marriage in a ceremony called *kedushin*, from the word *kadosh* (holy), an act that symbolizes their being set aside exclusively for each other. *Kashrut* sets Jews
aside from others by requiring that they eat differently. It also has the
effect of unifying the Jewish people by enabling all Jews to sit at a common table. *Kashrut* teaches restraint and self-control. Some things are
simply not kosher.

HISTORY

The laws of *kashrut* flow from texts in Genesis, Leviticus, and
Deuteronomy that provide extensive lists of "clean" and "unclean" animals. But the sacred texts are only the beginning. The laws were ex-
panded over the centuries, first in the Talmud and later in the various
rabbinical codes of Jewish law, right up to today. With new foods on
the market, rabbis continue to issue rulings about what is kosher and
what is not.

If we follow the Biblical account closely, we see that original man,
Adam, was a vegetarian. God tells him that he can eat from "every herb
yielding seed" and "every tree in which is the fruit of a tree yielding
seed." Only when we come to the story of Noah, after the Flood, is
meat permitted. "Every moving thing that liveth shall be for you," God
tells Noah and his children.

In those few chapters in Genesis, we move from the ideal of the
Garden of Eden, where no meat is eaten, to the real, carnivorous
world of Noah. But Noah is not given free rein over animals. He is instructed to show animals compassion by not taking a limb or a piece of
flesh from a living animal for consumption.

Later in the Bible, when the Jews get the Torah, they are told that
this concession of eating meat comes with additional restrictions.
While Noah could eat all animals, the Israelites were given a long list
of animals that they could not eat. Off the menu went pigs, horses,
camels, rodents, lions, and other wild beasts. Birds of prey, like vul-

tures and eagles, were among the forbidden fowl. In the sea, eels, whales, dolphins, and all shellfish were deemed unkosher. When the listings of Leviticus II and Deuteronomy 14 are finished, Jewish cuisine is rather limited. On top of this, the rabbis added other restrictions, such as proper slaughter of animals and the strict separation of meat and milk.

Many Jewish scholars believe that vegetarianism is the ideal. Not only was that the case in Eden, but it is also part of the vision of the prophets who foretell the "end of days." In Isaiah 11, the prophet promises a world in which "the wolf shall dwell with the lamb . . . and the lion shall eat straw like the ox." Vegetarians will rule. But until then, Jews are told to revere life by keeping the laws of *kashrut*.

FOR THE CHICKENS

Isaac Bashevis Singer (1904–1991), the great Yiddish writer and Nobel laureate, was a committed vegetarian. He was once asked whether he was a vegetarian for health reasons. "Yes," he said simply, "for the health of the chickens."

NO HUNTING

The widespread Jewish aversion to hunting may have been summed up best by the Jewish-born poet Heinrich Heine (1797–1856): "My ancestors did not belong to the hunters so much as the hunted," he wrote, "and the idea of attacking the descendants of those who were our comrades in misery goes against my grain."

KOSHER AMERICAN STYLE

Keeping kosher is a complex system that means different things to different people. "No two people keep kosher the same way," one friend told me. To some, keeping kosher means abstaining from the forbidden animals specifically mentioned in the Bible, like pig and lobster. To others, it means buying only kosher meats. For some, it means keeping separate dishes: one set for milk, one for meat. For others, it means keeping kosher at home but eating non-kosher outside the home. For still others, it means eating only products with a kosher symbol, such as an "OU" or a "Star K," both at home and outside.

However one chooses to do it, keeping kosher today is easier than in past generations. Numerous mainstream products on the market are produced under rabbinic supervision. Breads, crackers, sauces, cheeses, yogurts, pasta, meats, poultry, and condiments all have kosher versions. And while there is no way to make bacon or shrimp kosher, there are imitation varieties made from soy and other kosher ingredients that I'm told taste almost like the real thing. Foods that were once verboten in kosher homes are now standard. In 1997, that quintessential American snack, Oreos, got the OU certification. There was rejoicing in many Jewish homes. I, like many Orthodox, grew up only hearing about "America's favorite cookie" but never tasting it. Oreos contained lard—it was right there on the list of ingredients. But Nabisco cleaned up its act and got the OU, and now the cookies fill lunch boxes where once they were not welcome.

Kosher restaurants have also proliferated. Just about every major American city, from Houston to Boston, has at least one. The Manhattan Yellow Pages lists twenty-five. And they're not all delicatessens, either. There are kosher Indian, Mexican, Italian, Chinese, Japanese, and Thai restaurants. Kosher pizza shops are also popular—but don't expect prosciutto on your pizza.

At the fancier kosher restaurants, like the Manhattan steakhouse Le Marais, it's not uncommon to see one person with a *kippah* sitting at a table of non-Jewish businessmen. A persuasive kosher person can get clients or business associates to join in at a good kosher restaurant—at least once. The more common scenario is to find a person who observes *kashrut* (with or without a *kippah*) with business associates at a fancy non-kosher restaurant, feverishly trying to find the one thing on the menu that comes closest to being kosher. One friend told me about spending an evening at a Japanese restaurant moving sushi from one corner of the plate to another. "I had no idea what any of it was," he said. Occasionally, he would drop a piece into his napkin or on the floor. He ate nothing all night. Other observant people have learned to cope in such situations by ordering vegetables or seafood that is kosher (even if it is not prepared in a kosher kitchen). Most Orthodox rabbis will tell you that vegetables and fish prepared in a non-kosher kitchen are forbidden. No doubt these rabbis are doing their job, but they are a bit out of touch; they don't normally have to do business at non-kosher restaurants the way so many of their congregants must.

Reform rabbis, of course, do. I was once at a convention of Reform rabbis in Minneapolis and ate lunch at a non-kosher restaurant with a rabbi who ordered something I wouldn't dream of eating there: a hamburger. I sat there eating tuna salad while the rabbi ate non-kosher meat. My Orthodox rabbi would not have approved my dining in this non-kosher establishment, but, I reasoned, at least I wasn't eating a hamburger.

Among the Reform, *kashrut* is a matter of personal choice for both rabbis and laypersons. The 1999 Reform "statement of principles" says that some traditions abandoned by Reform, such as *kashrut,* "demand renewed attention," but there is no requirement to keep kosher. Conservative Judaism requires adherence to *kashrut* standards, but a recent study found that only 15 percent of Conservative Jews keep kosher homes. One of the defining characteristics of Orthodoxy, however, is *kashrut* observance. If someone identifies as Orthodox, most would assume that the home is kosher. Yet, many modern Orthodox Jews are more lax about *kashrut* when eating outside the home. They will not eat non-kosher meat or poultry and will favor the items on the menu that are fish or vegetarian dishes. While Orthodox rabbis frown on this practice, they admit that an earlier generation of Orthodox rabbis accepted such compromises for their congregants if not for themselves. Things have changed, however, the rabbis argue, noting the proliferation of kosher restaurants and kosher supermarket items; there is no longer an excuse for the lax standards of the past.

WHY KOSHER?

In the Bible, no reason is given for the kosher laws. In rabbinic literature, *kashrut* is included among those laws for which there is no rational explanation given—a category known in Hebrew as *chukkim.* Why should some foods be permitted and others forbidden? Why are some foods okay to eat alone but rendered unkosher when mixed together? What difference does it make what a person eats?

These are not new questions. They were addressed by Jesus in the New Testament gospel of Matthew: "Not that which goeth into the mouth defileth a man; but that which cometh out of the mouth" (Matthew 15:11). The laws of the Hebrew Bible, given to a desert tribe, came to be considered outdated and irrelevant by first-century Christians, who said that the essence of the teaching of Abraham and Moses was not about ritual but about faith.

The Jews argued—and still argue—that both faith and ritual are essential. Jewish philosophers have struggled to explain such ritual requirements as *kashrut.* Some argued that there were physical benefits associated with eating kosher; others said that the benefits were purely spiritual. Maimonides, in his *Guide to the Perplexed,* written in Egypt in 1190, understood the dietary laws as a means of keeping the body pure and healthy. The meat of forbidden animals, he said, was unwholesome.

Nachmanides, who lived in thirteenth-century Spain, saw the dietary laws as being of benefit to the soul rather than the body. Predatory animals are forbidden, he explained, because of their violent character. Likewise, a milk and meat mixture is off limits because the combination represents an insensitivity to life. Milk, the symbol of sustaining life, should not be mixed with the meat of a dead animal.

Modern Jewish philosophers tend to side with Nachmanides that the benefits of *kashrut* are essentially spiritual. To adopt Maimonides' reasoning that *kashrut* represents a healthier lifestyle is to risk being contradicted by science. In an age of refrigeration, sanitary food preparation, and government regulation, many of the reasons once given for *kashrut* no longer apply.

What the rules of *kashrut* provide is a discipline that at once sets Jews apart and connects them to the sanctity of all living things.

VARIATIONS ON A THEME: HEAVENLY DISHES

Rabbi Bob Alper, a former pulpit rabbi turned comedian, is fascinated by people who keep kosher at home but eat non-kosher foods out. "What are they thinking?" he asks. "Well, at least their dishes will go to heaven."

Speaking of dishes, I've heard of some Jewish homes with three sets of dishes—meat, milk, and Chinese. These people are otherwise kosher but give it all up to eat Chinese food. How does this happen? My friend Jack, a writer who grew up in a Conservative home in Detroit, told me this story:

"We kept kosher at home, separate dishes and all. But we had a weakness for Chinese food. My mother would order out, but she had one rule: we had to eat the Chinese food in the den. But the den was cold, so in the winter we brought the Chinese food into the dining room. Then she developed another rule: we had to eat it on paper plates. Eventually, we got dishes. We just had to keep them separate."

As with Shabbat, there are people who observe a fifty-mile *kashrut* rule. If they're on vacation or traveling on business, they feel released

KOSHER IS IN THE DETAILS

Jews who keep kosher are often accused of being overly concerned—even obsessed—with the details. They check the labels on the packages for questionable ingredients and carefully count the hours between meat meals and milk meals. They seem to accuse every food of being *treif* until it is proved kosher.

While the charge of obsession may be true, there is sometimes power in the details, as is obvious in the following story about the late Rabbi Louis Finkelstein as told by Rabbi Maurice Lamm. Rabbi Finkel-

from *kashrut*, especially if they're in Maine (must taste the lobster) or in Maryland (oh, those crabs). Closer to home, they're kosher.

My friend Barry, a Jewish educator, told me about being in a non-kosher restaurant in Boston with his two aunts, who keep a strictly kosher home. One of the aunts couldn't decide. She contemplated the chicken, but then she exclaimed, "I can't have *goyishe* chicken. Waiter, I'll take the scallops."

Some habits die hard. A family outside of Kansas City doesn't keep kosher in the traditional sense, but they do have separate dishes for milk and meat. When they eat bacon, which is with some regularity, they eat it on their meat plates.

At the other end of the *kashrut* extreme are Hasidic families who don't want non-kosher animals around in any form. My friend Reuven from Minneapolis doesn't allow his kids to have—as toys—any stuffed animals that aren't kosher. Toy cows and sheep and chickens are okay, but no horses, elephants, or lions are permitted. Miss Piggy cannot cross his threshold. "We're looking for good role models," Reuven told me.

stein, the former chancellor of the Jewish Theological Seminary in New York City, visited the great conductor Andre Kostelanetz, whose wife brought out a platter of cookies. The rabbi expressed his thanks but declined, explaining that even a small ingredient could render them unkosher. The conductor asked what a tiny bit of *treif* could possibly do to his soul. "Tell me, maestro," Rabbi Finkelstein responded, "what would the final crescendo of Beethoven's Fifth Symphony sound like if you took out just one bar?"

The maestro understood.

ECO-KOSHER

In the 1970s, Rabbi Zalman Schacter-Shalomi set a new standard for *kashrut* when he coined the term "eco-kosher." He asked people to consider whether additives or chemicals were used in the preparation of the meal, whether the animals they were about to eat were treated humanely—not only at the moment of slaughter, but before. In the eco-kosher system, free-range chickens may be preferable to kosher chickens raised in a dark, airless cage. Even better would be free-range kosher chickens that have been ritually slaughtered. And even better, in this system, would be no chickens at all. Eco-kosher holds vegetarianism up as a high ideal and ultimate Jewish goal, since eating fish and animals is harmful to our fellow creatures. Eco-kosher is also concerned about whether the clothes one wears are kosher. Were they manufactured in a shop where underage youth were employed or where taxes were not paid? Is that leather on your belt or on your shoes really necessary?

In a real way, Rabbi Schacter-Shalomi's life reflects this ethic of eco-*kashrut*. A former Lubavitch Hasid, he broke with the Hasidic movement because he felt that it was too narrow in its worldview and unjust to women and non-Jews. His family name was Schacter, which means slaughterer. But he added Shalomi, from the word *peace,* to indicate a transformation to the peaceful gatherer.

The Basics

BIBLICAL ORIGINS "These are the creatures that you may eat from among all the land animals. . . . (Leviticus 11:2 and on). "You shall not eat anything abhorrent. These are the animals that you may eat. . . ." (Deuteronomy 14:3 and on). "That is why the children of Israel to this day do not eat the thigh muscle that is on the socket of the hip. . . ." (Genesis 32:32). The Orthodox and the Conservative consider these laws binding today; the Reform do not.

FRUITS AND VEGETABLES All things that grow—everything from artichokes to zucchini—are kosher. Flowers, nuts, and roots are also kosher.

DAIRY PRODUCTS Milk from a kosher animal is kosher, as are soft cheeses such as cream cheese and cottage cheese. Yogurts are also kosher, provided they do not have any non-kosher additives such as gelatin. With regard to hard cheese, there is a difference of opinion. According to the Orthodox, all hard cheeses need rabbinical supervision, since the hardening agents, such as rennet, are often derived from the stomach lining of non-kosher animals. Conservative scholars, however, say that all cheeses are permitted, since rennet is so transformed that it is not considered a food; often, they add, rennet used today is artificial and therefore kosher.

WINE The Orthodox require rabbinical supervision of all wines and grape products. The requirement grows out of medieval fears that the wines of non-Jews are used for pagan libations, thus rendering them unfit for consumption by Jews. Conservative rabbis have ruled, however, that such fears are today unfounded, and all wines are permitted, even without rabbinic supervision. Still, even according to the Conservatives, it is preferable to use kosher wines, especially those from Israel, for liturgical purposes, such as sanctifying the Shabbat during *kiddush*.

FISH Fish that have fins and scales are kosher, including trout, salmon, tuna, mackerel, bluefish, and anchovies. Shellfish, such as crabs, lobster, and clams, are unkosher. So are eels, whales, and dolphins.

MEAT Animals that chew their cud and have split hooves are kosher, provided they are slaughtered and prepared according to the laws of *kashrut*. These include cows, sheep, moose, deer, and yak. Among unkosher animals are pigs, lions, camels, horses, and rodents.

FOWL Chickens, turkeys, ducks, and geese are all kosher and are treated like meat products; kosher slaughtering and preparation are required. Birds of prey are not kosher, including eagles, herons, ostriches, owls, and vultures.

PARVE These foods are neither milk nor meat and therefore can be

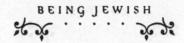
eaten with either. They include all things that grow (fruits, vegetables, roots) and all fish that is kosher.

SLAUGHTERING To be fit to eat, it is not enough for an animal to be in the kosher category. The animal must be slaughtered according to Jewish law by a ritual slaughterer, known as a *shochet*. The methods, while ancient, are designed to minimize the pain felt by the animal. Sharp knives and swift action are required. An animal that is shot to death or that dies in an accident or of natural causes is not kosher. Hunting is not a Jewish sport.

KASHERING After slaughter, the meat must be washed and salted (to draw out the blood) in a process known as *kashering*. The term is also used to describe the process of transforming utensils or even a whole kitchen from non-kosher to kosher.

PREPARATION Kosher meat must be prepared in a kitchen where all the knives, cutting surfaces, and pots are kosher. Finally, the food must be served on a kosher plate and consumed with kosher flatware.

MILK AND MEAT *Kashrut* requires the separation of milk and meat products. The law is derived by the rabbis' interpretation of a thrice-repeated verse in Exodus and Deuteronomy: "You shall not boil a kid in its mother's milk." Milk and meat (including fowl) cannot be cooked or served together. To reinforce the separation, separate dishes were mandated for the different categories. The rabbis also imposed a waiting period between the consumption of meat and of milk to give the body a chance to digest the meat. Traditions vary, but the waiting time ranges from one hour to six hours.

CHAPTER SEVENTEEN

The Jewish Home

Many consider the synagogue to be the center of Jewish life. Synagogues often even call themselves just that: the Jewish Center. But the real heart of Jewish life is the home. It is in the home where Judaism is fully experienced—through books, ritual objects, religious observances, conversations, study, and prayer. If there are children in the house, then the home becomes the most important educational sphere. The way adults talk and act—toward their children and toward each other—teach children more than any synagogue or classroom can.

Some of the moments of greatest religious significance take place primarily in the home (and only by default in the synagogue). They include lighting the Hanukkah candles, enjoying a Sabbath meal, participating in a Passover seder, and, in the case of the death of a loved one, sitting *shiva*. Jews have come to call the prayer room of the synagogue the "sanctuary," but the real sanctuary is the home. It must be a place where each member of the family finds refuge from the pressures of the outside world. When I first became a reporter at the *New York Times*, I became friendly with Ken Briggs, the paper's excellent religion writer, who is an ordained Methodist minister. No one understood the dynamics of working for a daily paper like Ken. "Some days you're on top, usually when you're on Page One," he would say. "Some days you're on the bottom. The editors ignore you, no one returns your calls, even the copy boys won't talk to you." In journalism and in so many other professional fields, our self-esteem easily gets tied up with our success at work. But my friend Ken had a family. "You know," he'd add, "no matter what happens at work, when you go home at night, you're 'Daddy.' Your child doesn't care how much money you made or how many Page One stories you had or whether you screwed up. Love for Daddy is unconditional." That's the ideal of home for me—not just for mothers and fathers, but for kids too.

Reaching that level of unconditional acceptance is hard; working for it is essential. And while we're working on it, it is important to share it—essentially to export it to others. The Jewish home is a private, sacred space, but it also has a communal role. A great Jewish virtue is the *mitzvah* of *hachnasat orchim,* the welcoming of guests. The truly Jewish home both shines within and radiates without, providing a warmth for all who enter.

MEZUZAH

ORIGINS "And these words, which I command you this day, shall be in your heart . . . and you shall write them upon the doorposts of your house, and on your gates" (Deuteronomy 6:6–9 and 11:18–20).

The outward sign of a Jewish home is a *mezuzah,* a small box or cylinder attached to the doorpost that contains fifteen biblical verses inscribed by hand on parchment. The verses proclaim the oneness of God and tell of God's promise to those who follow the commandments. "I will give you rain for your land at the right season . . . and you will eat and be satisfied," the Scripture promises. As you enter a house it is customary to lightly touch the *mezuzah* with your right hand and kiss the spot. Kissing the *mezuzah* makes you aware that you are entering a sacred space, the kind of sanctuary that a home should be.

The *mezuzah* serves as a form of Jewish identity as well as, in Jewish folklore, a kind of amulet or sentry box that protects those within the house. The important part of the *mezuzah* is not the shell (which is the decorative casing and is often made of ornate silver, blown glass, or plain plastic) but the inner workings. The scroll must be written on parchment by the hand of a scribe. The parchment is rolled into a cylinder, and the Hebrew letters *shin, daled,* and *yud* are printed on the back. The letters form one of the names of God and also are an acronym for the Hebrew words that mean "Guardian of the Door of Israel."

The *mezuzah* is placed one third of the way down from the top of the door in a slanting position at a 45-degree angle to the floor. The slanting of the *mezuzah* is in itself a sign of compromise, which suggests a method of resolving conflicts within the family. Medieval scholars differed on whether the *mezuzah* should be horizontal or vertical. An understanding was struck in which it was put at a slant, showing concern for both opinions.

As a Jewish practice, *mezuzahs* belong on the doorposts of the house. One modern adaptation is to wear a *mezuzah* as jewelry, usually made of silver and hanging from a chain. Although it has become a form of Jewish identification, such jewelry has no religious significance. I learned another modern *mezuzah* custom from my friends Ray and Amy, a couple from Tucson who were on sabbatical in Israel with my family. Ray and Amy have been on a journey toward greater Jewish learning and observance throughout their fifteen-year marriage. When they first decided to put *mezuzahs* on the doorposts of their Tucson home, they filled the casings not with Biblical verses written in Hebrew by a scribe but with more personal prayers and hopes written by them and their children. "May this be a Jewish house where love and caring prevail." Later, they added the biblical verses, which say much the same thing but in a more traditional way.

HOSPITALITY

ORIGINS "And the Lord appeared to him [Abraham] by the tere-
binths of Mamre, as he sat in the tent door in the heat of the day;
and he raised his eyes and looked, and, lo, three men stood by him;
and when he saw them, he ran to meet them from the tent door, and
bowed himself to the ground, and said, My Lord, if now I have
found favor in thy sight, pass not away, I pray thee, from thy servant;
let a little water, I pray you, be fetched, and wash your feet, and rest
yourselves under the tree. And I will fetch a morsel of bread, and
comfort your hearts" (Genesis 18:1–5).

The biblical model of hospitality is Abraham, who sat outside the door
of his tent waiting for guests to arrive. From the Genesis account of
Abraham interrupting his communion with God, the Talmud concludes: "It is greater to invite in guests than to receive the divine presence." In Jewish folklore, Abraham's home had four openings, one
facing each direction, so that he could greet guests coming from every
direction. In the account in Genesis, when Abraham sees guests approaching, he runs to greet them, bows, and beseeches them to stay a
while. He goes on to promise them "a morsel of bread," but in the account that follows he brings them cakes, bread, butter, and a young calf
"tender and good."

Home is at once a sanctuary for the family and a place for the wayfarer. In Hebrew, such hospitality is known as *hachnasat orchim*, welcoming the guests, and refers to entertaining the poor rather than
simply inviting over friends. The traditional definition of the poor were
those without enough food for themselves and their families. But there
are different types of poverty. There is merit in inviting to one's table
those who are traveling away from home as well as those who are single and long for a family environment. On the Sabbath or on a festival,
it is especially important to have as guests those who would otherwise
not experience the joy of the day. No festive table is complete without
a guest. Living as we do on a college campus, we enjoy hosting stu-

dents for a Sabbath meal. Many are away from home and welcome the opportunity to connect with a family.

In some synagogues, home hospitality is so institutionalized that the rabbi makes an announcement in synagogue offering visitors a place for a Sabbath meal. After the services, visitors are put together with host families.

The issue of having guests is one that Shira and I often discuss. Sometimes we just want to be alone, arguing, "Our family comes first." There are times when this is true; we don't want intrusions. On the other hand, putting our family first sometimes *demands* having guests. The example we set to our children about hospitality is an important one. What we get in return for having guests is an incalculable enrichment of our lives. We've had elderly widows and young college students, single mothers and traveling salesmen. Every person has a story to tell, and many have Sabbath traditions and songs that are different from our own. For those of us who are fortunate enough to have a family, it is imperative to remember that there are many, many people who are alone.

I feel a special obligation to perform this *mitzvah* because I have so often been on the receiving end. When I travel abroad and know I will be away from my family on Shabbat, I am not shy about calling in advance to find a family that will host me. The Lubavitch Hasidim, who have an international network of community centers known as Chabad houses, are a great resource in this effort. They have helped me find a Shabbat meal while traveling everywhere from Casablanca to Moscow to Rome to Harare. While I was in Italy recently, the Lubavitch arranged for me to eat with a family in Rome. As planned, I met the man, an executive of Italian television in his forties, at the Great Synagogue, and then walked through the streets with him to his apartment. As we walked past the cafés and bars the man told me how he and his wife were *ba'alei teshuva*, returnees to Judaism, who had become more religiously observant in recent years. We ascended the stairs to his apartment, and I entered what seemed to be a fashionable art gallery. On the walls of his home were three tiers of drawings and paintings, most of them in a classical style. But one wall caught my eye. A dozen charcoal sketches of a beautiful full-breasted nude reached to the ceiling. I tried not to stare.

The man made the traditional blessings and helped his wife serve a scrumptious Sabbath meal, with a Mediterranean flavor (she was Sephardic). His wife, who wore a long Orthodox-style dress and head covering, told me of her spiritual transformation to tradition. "That," she said smiling while pointing to the wall of nudes, "used to be me."

HONORING PARENTS

ORIGINS "Honor your father and your mother, that your days may be
long in the land which the Lord your God gives you" (Exodus
20:12). "Every one of you shall fear his mother and his father, and
you shall keep my sabbaths. I am the Lord your God" (Leviticus
18:3).

In a traditional Jewish home, a child does not sit in his mother's or father's place. This might seem like a trivial rule, but from it flows a whole attitude toward parents. Parents occupy a special place in the Jewish family. While by no means divine or beyond question, they are said to be partners with God in creation and, in the mind of the Talmud, are linked to the divine. From the Talmud: "Our masters taught: There are three partners in a person: the Holy One, the father, and the mother. When a person honors father and mother, the Holy One says: I account it to them as though I were dwelling among them and they were honoring me."

Honoring parents is, of course, the fifth of the Ten Commandments. The rabbis see poetic symbolism where the commandment is placed in the Decalogue. The first five commandments—the injunction against idol worship, the requirement to honor the Sabbath, etc.—are generally regarded as those governing the behavior toward God. The commandments of the second set—don't kill, don't steal, don't commit adultery—regulate behavior between human beings. Honoring one's parents, then, takes on a greater, almost divine, significance as a bridge between God and humankind.

The Talmud comments on the two biblical expressions concerning parents, one to "honor" parents and the other to "fear" them. "What is 'fear' and what is 'honor'?" the Talmud asks. "'Fear' means not to stand in their place, not to sit in their place, and not to contradict them. 'Honor' means to feed them, clothe them, escort them in, and escort them out."

The Talmud talks about the extent to which one must go to fulfill this *mitzvah*. A discussion begins, "To what extent must one honor parents?" The sage named Ula says, go and look at the example of a Gentile from Ashkelon, a Roman whose name was Dama ben Natina. On one occasion, merchants came and offered him 600,000 gold coins if he could immediately produce a certain jewel. Dama ben Natina said that the jewel was in safekeeping under the pillow of his father. "Wake him," they insisted. Dama ben Natina refused. "I will not disturb his sleep for all your money." The text goes on to give other examples of acts of parental honor. One nobleman, dressed in gold robes and standing among the elders of Rome, was suddenly accosted by his mother. She approached, tore his clothes, and spit in his face. The nobleman did not flinch. "He did not shame her," the Talmud says.

The mother of one of the rabbis of the Talmud, Rabbi Tarfon, tells of her son's greatness in this regard. Once she went out on the Sabbath for a walk, and the strap of her sandal broke. Her son put his hand under her foot and let her walk on it until she reached her destination. The rabbis listen, but are unimpressed. They comment: "Even if he had done this a thousand times, he would not approach one half of the honor to parents that the Torah demands" of a child.

The demands on children vis à vis their parents seem so great that one rabbi in the Talmud, an orphan, exclaims somewhat facetiously that he is lucky to never have known his parents. Rabbi Simeon b. Yohai concludes: "The most difficult of all the *mitzvot* is 'honor your father and mother.'"

What Jewish parents really want from children is not subservience but *nachas,* a Yiddish term that might best be translated as a combination of joy and pride. *Nachas* is a special kind of pleasure that is experienced without even a trace of jealousy. If your best friend wins the lottery, you may be happy for him, but you might be jealous. If your child gets an A, you experience a joy that is without jealousy—that's *nachas.*

In every family conflicts arise. As much as our parents may want us to be like them, we grow up in a different generation and a different time. My parents grew up in the 1930s, I in the 1960s, and my children at the turn of the new century. Our culture, our music, our mores, our clothes, our sense of style are all different. My parents had the Andrews Sisters, I had Phil Ochs, and my children have Britney Spears and Michael Nyman (my older son loves movie scores). What Judaism provides is a set of consistent values. I didn't sit in my parents' place, and my children don't sit in mine.

Is there room for dissent? What if children disagree with parents? What if a parent's vision for the children's future is different from theirs? Can a parent tell a child whom to marry, where to live, what profession to pursue? Does the child have to listen?

The answer goes back to the Ten Commandments. It does not say "always listen" to your parents. It says "honor" and "fear." Sometimes children can disagree, but they must always do it with respect and even a bit of fear.

SEX WITHIN MARRIAGE

ORIGINS "Hence a man leaves his father and mother and clings to his wife, so that they become one flesh" (Genesis 2:24).

Judaism has such a positive view toward sex that sex is regarded as a holy act—under the right circumstances. The right circumstances are within marriage. The rabbinical term for marriage, in fact, is *kedushin,* which is the Hebrew word for holy. Marriage is a holy union; sex outside marriage is wrong.

Within the context of marriage, sex is not only for procreation but for pleasure, and the rabbis of the Talmud put special emphasis on the pleasure of the woman. Sexual pleasure is a woman's right under her marriage contract, the *ketubah*. In one Talmudic passage, the rabbis set out the man's obligations based on his line of work in a surprisingly systematic way. "The duty of conjugal rights as enjoined in the Torah is: every day for those who have no occupation, twice a week for laborers, once a week for ass-drivers, once every thirty days for camel-drivers, and once every six months for sailors" (Mishna Ketubot 5:6). In a discussion that follows, the rabbis suggest that a wife must consent to a change in her husband's profession if it is to affect their sex life.

The rabbis of the Talmud developed a rather positive and open attitude toward sex and rejected the view, later prevalent in Christianity, that marriage was just a concession to baser passions. Typical of the Christian attitude were the writings of Paul, himself a celibate, whose famous line from the New Testament book of Corinthians was "it is better to marry than to burn with passion."

In the Jewish view, Friday night is a particularly meritorious time for married couples to have intercourse, joining the bliss of the Sabbath with the bliss of the marriage. In the marital bed, whatever feels good to the couple is permissible as long as it is consensual and not harmful. Among the rabbis of the Talmud, some counseled for restraint, saying that the missionary position was the preferred method; others allowed for greater variation. The sixteenth-century Polish authority Rabbi Moses Isserles writes that a man can do "as he pleases with his wife. He can kiss any part of her body; and he can have intercourse both in the usual way or in an unusual way or on her limbs, provided that he does not spill his seed."

But a woman's happiness is paramount. Sex in the marital bed is a celebration—a time for joy, laughter, and spontaneity. One medieval rabbinic text, the *Iggeret ha-Kodesh*, instructs the husband on the act of foreplay: "Speak to her so that your words will provoke desire, love, will, and passion." The writer further counsels: "A man should never force himself upon his wife and never overpower her . . . see that your wife's intentions combine with yours. Do not hurry to arouse her until she is receptive. Be calm, and as you enter the path of love and will, let her insemination come first."

The notion that the woman should be allowed to reach orgasm first is found in numerous rabbinic sources. One passage of the Talmud (Niddah) even suggests that if the woman reaches orgasm first, the child of the union will be a male. Notwithstanding the bad science here, one can see how the practice demonstrated a concern for pleasing women in the marital bed.

Likewise, a woman must concern herself with her husband's sexual pleasure. In one passage in the Talmud (Shabbat 140b), Rabbi Huna is said to have instructed his daughters on how to please their husbands. A woman who turns away from her husband in bed is called a "rebellious wife."

Does all this sound too good to be true? In a way, it is. There is a major caveat to the celebration of Jewish marital sex that severely curtails sex—the laws of "family purity." The source of these laws is in Leviticus 18:19: "Do not come near a woman when she is impure with her menstrual flow to uncover her nakedness." The rabbis of the Talmud not only outlawed sex during the woman's period but extended the time of separation an additional seven days to ensure that there is no confusion that might lead to intercourse during the menses. Following the separation, a woman must go to the *mikveh,* or ritual bath, before being permitted once again to her husband.

The stringency of the rabbis in effect nearly doubles the biblical time during which religious couples must abstain from sex, from five to fourteen days. Another discipline that the rabbis add during this time is to prohibit even casual contact that might lead to sexual arousal. Strictly interpreted, during the two-week time of separation husband and wife are not supposed to touch each other, drink from the same glass, or share the same bed. For this reason, twin beds are the norm in many Orthodox households.

These are some of the toughest Jewish laws to observe. Many explanations are given from the standpoint of symbolism, tradition, and even feminism. Symbolically, each month that the egg is not fertilized, a chance for a new life is lost. Going to the *mikveh* purifies one from that encounter with a lost life and offers the promise of new life possibilities. The argument from tradition is a powerful one. It recognizes that Jewish women have done this for centuries, often in times of adversity. The *mikvehs* of Europe were dank and cold and threatening places, right out of an Isaac Bashevis Singer story. Women made sacrifices to go. The *mikvehs* of today, incidentally, are luxurious by comparison. Some are built like spas, with Jacuzzis and hair dryers. Finally, the Orthodox feminist argument turns on its head the idea of separation during menstrual periods. Rather than a time of women's impurity, it is a time of women's empowerment, a time when they cannot be treated like sexual objects but must be seen as beings above their sex.

As with the kosher food laws, the justifications for family purity laws on the grounds of health go only so far. Indeed, there may be health benefits to such abstention, but observing these laws is ultimately an act of faith. Just how a couple observes them is their own business. By tradition, a woman goes to the *mikveh* at night, under the cover of darkness, rather than in the daytime. Discretion is paramount. To talk about one's observance of these laws is tantamount to detailing one's sex life. And, as with the kosher laws, there are variations on the *mikveh* theme. No two couples observe the laws surrounding *mikveh* in precisely the same way. There are those who do not even touch during this time, but there are also those who sleep in the same bed but do not have intercourse. Some abstain for five days but do not count the additional seven. And others count all twelve days but don't go to the *mikveh* at the end. There are Orthodox couples who ignore these laws as too difficult, and Conservative and Reform couples who embrace them as a healthy religious discipline.

BIRTH CONTROL

ORIGINS "Be fruitful and multiply, replenish the earth and subdue it" (Genesis 1:28).

The practical consequence of the laws of "family purity" is to make sex more likely to produce a child because the two weeks when sex is permitted are the most fertile times of the monthly cycle. The "natural" method of birth control practiced by observant Catholics—in which couples have sex during the *least* fertile times of the month—is not an option in traditional Judaism. And traditional Judaism does not routinely permit the use of artificial birth control devices unless the life of the mother would be endangered by pregnancy. Most Orthodox rabbis tend to interpret that standard very liberally especially once a family already has children—preferably one of each gender. They will permit the use of various devices (such as the diaphragm) and medications (the birth control pill) if the birth of yet another child would put undue emotional stress or financial hardship on the family. The use of condoms is seen as more problematic because they waste seed in a manner similar to that outlawed in the Genesis story of Onan, who sinned by spilling "his seed on the ground" (Genesis 38:9). Ultra-Orthodox and Hasidic rabbis tend to be more stringent, discouraging all birth control devices unless pregnancy would result in a direct danger to the mother's life. This attitude toward birth control explains the larger family size among the ultra-Orthodox.

FORBIDDEN SEX

By strict Orthodox standards, all sex outside of marriage is forbidden. For the other branches of Judaism, distinctions are drawn between different sexual activities outside of marriage. As young people increasingly postpone marriage in order to complete their schooling and start their careers, few rabbis today are surprised when a young man and his fiancée come to set a wedding date and put down the same address on their application. And masturbation, once regarded as wasting a limited supply of seed, is widely acknowledged as a healthy and harmless release of sexual tension.

With psychological studies showing that homosexuality is a condition of birth as much as a conscious choice, more and more religious leaders see the value of committed, monogamous homosexual relations, especially in an era of promiscuity and disease. Gay synagogues, once seen as at best a curiosity and at worst an offense, have emerged as a respected force in many urban Jewish communities. Most major American cities with large Jewish populations—New York, Los Angeles, Houston, Atlanta, Boston—have a gay synagogue.

The Reform seminary, Hebrew Union College–Jewish Institute of Religion, ordains sexually active, publicly professing gays as rabbis. Many Reform rabbis will perform commitment ceremonies for gay couples. The Conservative rabbinical seminary does not ordain gays, but there are many within the movement who advocate such ordinations, arguing that justice demands such a change. Numerous Conservative synagogues have active outreach programs to involve gays in synagogue life.

The Orthodox, however, hold fast to the verse in Leviticus 19 that declares that for a man to lie with a man is "an abomination." They make no allowances for modern psychological research. Nonetheless, there are many young Orthodox men and women who quietly live a gay lifestyle. Some of them find a religious home at New York's gay and lesbian synagogue, Congregation Bet Simchat Torah. Worshipers at the two-thousand-member synagogue range from Hasidic youth struggling with their sexuality to secular Jews searching for a spiritual dimension to their lives.

CHAPTER EIGHTEEN

Outside the Home

When I walk with my twelve-year-old daughter, Emma, in the upper Manhattan neighborhood where we live, she has one rule: I am not allowed to pass a beggar without giving some money. Sadly, there are many needy people, and we pause and give a coin or two to each. But Sabbath is a problem because one of the ways in which our family observes the day is to refrain from carrying money. Shabbat is not a time for commerce, we've taught our children. But this is not commerce; this is charity, Emma argues. At first, Emma made me stop and explain to each homeless person, "We wish we could help you, but it is our Sabbath and we don't carry money." (This being New York, some of the beggars even responded with *"Gut Shabbos!"*) Then Emma hit on a new idea. Before leaving for synagogue Saturday morning, she butters some bagels or takes a bag of potato chips or a box of raisins with her. When we encounter the homeless, Emma offers them food.

I like to think that Emma's undaunted charitable impulse grows out of the Jewish rituals that she's learned at school and at home. To be a Jew in the world means translating Jewish ritual into action. Here are some ways in which that is supposed to happen:

• We pray so that that we can hear others pray. Prayer opens our hearts to the needs of others.

- We eat kosher foods so that we are sensitive to animals and all of God's creation.
- We observe the holidays so that we remember God's historic kindness to the Jewish people.
- We observe the Sabbath as a day of rest as a way of recognizing that others must rest too.

The expression "charity begins at home" has two meanings. The obvious is that you take care of your own first. But a more profound understanding of the phrase is that you learn at home how to do charity outside the home. In Judaism, charity is not simply a good deed but a *mitzvah*, a ritual in itself. Even a poor person, who depends on the public's generosity, is obligated to give charity.

In Hebrew, it is called *chesed*, acts of benevolence that occupy a special place in Jewish law. Most everything else in Judaism has limits: there are seven days of mourning, two days of Rosh Hashanah, four corners on a *tallit*, twenty-five hours to Shabbat. But the acts of *chesed* have no limits.

"The world is built on *chesed*," the Talmud says. If people do not take care of each other, humankind cannot exist. There are two categories of *chesed*. One is *tzedakah*, or charity, which involves giving money to the needy. The other is *gemilut hasadim*, which are acts of kindness. While charity consists of material help, kindness costs nothing. Kindness can simply be a word of advice, a helping hand, or a look of encouragement.

CHARITY

ORIGINS "There shall be no needy among you" (Deuteronomy 15:4).

There is a story of a Hasidic master, Rabbi Meyer Hurwitz, who taught that the obligations of almsgiving were as great as the obligations of daily prayer. Just as a pious Jew does not eat until he or she

prays, Rabbi Hurwitz would not eat until he did an act of charity. Usually this was easy. A beggar would approach him on his way to the synagogue. A congregant would need a word of encouragement. He would visit a sick neighbor or one in mourning. But one day, no one approached him. No one in his town was ill, and no one was in mourning. He went to his study and refused to eat all day. How could he take God's food, he said, if he did not imitate God by giving to others?

Judaism has a hierarchy of charity that begins with the "needy among you," in the words of Deuteronomy, and flows out to the world. First, the Talmud says, one gives to the poor of one's family, then to the poor of one's town, and then to the poor of other towns.

Feeding the poor is a priority. If supplicants ask for food, it is not right to investigate their financial status, the rabbis say. Feed them. If they ask for clothes, it is okay to investigate to make sure they are truly in need.

In another Talmudic discussion of charity, the rabbis ask who you give to first: a poor man or a poor woman? The answer is dated and certainly belongs to a different era, but it is worth repeating for its sensitivity. Who do you give to first? It depends, the rabbis say, on whether you are giving food or clothes. If you are giving food, give to the man first; it is more often his responsibility to feed his family. But clothes go first to the woman; a woman poorly dressed will suffer greater embarrassment.

VISITING THE SICK

The tradition says that the divine presence dwells among the sick because God shares in their suffering. To be at the bedside of an ill person brings comfort and, on a mystical level, is a healing act in itself. It is sometimes called the ministry of presence. You don't even have to say anything; the important thing is being there. We bring the sick a connection to the outside world, a sign that they are not forgotten, and, most important, hope.

In some ways, visiting the sick is seen as an act of curing, not just kindness. The Talmud (Bava Mezia 30b) says that one who ignores a sick person hastens his death, while one who visits takes away one-sixtieth of the illness. Because the sick need visitors so badly, there are Orthodox rabbinic opinions that permit travel on the Sabbath so that the sick person will not be alone. For example, it is widely accepted in Orthodox circles that a man can accompany his pregnant wife in labor to the hospital in a car on the Sabbath. The distress that a woman might feel by being alone could result in harm to her or the fetus. The only others for whom these travel restrictions are relaxed are the doctor treating the sick; the visitor too has medicinal powers.

PRAYING FOR THE SICK

A Jewish name is completed with the father's name: Isaac ben (son of) Abraham, Dina bat (daughter of) Jacob. On Jewish legal documents, such as a marriage contract, the father's name is used as the family name. When it comes to praying for the sick, however, the mother's name is used: Isaac ben Sarah or Dina bat Rivka. When appealing for mercy for the sick, the rabbis suggest, the appeal should be made in the mother's name, for the mother has greater merit in heaven.

When I visit a sick person I always ask for the name of the mother. People are often taken aback. "I'm not a religious person, but my mother's name is Sylvia," a former student who had cancer told me from his hospital bed. It was almost as if the mere mention of his mother's name had softened him. He added quietly: "Pray for me."

VISITING THE BEREAVED

Visiting a house of mourning during the week of *shiva* is a difficult task. It is hard to face someone in such a moment of sorrow. It is hard to know what to say. The etiquette of *shiva* actually makes it easy for the visitor; the visitor enters the house quietly, takes a seat near the mourner, and says nothing until the mourner speaks first. The mood of the mourner shifts often; he or she will sometimes want to talk about the deceased and will sometimes want news of the outside world, the job, politics, or friends. The visitor should follow the mourner's cues. In the moment of sorrow, the greatest kindness is one of presence.

LENDING MONEY

Our financial lives are governed by big, impersonal banks that make decisions on the basis not of who we are but of what we have. If we

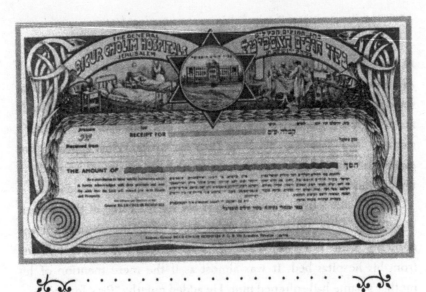

need a loan, the bank doesn't care if we're good people; they want to know if we're a good risk.

There has long been a tradition in the Jewish community of Jews helping Jews. Free-loan societies that lent money without interest were set up so that Jews in need could get low-interest or no-interest loans. Wealthier members of the community were always willing to help out the less fortunate. According to the Torah, it is improper to charge interest. While there are ways around this law (and it could have the effect of discouraging lenders), there is much wisdom to it. The reward for lending money to friends is the knowledge that you are enabling them to get back on their feet and become self-sufficient once again.

HELLO

"You should greet everyone with a good countenance," the Talmud counsels. A smile might seem like a small thing, but many people are afraid to connect with others. But given a chance, even a simple "hello," they will respond. The story is told about a neighbor of Rabbi Israel Salanter, the great nineteenth-century Lithuanian preacher. It was the ten-day penitential period from Rosh Hashanah to Yom Kippur, a time of great solemnity. The neighbor went around with a long face; he was serious, clearly worried about his fate. But Rabbi Salanter rebuked him. "Your face is not a *reshut hayachid*, a private domain," he said. "Your face is a *reshut harabim*, something that belongs to the public. You have a responsibility to show happiness, no matter what's going on inside." And just as one's moodiness is contagious, so is one's cheerfulness and joy.

The Rachman Strivka, the contemporary leader of a small Hasidic sect in Brooklyn, put it another way. He told a follower, the father of six, to get over his depression. He said: "It's a *mitzvah* to be *samayach*— happy—and an even bigger *mitzvah* to pretend to be *samayach*."

HELPING THE AGED

Judaism has a special reverence for the elderly. My favorite sign on the buses in Israel is a sticker near the front seats with a quote from the Torah: "In the presence of age, rise." It's a more poetic way of saying (as they do on the New York subways), "Please give this seat to the elderly or handicapped." Our society glorifies the young and healthy and lives in fear of growing old. We tend to put our elderly into institutions rather than revere them in their homes and in our public places. In our community, there are both college students and elderly residents. Our synagogue has established a "buddy system" whereby young people stay in touch with the older persons. They might call them during the week or on a particularly cold or hot day. My wife has informally adopted an eighty-year-old woman in our synagogue named Regina. Shira often takes her food shopping or drives her to see friends. Their relationship makes me feel particularly good because Regina, once a neighbor of my late Aunt Minnie, used to take my brother and me to the park to play.

SENSITIVITY TOWARD ANIMALS

In Judaism, animals clearly serve humankind both as a source of food and as a source of labor, but they are not to be abused and are to be treated with kindness. When Noah loaded the animals, two by two, into the ark, he was clearly acting in self-interest, but he also had an obligation to his creatures. According to one rabbinic tale, Noah never slept on the ark because he was so busy feeding the animals, each according to its needs. One of the seven laws given to Noah after the Flood was that he refrain from eating meat torn from an animal. There are numerous examples in the Torah of kindness to animals. Animals could not be muzzled while working in the field (Deuteronomy 25:4) lest they have to work without reward. Likewise, an ox and a mule should not be harnessed together (Deuteronomy 22:10), since being of unequal strength and size, both would suffer. While the latter two are prohibitions, there is also a positive command: When a man comes across a bird's nest, he cannot take the eggs without first sending the mother away. It can be debated whether the mother bird experiences pain by seeing her eggs taken, but certainly the law is intended to teach compassion for all things.

Finally, animals are included in the rest mandated on the Sabbath. In the Ten Commandments, the requirement to rest on the Sabbath is for "you, your son or your daughter . . . your ox or your ass, or any of your cattle." There is a fanciful rabbinic story that tells of a pious Jew who became poor and had to sell the cow that he had used to plow his fields to a Gentile. The cow, however, refused to work for its new owner on the Sabbath. The Gentile summoned the Jew and told him to take back his lazy cow. The Jew approached the animal and whispered in its ear, "When you were mine, you ploughed all week and rested on the Sabbath, but now you belong to another. Rise up, rise up and plough." Immediately the beast stirred and rose to plow. Seeing this, the Gentile grew fearful. He said, "If a beast, who has no speech and no sense, can recognize its maker, shall I not?" The story ends with the Gentile becoming a proselyte and eventually a learned Jew.

CHAPTER NINETEEN

Study

ORIGIN "This book of the Torah shall not depart out of your mouth, and you shall meditate on it day and night, that you may be careful to do all that is written in it; for then you shall make your way prosperous, and then you shall have good success" (Joshua 1:8).

As a boy I heard a story about a shopkeeper who made a promise to study a new Jewish text each day. This man was not a rabbi or a scholar, but a simple man with a business and a family. One Friday night, the man came home to find his apartment dark. The automatic clock that shut off his lights on the Sabbath had gone off, and the Sabbath candles on the table had burned out. He could not turn on a light, even for Torah study, because that would be a violation of the Sabbath. Determined not to miss a day of study, the man pulled his chair to a window and read the Talmud by the light of the moon.

The story stands out in my mind because the man was so uncompromisingly devoted to his ideals, both Sabbath observance and Torah study. He had a passion for study that even darkness could not crush.

Torah study is a daily encounter and, for many, an act of religious devotion. But just what are we to study? What is Torah? And what relevance can texts written thousands of years ago have for our daily lives?

To answer the question, we have to examine just what is meant by Torah, for it has many meanings.

257

SCROLL On the most basic level, Torah is the handwritten scroll that contains the Five Books of Moses and is kept in the ark in the synagogue. The scroll is written by a scribe in Hebrew calligraphy with a feather pen (from a kosher animal) on parchment, in a process that often takes a full year. The scroll is covered with a velvet mantle and is dressed with silver ornaments when taken out into the congregation. It is read from publicly four times a week: on Mondays, on Thursdays, and twice on Saturdays.

CHUMASH Torah in printed form is called the Chumash, a book used in the synagogue to follow the reading from the scroll or used at home or in school to study. Chumash comes from the Hebrew *chamesh,* meaning five, and refers to the Five Books of Moses, also known as the Pentateuch. Chumash is often printed with commentaries. The most popular commentary in Hebrew is by the eleventh-century scholar Rashi; there are many others in a popular compilation of medieval exegetes known as the *Mikraot Gedolot.* In English, there are numerous editions with commentaries, including one from the Jewish Publication Society, as well as the Hirsh, Hertz, Plaut, and Stone editions.

TANACH Torah can also mean all of Jewish Scripture, including the prophets and later writings included in the Jewish canon. The Hebrew term for this is Tanach—an acronym for Torah, prophets (*nevi'im*), and writings (*ketuvim*)—and it is also known as the Written Torah.

TALMUD The most elastic term of Torah encompasses all of Jewish learning, both the written and the oral traditions. The Written Torah is used to refer to the entire Hebrew Bible. The Oral Torah is used to refer to the Talmud (which, despite its name, is written down) and all the conversations and study that flow from it and other written sources.

According to the Orthodox understanding, on Mount Sinai, Moses received both the Written Torah and an Oral Torah that explained it.

When, for example, the written law said, "an eye for an eye," the Oral Torah adds this: Don't gouge out an eye, rather collect monetary compensation. Or when it said, "don't boil a kid in its mother's milk," the Oral Torah explained the regulations of *kashrut*. To study these texts and interpretations, to the Orthodox mind, is to study Torah. The two are inseparable. This is the approach of the religious academy, known as the yeshiva, where Torah study is regarded as an act of religious devotion.

However, non-Orthodox scholars see a clear separation between the Torah and its offspring, the Talmud and the oral traditions. These scholars trace how the laws were added, updated, and even abrogated by rabbis over time. This approach, known as the historical and critical method, is embraced by the non-Orthodox rabbinical seminaries and most Jewish studies departments of universities. By necessity, this intellectual method does not treat the texts with the same reverence as the yeshiva approach. You cannot both critique and fully revere texts at the same time. The faith-based yeshiva approach, on the other hand, often must fly in the face of historical fact.

The terms *Oral Torah* and *Written Torah* derive from an Orthodox understanding that the Oral Torah was passed down through the generations until the time of the second century, when, fearing it would be lost, the emerging rabbinate wrote much of it down. Even though it was written down nearly two thousand years ago, the Talmud is still called the Oral Law.

My favorite definition of the Talmud is that it is not simply a book but a library of Jewish law, lore, custom, and superstition. Its range of topics is vast, from laws of compensation of accident victims to agricultural practices, from domestic issues like marriage and divorce to ritual practices like daily sacrifice and festival observances. There are more than sixty books, known as tractates, some of them as short as three folio pages (dealing with the laws of first-fruit offerings) and some as long as 157 pages (dealing with the laws of the Sabbath). And there are two versions, one compiled in Israel (known as the Jerusalem Talmud) and the other compiled in Babylon (the Babylonian Talmud). When people refer simply to the Talmud, they mean the Babylonian version, which is considered more complete and authoritative.

The Talmud has a staccato, stream-of-consciousness style; a discussion of prayer can suddenly turn into a discussion of demons. The traditional edition also has no punctuation, so that the entire book can be read as one run-on sentence with nary a comma or a period in sight. To add to the difficulties of reading it, Hebrew has no capital letters, so it is hard to know when sentences start and end. There are modern, punctuated editions of the Talmud, notably the Steinsaltz edition, as well as several editions in English.

I once began an article in *The New York Times* about women's Talmud study like this:

imagine reading a book without any commas periods or other punctuation marks imagine reading without capitalization or vowels that is what reading the talmud is like but also imagine that you have mastered the keys to this complex library of jewish knowledge with its own set of rules

Suddenly, things make sense. Suddenly you understand not only the words and the concepts but have joined an intellectual process that has shaped more than 2,000 years of Jewish spiritual life and religious law. You are not merely a reader; you are a player.

That first paragraph had to go to the highest echelons of the *Times*'s newsroom to get a dispensation from the paper's strict rules of grammar and punctuation.

One popular place to begin Talmud study is with the Mishna of *Pirkei Avot* known as *Ethics of the Fathers*. I studied this volume with my son Adam as he prepared for his bar mitzvah because it serves as a blueprint for all Torah study. The sixth chapter, compiled in the Mishna in about the year 200, begins:

> Whoever occupies himself with the study of the Torah for its own sake merits many things . . . he is called friend, beloved. . . . The Torah invests him with humility and reverence; it enables him to become righteous, godly, upright, and faithful; it keeps him far from sin, and draws him near to virtue. . . . He is like a fountain, that ever gathers force, and like a never-failing stream. He becomes modest, patient, and forgiving of insults. The Torah . . . raises him above all creatures.

How does one study Torah? The Mishna says that Torah is "acquired" in forty-eight ways, each one of them a good lesson for life:

> Study, attentive listening, audible rehearsing, mental alertness, intuitive insight, awe, reverence, humility, cheerfulness, attendance on scholars, close association with colleagues, discussion with students, sedateness, knowledge of Scriptures and Mishna, moderation in business, moderation in worldly interests, moder-

ation in pleasure, moderation in sleep, moderation in conversation, moderation in merriment, patience, a good heart, intellectual honesty, uncomplaining acceptance of chastisement, knowing one's place, being content with one's lot, setting a limit to one's words, claiming no credit for oneself, being beloved, loving God, loving humanity, loving righteousness, loving equity, loving reproof, shunning honors, taking no pride in one's learning, not delighting in dictating decisions, bearing the yoke of one's colleague, judging him favorably, directing him to truth and peace, being composed in one's study, asking and answering. Listening and adding to one's knowledge, learning in order to teach, learning in order to practice, making his teacher wiser, noting with precision what one has learnt, and reporting a thing in the name of the person who said it.

After Adam's bar mitzvah, we took up the study of the tractate B'rachot, which he'll probably remember more vividly. In this tractate, which primarily deals with the technical laws of prayers and blessings, there are flights of fancy, including one long discussion about demons, how many there are, and whether one can see them. Want to see one? The Talmud gives a formula: Take the embryonic sac of a black cat that is the firstborn daughter of a firstborn black cat, dry it out, burn it, take its ashes, and rub them into your eyes. You will see them. But it comes with a warning: One rabbi tried it and came to great harm.

On another page, the Talmud says that God gets angry every day. "And how long is His anger?" The answer is *rega,* the Hebrew word for moment. And how long is a *rega?* One opinion, is that a *rega* is 1 / 58,0000 of an hour, and the other is that *rega* is as long as it takes to say *rega.* Adam and I took turns seeing how fast we could say the word.

Such stories of the Talmud are part of the Talmud known as *aggadah.* Anyone who believes that Talmud study is dry and legalistic should consider that one-third of the Talmud is *aggadah,* which consists of ethics, history, philosophy, tales, and proverbs. The other two-thirds, dealing with legal matters, is known as *halacha*. The *aggadah* portions were compiled in a famous text, the Book of Legends (Sefer Ha-Haggadah), first published in Odessa in 1908. In a famous essay on the subject, one of the editors, Hayyim Nahman Bialik, described *aggadah* as the poetry of Judaism. *Halacha*, he added, is the prose. He lamented that the legalistic prose has often overwhelmed the poetry.

To ensure that Torah is studied every day, verses from the Talmud as well as the Scripture are incorporated into daily prayer. They tend to be more tame than the ones about demons. For example, quoting from a mishna in Peah, the prayer book says: "These are the things for which no limit is prescribed." The first three things without limit mentioned are the size of offerings to the Temple and to the poor. The last two are "the practice of kindness and the study of Torah"; for these, the sky is the limit.

The daily prayer book begins with the blessings that one says on the study of Torah. Usually blessings are said before the act; if one is about to eat an apple, one utters the blessing on fruit and then eats. But the Torah blessings are said for the whole day. Torah study should be a feature of daily life.

DAILY STUDY

Torah study is immeasurably enhanced by studying with others. One can, of course, study in classes led by a teacher. But often equally effective is studying in partnership with another student, in a system known as *havrutah*. The *havrutah* method of study is the approach taken in the classic Orthodox European yeshiva. Boys or young men sit in the study hall in pairs and prepare the text, usually the Talmud, by breaking it down word by word and concept by concept. In its structure, the Talmud is a record of the debates of the great academies of Babylon and Palestine. Through *havrutah* study, students of the Talmud can actually enter into the debates of old. The *havrutah* model, still used by the Orthodox, has been adopted by the non-Orthodox seminaries. Insights are shared, questions resolved, and texts unraveled. But perhaps most important, studying with the right study partner often provides momentum. It keeps one engaged and moving forward. Of course, finding time to study is difficult, and coordinating with another student makes the task even more challenging. But short of sitting down together, it is also possible to study together by creating a synchronized study model, known as *daf yomi,* which means a page a day. People far away from each other can feel connected and part of a learning community simply by studying the same text, page by page.

The concept of *daf yomi* was first proposed in 1923 by Rabbi Meir Shapiro before a gathering of rabbis in Vienna. He urged both rabbis and laymen to tackle a page of Talmud each day. He noted that if they all started from the first page of the first tractate and continued from there, covering all 2,711 pages, they would finish the entire Talmud in seven and a half years. The idea caught on. *Daf yomi* is now in its eleventh cycle. Tens of thousands study the Talmud in this fashion, most of them in classes but some on their own or on the telephone (there's an 800 number) and on the internet (www.dafyomi.com). In 1997, when the tenth cycle of Talmud study in this fashion was completed, the event was marked by huge gatherings of Talmud students in major cities in Israel and the United States. At the Yad Eliyahu Stadium in Jerusalem, some ten thousand people gathered. Madison Square Garden in New York was sold out; all twenty-six-thousand seats were taken. More people participated in this system of study than Rabbi Shapiro or anyone could have predicted.

The idea of this kind of synchronized study has caught on. In 1999, the United Synagogue of Conservative Judaism encouraged the members of its 770 congregations to read a Bible chapter each day. At that rate, it would take two and a half years to finish all twenty-four books of the Hebrew Bible. One friend of mine, a journalist, is part of a small study group that reads a page of the *Encyclopaedia Judaica* each day. Once a week, members e-mail each other with insights and lessons.

Midrash

One additional tool of Torah study is *midrash*. This method, employed by the rabbis of the Talmud to investigate Scripture, often involved wordplay and creativity. The rabbis frequently used the text to find the answers they were looking for all along. For example, it is forbidden by Torah law to light a fire on the Sabbath. Yet, if someone is ill, it is permissible to light a fire to keep the person warm. Why? The rabbis find a proof in the text, in this case Leviticus 18:5: "You shall therefore keep my statutes and my ordinances, by doing these a man shall live." The *midrash* takes the words "shall live" and says that one should "live by the rules and not die by them." Therefore, one may break the Sabbath (or almost any other law) in order to keep a person alive. This process can be viewed in two ways. One is that the text intended this all along. That is, from the start, the intention of God in writing the Scripture was that the Sabbath can be broken to save a life; the exemption was simply hidden in the text. Or it can be viewed as the situation changing. The law as first stated was unreasonable. Therefore, the rabbis found a new meaning in an old text to get the result they needed.

Midrash is employed in the Talmud but is not limited to it. In fact, people do *midrash* today. I've seen this in both the Orthodox yeshiva world and the liberal Jewish community as well. People use *midrash* to tease things out of the text. There is a growing body of women's *midrash*, for example, that develops teachings about women whose stories have for so long gone untold. Feminist scholars use *midrash* to explain the acts of Sarah when she told Abraham to expel Hagar or to talk about the feelings of Dina, the daughter of Jacob, when she was raped.

Midrash is important because it puts in a Jew's hands the ability to bring ancient teaching in line with contemporary thought and practice.

As I've tried to demonstrate in these pages, Torah is not monolithic. It comes in written and oral versions. It can be approached intellectually or spiritually. It comes as poetry and prose. New ideas can be found in old texts through the process of *midrash*. It is handed down from generation to generation, and in the process, Torah is enhanced, enriched, and sometimes altered.

The story about Gabriel teaching Torah to fetuses in the womb—the story with which I began this book—is part of that Torah tradition. Every Jewish schoolchild is told the story and can repeat it: The angel Gabriel sits in the womb with the soon-to-be-born child and teaches it all of Torah. Right before it is dispatched into the world, the fetus is struck on its upper lip, and all of the teachings are forgotten. Once I began to look through the sources, however, I could not find this version. This story was not written down. The closest thing was from a medieval text called *Seder Yetzirat Ha-Vlad*, "The Creation of the Embryo." In this version, the soul of the fetus is visited by two angels, taken on a journey, and shown, not Torah, but heaven and hell. These are your choices, the soul is told; it all depends how you live your life. It read like the R-rated version of the story I so loved.

I puzzled over these two versions—the written tradition and the oral tradition—and realized that they were both valid. A story told has as much power than a story written, if not more. The written version is a morality tale that warns of fire and brimstone, reward and punishment. The oral tradition provides an educational initiation story of great warmth. One version might be said to represent the worldview of the Hasidim, and the other of the Mitnaggedim, the more legalistic, yeshiva approach. One might be said to represent the rigid Orthodox and the other the relaxed Reform. One might represent the learning-as-devotion school; the other, the practitioners of the historical and critical method. The fact that both versions of the Gabriel story exist in contemporary Jewish culture is yet another reminder that there is no one way to interpret Judaism. There is no one way to live the Jewish life. There is a tradition that came before us, but there are also many versions that lie ahead. There are an infinite number of variations on the theme of being Jewish. I have tried to lay out the foundations, and from there, each of us can create our own Jewish future.

BIBLIOGRAPHY

Abramowitz, Yosef, and Susan Silverman. *Jewish Family and Life*. New York: Golden Books, 1997.

Alper, Robert A. *Life Doesn't Get Any Better Than This*. Missouri: Triumph Books, 1996.

Artson, Bradley Shavit. *It's a Mitvzah!* New Jersey: Behrman House, 1995.

Berman, Louis A. *Vegetarianism and the Jewish Tradition*. New York: Ktav Publishing, 1982.

Biale, David. *Eros and the Jews*. New York: Basic Books, 1992.

Biale, Rachel. *Women and Jewish Law*. New York: Schocken, 1984.

Birnbaum, Philip. *Daily Prayer Book*. New York: Hebrew Publishing Company, 1987.

Cardin, Nina Beth. *Out of the Depths I Call to You*. New Jersey: Aronson, 1992.

Cohen, Tamara, ed. *The Journey Continues: The Ma'yan Passover Haggadah*. New York: Ma'yan: The Jewish Women's Project, 2000.

Dershowitz, Alan M. *The Vanishing American Jew*. New York: Little Brown, 1997.

Diamant, Anita, and Howard Cooper. *Living a Jewish Life*. New York: HarperCollins, 1996.

Donin, Hayim. *To Be a Jew*. New York: Basic Books, 1972, 1991.

Dresner, Samuel H. *The Jewish Dietary Laws*. New York: Burning Bush Press, 1959.

Encyclopaedia Judaica. Jerusalem: Keter Publishing House, 1978.

Gaster, Theodor H. *Festivals of the Jewish Year*. New York: William Morrow, 1952.

Gillman, Neil. *Conservative Judaism*. New Jersey: Behrman House, 1993.

———. *The Death of Death*. Vermont: Jewish Lights Publishing, 1997.

Gold, Michael. *Does God Belong in the Bedroom?* Philadelphia, Jewish Publication Society, 1992.

Goldberg, J. J. *Jewish Power*. New York: Addison Wesley, 1996.

Gordis, Daniel. *Becoming a Jewish Parent*. New York: Harmony Books, 1999.

Greenberg, Blu. *How to Run a Traditional Jewish Household*. New York: Fireside, 1985.

Greenberg, Irving. *The Jewish Way*. New York: Summit, 1988.

Hammer, Joshua. *Chosen by God*. New York: Hyperion, 1999.

Hammer, Reuven. *Entering the High Holy Days*. Philadelphia: Jewish Publication Society, 1998.

Harris, Lis. *Holy Days*. New York: Simon & Schuster, 1985.

Hartman, David. *A Heart of Many Rooms*. Vermont: Jewish Lights Publishing, 1999.

Heilman, Samuel. *The Gate Behind the Wall*. New York: Summit, 1984.

Helmreich, William B. *The World of the Yeshiva*. New Haven: Yale University Press, 1982.

Hertzberg, Arthur. *The Zionist Idea*. Philadelphia: Jewish Publication Society, 1959.

Israel, Richard. *The Kosher Pig: And Other Curiosities of Modern Jewish Life*. Los Angeles: Aleph Design Group, 1994.

Jacobs, Louis. *The Jewish Religion*. New York: Oxford University Press, 1995.

———. *The Book of Jewish Practice*. New Jersey: Behrman House, 1987.

Joselit, Jenna Weissman. *The Wonders of America: Reinventing Jewish Culture 1880–1950*. New York: Hill & Wang, 1995.

Klagsbrun, Francine. *Jewish Days*. New York: Farrar Straus Giroux, 1996.

Klein, Isaac. *A Guide to Jewish Religious Practice.* New York: Jewish Theological Seminary, 1992.

Klinghoffer, David. *The Lord Will Gather Me In.* New York: Free Press, 1999.

Lamm, Maurice. *The Jewish Way in Death and Mourning.* New York: Jonathan David Publishers, 1969.

———. *Living Torah in America.* New Jersey: Behrman House, 1993.

Lamm, Norman. *The Shema.* Philadelphia: Jewish Publication Society, 1998.

Montefiore, C. G., and H. Loewe. *A Rabbinic Anthology.* Philadelphia: Jewish Publication Society, 1960.

Newman, Louis I. *The Hasidic Anthology.* New York: Schocken Books, 1963.

Salkin, Jeffrey K. *Putting God on the Guest List.* Vermont: Jewish Lights Publishing, 1992.

Schneider, Susan Weidman. *Jewish and Female.* New York: Simon & Schuster, 1984.

Strassfeld, Michael. *The Jewish Holidays.* New York: Harper & Row, 1985.

———, and Sharon Strassfeld, editors. *The Third Jewish Catalog.* Philadelphia: Jewish Publication Society, 1980.

Telushkin, Joseph. *Jewish Literacy.* New York: William Morrow, 1991.

———. *Jewish Humor.* New York: William Morrow, 1992.

———. *Jewish Wisdom.* New York: William Morrow, 1994.

Waskow, Arthur. *Seasons of Our Joy.* New York: Bantam, 1982.

———. *Down-to-Earth Judaism.* New York: William Morrow, 1995.

Wieseltier, Leon. *Kaddish.* New York: Knopf, 1998.

Wouk, Herman. *The Will to Live On.* New York: Cliff Street Books, 2000.

Zornberg, Aviva Gottlieb. *Genesis: The Beginning of Desire.* Philadelphia: Jewish Publication Society, 1995.

INDEX

LIST OF ILLUSTRATIONS

ABOUT THE AUTHOR

ARI L. GOLDMAN, one of the nation's leading religion journalists, was a reporter for the *New York Times* for twenty years. He left the *Times* in 1993 to teach journalism at Columbia University, where he has trained a new generation of religion writers. Professor Goldman was educated at Yeshiva University, Columbia, and Harvard. In addition to *Being Jewish,* he wrote a best-selling memoir, *The Search for God at Harvard,* and a popular book about Jewish mourning rituals called *Living a Year of Kaddish.* Goldman has been a Fulbright Professor in Israel and a Skirball Fellow at Oxford University in England. He recently began writing a regular religion column for the *New York Daily News.* He lives in New York with his wife and their three children.